THE BUILDER

THE BUILDER

MBS: Shaping Peace and Power at a Defining Moment in History

Frederic E. Teboul and Thierry Pastor

Forewords by Alan Dershowitz *and* Ahdeya Ahmed Al-Sayed

Skyhorse Publishing

Skyhorse Publishing books may be purchased in bulk at special discounts for sales promotion, corporate gifts, fund-raising, or educational purposes. Special editions can also be created to specifications. For details, contact the Special Sales Department, Skyhorse Publishing, 307 West 36th Street, 11th Floor, New York, NY 10018 or info@skyhorsepublishing.com.

Skyhorse® and Skyhorse Publishing® are registered trademarks of Skyhorse Publishing, Inc.®, a Delaware corporation.

Visit our website at www.skyhorsepublishing.com.

Please follow our publisher Tony Lyons on Instagram @tonylyonsisuncertain

10 9 8 7 6 5 4 3 2 1

Library of Congress Cataloging-in-Publication Data is available on file.

Hardcover ISBN: 978-1-5107-8425-3
eBook ISBN: 978-1-5107-8426-0

Cover painting by Sergio Kopeliovich
Cover design by David Ter-Avanesyan

Printed in the United States of America

To Amalya, Bella, Nélya, and Sacha

Contents

*All success stories start with a vision, and successful visions
are based on strong pillars.*

H.R.H. the Crown Prince Mohammed bin Salman bin Abdulaziz Al Saud

Foreword
by Professor Alan Morton Dershowitz[1]

In the Arab-Muslim tradition, it is customary to greet one's interlocutor with the phrase *Salām 'alaykum*—literally, "peace be upon you." The conventional response is *Wa-'alaykum as-salām*, "and upon you, peace." This ritual exchange embodies a profound aspiration: that human interactions might be founded upon peace, mutual recognition, and shared dignity. It is a symbolic gesture—one that speaks not only to religious or cultural values, but to a universal longing for harmony among individuals and peoples. Yet the world as it is—complex, fractured, and often cruel—rarely aligns with such noble intentions. Far from being the norm, peace is more often the exception. Across history and into the present, we are confronted with a sobering reality: that conflict, rather than dialogue, remains a persistent feature of human affairs. Time and again, it has appeared easier to resolve differences through violence than to uphold the fragile edifice of peace—easier to destroy than to preserve, to sever than to reconcile. The twentieth century alone bears witness to this tragic tendency. It is estimated that over 230 million people[2]—combatants and civilians alike—perished in armed conflicts during that century. This staggering number, which excludes the even greater multitude of those wounded

---

1   Born on September 1, 1938, after studying at Brooklyn College and Yale University, Alan Morton Dershowitz became the youngest Professor of Law in the history of Harvard University in 1964, a position he held until 2013. He has also had a distinguished career as an attorney-at-law, during which time he was called upon to handle high-profile criminal and constitutional cases. Alan Dershowitz is renowned for his personal commitment to defending individual rights and freedoms. Known for his outspoken positions, he has published numerous articles and books, including many bestsellers.

2   Center for International & Security Studies at Maryland, "Deaths in Wars and Conflicts in the 20th Century," June 20, 2006, https://cissm.umd.edu/research-impact/publications/deaths-wars-and-conflicts-20th-century#:~:text=%2D%20An%20itemized%20total%20sum%20of,of%20this%20sum%20are%20provided.

or permanently displaced, is roughly equivalent to the entire population of Pakistan today, the fifth most populous nation on earth. It is a sobering comparison that underscores the scale of human devastation wrought by war. I abhor violence in all its forms. Yet over the course of my life, I have repeatedly been forced to confront its most vile and intimate expressions. Violence, regrettably, remains an enduring facet of the human condition—a dark mirror held up to our species, reflecting not only the fragility of peace but the recurring failure to sustain it.

War still rages in the Middle East, a region already plagued by so many long-standing crises. The shattering of peace efforts, which once promised brighter days ahead, fills me with sorrow. How fervently I wished for sustainable peace in this volatile region. Given recent events, such hopes now appear tenuous. Nevertheless, a faint beacon of optimism persists within me. I believe that visionary leaders could potentially bridge divides and foster peace. But is genuine peace merely an unreachable ideal? The realities of today lean toward this pessimistic interpretation. Conflict often seems more palpable than coexistence. Yet, I maintain that the right leaders could unite fractured voices, championing peace as a testament to the enduring spirit of humanity amidst a fractured world. To me, the concept of peace is inextricable from the essence of humanity.

My professional journey as an attorney-at-law and as a Professor of Law at Harvard Law School has profoundly shaped my analytical and problem-solving mindset. Throughout my career, I have been a staunch defender of individual rights and liberties. My numerous publications, including articles and books, have often sparked vigorous debate among my peers. I have unwaveringly adhered to my principles, perhaps because of this, even though my perspectives may not have always been fully grasped. In this respect, I find a certain, if unlikely kinship with the protagonist of this book.

My writings about the complex and heart-wrenching conflict between Israel and Hamas (and its supporters) reflect my deep concern over the human and humanitarian crises it has spawned, affecting countless individuals both directly and indirectly. In my latest endeavor, I strive to shift the focus to a particular political leader who might be instrumental in forging peace, though I question whether this alone will suffice.

Throughout my life, I have been acutely aware of the profound impact of language. In light of this, I wish to amend a previous assertion: the world does not merely need advocates for peace, but rather dedicated *builders* of peace.

I yearn for a world where peace—Shalom and Salam—reigns supreme, transcending tension and conflict. I harbor no illusions about the eradication of violence, but I am confident that every crisis harbors a potential resolution. I envision an international body that convenes individuals from diverse faiths, united in their dedication to dialogue, coexistence, tolerance, and understanding. Such interactions foster enlightenment. I believe this congress aligns with the sentiments expressed by His Royal Highness, Crown Prince and Prime Minister, Mohammed bin Salman bin Abdulaziz Al Saud.

Yet, I recognize the barriers posed by misconceptions. Learning of this book, which offers a fresh perspective on the Kingdom of Saudi Arabia and its Crown Prince, diverging from prevalent Western narratives, I felt compelled to study, comment upon, and bring to a wider audience its unique insights. This book elucidates the Crown Prince's vision, detailing his economic, societal, and diplomatic reforms—a portrayal hitherto unseen in much of Western literature. In this comprehensive examination, it becomes evident that much of Western analysis hinges on misconceptions about, and incomplete understanding of, his daring societal reform efforts.

The core argument is that the West often fails to delve deeper into the psyche and decision-making processes of the Crown Prince. This oversight leads to a stark contrast between his perceived image in Europe and North America, and the genuine respect and admiration he commands both from his own people and in regions such as Asia, Africa, Latin America, the Arab-Muslim world, and Russian-speaking territories.[3]

We often underestimate the efforts he has made to initiate reforms, including the difficult discussions and negotiations both within his country and internationally, aimed at fostering modernization and pursuing peace—social, societal, and religious. I fully believe in the sincerity of his commitment to this mission.

The enduring crises in the Middle East have left indelible scars on its

---

3   This popularity is linked to all the humanitarian actions of the Muslim World League (MWL), Al Rabita, and the King Salman Humanitarian Aid and Relief Centre undertaken around the world and not only in regions of Islamic culture. This point will be developed later in the book.

populace. While many dedicated individuals strive for resolution, past Western interventions have largely proven ineffective. Engaging with numerous stakeholders from the region, it becomes evident that the overarching desire is for sustainable peace, unhindered by national, confessional, or other delineations. The horrors of war, which I vehemently denounced at every juncture of my life, persist despite the genuine efforts of many global leaders. This prompts a question: is there a fundamental misalignment in our understanding?

Alas, many around the world have come to recognize the Crown Prince's pivotal role in his country primarily through one tragic event in Saudi history—the assassination of Saudi opposition journalist Jamal Ahmad Khashoggi by elements of the Saudi security forces at the Saudi Consulate in Istanbul on October 2, 2018. Following this, the alleged commando members responsible for the assassination were tried and received severe prison sentences in Saudi courts, and at least one senior official was dismissed and placed under house arrest. As the de facto leader of Saudi Arabia, the Crown Prince holds an implicit level of responsibility for that tragic incident. In September 2019, during a documentary by the Public Broadcasting Service (PBS), he took full responsibility for the tragedy, stating it occurred "under his watch,"[4] while firmly denying any prior knowledge of the "rogue operation."[5] A report dated February 11, 2021, from the office of the Director of U.S. National Intelligence, which was declassified two weeks later, reveals ambiguities concerning the circumstances of Jamal Ahmad Khashoggi's death at the hands of the commando team. The report articulates, "we do not know whether these individuals knew in advance that the operation would result in Khashoggi's death."[6]

Diplomatic misunderstandings, whether inadvertent or deliberate, can hamper any international initiative. Often, we might dismiss certain figures, deeming them ill-suited for peacemaking roles. Yet in the Middle East, only someone deeply attuned to the regional dynamics can truly spearhead peace

---

4   "The Crown Prince of Saudi Arabia," https://www.pbs.org/video/crown-prince-saudi -arabia-1jt2ey/, October 1, 2019.

5   Ibid.

6   Office of the Director of National Intelligence, "Assessing the Saudi Government's Role in the Killing of Jamal Khashoggi," February 11, 2021, https://www.dni.gov/files/ ODNI/documents/assessments/Assessment-Gov-Role-in-JK-Death-20210226v2.pdf.

initiatives. This is particularly true for efforts involving nations with complex diplomatic relations.

His Royal Highness, Crown Prince Mohammed bin Salman bin Abdulaziz Al Saud, appears to exemplify such a figure. His recent initiatives—some controversial—range from advocating for the Syrian Republic's reintegration into the Arab League, despite resistance from other Arab nations, to reopening diplomatic channels with the Islamic Republic of Iran. These actions suggest a genuine commitment to peace. His diplomatic endeavors to mediate the ongoing conflict between Saudi Arabia and Yemen's Houthi rebels, in conjunction with his partnerships with nations like the Republic of Sudan and organizations such as the Gulf Cooperation Council, vividly illustrate his profound dedication. Furthermore, his involvement in humanitarian missions underscores this commitment. Despite encountering numerous obstacles that frequently obstruct his initiatives, this young statesman embodies a pivotal dialogue partner, indispensable for advancing our collective aspiration for peace. It is precisely because of his and his nation's critical role in Middle Eastern peace efforts that Hamas may have sought to impede this process on October 7, 2023. We cannot allow that to reoccur.

The Vision 2030 program, launched by His Royal Highness, Crown Prince Mohammed bin Salman bin Abdulaziz Al Saud, in 2016, outlines ambitious economic, societal, and diplomatic targets. What he has embarked on since then illustrates an encouraging trajectory, the audacity of which might be undervalued by Western observers. His strategic decisions demonstrate the foresight of a visionary leader, even if not universally recognized as such. Engaging with him is not merely an option; it is an imperative. Given the Crown Prince's vast influence, expertise, and pragmatism, he remains a unique force capable of navigating conflict zones and challenges. Envisioning peace in the Middle East without his involvement is counterproductive. While external assistance will surely be required, he stands out as an important ambassador for sustainable peace, both regionally and globally. As Victor Hugo said, *"Nothing is more powerful than an idea whose time has come."*

Foreword
by Ahdeya Ahmed Al-Sayed[1]

In these uncertain times, we are once again reminded of a pervasive issue plaguing our world, increasingly marred by violence: intolerance. It reigns supreme within communities that struggle to set aside differences, often rejected for a multitude of unfounded reasons. Nations fail to understand each other, leading to misunderstandings that inevitably impact international relations. Such ignorance tarnishes the reputations of leaders whose significant achievements remain unrecognized.

I am an Arab woman and a Muslim, hailing from the Arabian Gulf nation that witnessed the so-called Arab Spring a decade ago. How often have I faced derogatory remarks about my homeland, the Kingdom of Bahrain? This small island monarchy, home to a cosmopolitan population, is frequently subjected to outdated criticisms regarding the living conditions of both Bahrainis and foreign residents. Additionally, the country's connection to Saudi Arabia via a bridge over the Gulf is often portrayed by detractors as a controversial point of entry, disregarding the significant societal advancements occurring within the Kingdom. These transformative changes, driven by a courage largely

---

1   Ahdeya Ahmed Al-Sayed is the former president of the Bahrain Journalists Association. She obtained her master's degree in Mass Communication from the University of Leicester, UK. She worked as media advisor for Bahrain's government, Ministry of Cabinet Affairs and Ministry of Information. She also served as spokesperson for Bahrain's parliamentary and municipal elections in the year 2006. She joined a Bahraini local newspaper as a journalist and Bahrain Television as a political TV shows host in 1991. She currently writes for several regional newspapers and has been the most active journalist in the Arabian Gulf region defending and advocating for signing peace agreements with Israel to create a more stable and secure Middle East, where all religions coexist in peace. She won the 2019 Female Arab Journalist of the Year award given by the London Arabia Organisation. In 2024, she received the Women Making Waves Award from Women's Voices Now.

unrecognized in the West, arise from a profound misunderstanding of Saudi Arabia's customs and traditions.

The Saudi Crown Prince is not merely a visionary; he is a decisive leader who has transformed Saudi Arabia virtually overnight. Such profound changes require the extraordinary courage possessed by only the greatest leaders. His bold decisions have significantly elevated the status of women in society, empowering them and ensuring their rights are respected. Today's Saudi Arabia has opened its doors wider for women than ever before. Saudi women now regard their young Prince as their pillar of strength and protector. Current legislation is dedicated to safeguarding the rights of Saudi women, providing these highly educated and knowledgeable individuals with the life they deserve, both at home and in the workplace.

As a free woman and a journalist—a role not traditionally associated with an Arab and Muslim woman from the Arabian Peninsula—I have fought to establish myself in the media world. At the age of eighteen, I applied for a position as a trainee journalist at a local newspaper. My first byline appeared in December 1991, capturing significant public attention. It was then that I realized journalism is not merely a job; it is a vocation, rightly deserving its title as the fourth estate. In 1995, I made history by becoming the first political TV host on Bahrain Television, a pivotal moment in my career. This platform has allowed me to exercise freedom of the press and speech, significantly influencing public opinion.

I urge a fair and objective assessment of the societal progress in my homeland. The relentless criticism of its human rights record contradicts the truth about the Bahraini society that has for decades been a very modern state where women and men all have equal rights and opportunities. As a matter of fact, nearly 40 percent of Bahrain's Parliament is occupied by women, and 70 percent of journalists in Bahrain are women too. In addition, Bahrain also appoints women to the government, ministerial posts, and as diplomats. I myself, through elections, became the first woman to preside over the Bahrain Journalists Association, the union that defends the rights of journalists.

When my nation signed the Abraham Accords and I announced as journalist my support for them, I faced strong criticism from many people in my society who are strongly holding on to ideologies that resist change. In our societies, change must be gradually fed or presented to people, but in many cases, change had to be abruptly done because the change meant bringing happiness to the vast majority of the people. And what I woke up to one morning: Saudi Arabia's Crown Prince did it.

Because of the misconceptions of the West about this region, our countries in the Gulf need to work harder to convey the reality of this part of the world. The changes are tremendous but have happened gradually because a balance must always be created between how we advance and preserve our basis ethics, culture, and traditions that are very deeply rooted in us. This is what Crown Prince Mohammed bin Salman understands very well. Disrupting local customs and traditions would be a grave miscalculation in a society embracing modernity. The transition to modernity must be gradual, highlighting the crucial difference between evolution and revolution. Saudi Arabia is engaged in a transformative process aimed at improving living conditions, particularly for women.

However, some reforms face criticism in the West, being dismissed as mere demagogic maneuvers by the Crown Prince, and this way of looking at such a big transformation in Saudi Arabia is unfair as we, people who live around this country, simply view him as a leader who is extremely brave, courageous, and knows what we all need. Let's not forget that change and advancement in Saudi Arabia means that the whole region will grow, and that's what he expressed during the G20 Summit in 2018. The Crown Prince announced that Saudi Arabia will be completely different in five years. He achieved this promise. He strongly stated that the Middle East can be the "new Europe" and vowed to see the region thrive economically. The Crown Prince told a packed audience at the Future Investment Initiative forum in Riyadh that he would like to see the economic transformation of the region happen within his lifetime—and seven years after this statement, we witness that he kept to his word, and his country completely transformed. He said his "war" was restoring the Middle East to its past glory. "I believe the new Europe is the Middle East," Prince Mohammed said. "The Kingdom of Saudi Arabia in five years will be completely different."

The Crown Prince is driving Saudi Arabia's Vision 2030 plan for economic and social reforms. "If we succeed in the coming five years, other countries will join us, and this affirms why I believe that any change in Saudi Arabia is a change for the whole Middle East—a region that has been subjected to a rise in extremism while its leaders want to achieve peace and stability. In this historic speech, he cited Saudi Arabia's efforts to transform its oil-dependent economy, build more infrastructure, and fight terror. "All our projects are going ahead, reform is going ahead, our war on extremism is going ahead, our war on terrorism is going ahead . . . our efforts won't stop no matter how they try to constrain us," he said. And as a matter of fact, the war on terrorism was a promise made as he believed we, as a region, would not be able to advance without combating terrorism. As simple as I can say it, Saudi Arabia is being misinterpreted by many.

This misinterpretation reveals a deep ignorance among its critics. Saudi society is evolving, but these changes must be cautious, considering the deeply ingrained conservatism that preceded the Crown Prince's public responsibilities. The West fails to grasp the magnitude of negotiating with conservative religious leaders to foster a more flexible and modern religious approach granting rights and freedom to women previously unimaginable.

The Crown Prince has boldly undertaken reforms that are unprecedented in Saudi Arabia. The significance of these approved reforms is often underestimated, with some amounting to genuine revolutions. He is dedicated to modernizing the nation in accordance with the ambitious objectives of Vision 2030. Could this serve as a prelude to further structural reforms designed to meet the aspirations and expectations of the populace, the critical foundation for the achievement and success of these extensive reform initiatives?

His pursuit of peace stems from a profound and personal understanding of Islam, which rejects violence and advocates for harmony among people, placing tolerance—acceptance of differences—at the forefront of fundamental human respect. This principle is rooted in Quranic teachings that assert, "Tolerance is a strength, not a weakness." He is wholeheartedly troubled by the war in Gaza, a conflict with substantial regional and global ramifications. The prolonged duration of this conflict will increasingly undermine the ability of Israeli and Arab leaders in the region to govern effectively, subjecting them to public discontent and the heightened threat of rising extremism.

Pledging allegiance to His Royal Highness Prince Mohammed bin Salman by members of the Al Saud family and the Saudi people was grounded in their belief that he is the leader who will guide the Kingdom into a new era of progress, development, and prosperity. As a journalist, I can personally attest to the tangible changes taking place in Saudi Arabia, particularly in the realms of freedom of expression and the press, which have seen remarkable strides. Moreover, the introduction of entertainment in Saudi Arabia has brought joy and a newfound sense of freedom, especially among the youth, who make up nearly 70 percent of the population. On my first visit to Riyadh after the launch of the reform initiatives, I saw the joy in people's eyes—the freedom they felt was unmistakable. I had the chance to speak with young women in coffee shops and cafés; many expressed deep gratitude, saying that without Mohammed bin Salman and King Salman, they could have never dreamed of the opportunities they now enjoy. Women are driving, entering the workforce in greater numbers, and becoming visible contributors to society. These changes are not just symbolic—they represent real empowerment and transformation. Young men and women of Saudi Arabia today know that when qualified and with the standard of education required, they will pursue their dreams and reach their targets in their professional lives. When you walk into places, see young people, and ask them what just happened to their country, you sense how popular their Crown Prince has become. He is a leader who has given them a life many generations before them did not have the privilege of having. They have allegiance to their Prince.

On the geopolitical front, the war against the Houthis was not merely a military engagement to defend Saudi borders, but a broader strategic effort to safeguard the region from Iranian influence. The Islamic Republic of Iran, since the 1979 revolution and the rise of the Ayatollah regime, has pursued a policy of exporting its extremist ideology through proxies like the Houthis, Hezbollah, and even Hamas. Saudi Arabia stood firm, not only protecting itself but also its allies. In 2011, Bahrain invited the Peninsula Shield Force to combat an ayatollah-regime-backed movement to destabilize and hijack Bahrain. I, for months, witnessed how the Ayatollahs, through their proxies in Bahrain, attempted a coup in my beloved country, and I acknowledge and appreciate how the Peninsula Shield crossed the bridge and helped save my country from the dream of expansion. This commitment to regional stability highlights the Kingdom's leadership role in the Arab world. While Iran is grappling with economic failure and the daily oppression of its people, Saudi Arabia is undergoing a renaissance—economically, socially, and culturally.

The rapid growth of the entertainment industry has brought global celebrities and major events to the Kingdom, transforming its cultural landscape. As someone who once lived just twenty minutes from the Eastern Province, I never imagined witnessing such a change. This transformation will undoubtedly inspire neighboring countries to pursue similar paths of modernization.

AlUla has emerged as a global historical destination, and Riyadh Boulevard has become a hub for international stars and cultural events. These achievements are not superficial; they reflect a nation that is opening by listening to its youth and delivering on their aspirations. As a mother of three young men, I cannot just see the introduction of entertainment on such a high level merely as something trivial, but I see it as giving young people a life, freedom.

Saudi Vision 2030 has already surpassed several of its milestones ahead of schedule—for example, reaching the target unemployment rate of 7 percent in 2025—demonstrating the Kingdom's unwavering momentum and the bright future that lies ahead.

On May 13, 2025, President Trump begins his first international tour since his November 2024 election with a trip to the Middle East, which will take him to several Arab countries in the region. The first place he visits is Saudi Arabia, where he meets with the Crown Prince—a highly symbolic choice. He views the Kingdom as the cornerstone of his Middle East diplomacy and sees the Crown Prince as a key global leader, particularly in the pursuit of peace. His message aligns with sentiments previously expressed by former British Prime Minister Boris Johnson, who stated during the 2025 Saudi Media Forum that "the world should learn from Saudi Arabia's experience"[2] and recognize the country's rapid overall transformation, calling it an essential global player in today's major international challenges.[3] President Trump is laudatory for the changes he observes, eight years after his first official visit, both in terms of the modernization of the cities and the Saudi society as a whole. He declares himself impressed by the work accomplished by the Crown Prince and calls for deepening trade relations between the United States and Saudi Arabia, beyond

---

2   "Saudi Arabia set to become world's top tourism destination: Boris Johnson," February 19, 2025, https://www.argaam.com/en/article/articledetail/id/1791469.

3   "Boris Johnson at the Saudi Media Forum: The Kingdom Has Become a Global Political Hub," February 19, 2025, https://saudimf.sa/en/media-center/a103b985-37e5-444f-8c0b-0445d468a1d9.

the existing trade agreements whose total value is estimated at one trillion dollars. He praises the Kingdom's diplomacy in advancing peace,[4] a theme he emphasizes at length in his speech.

The Crown Prince's visionary approach, largely unrecognized in the West, is embraced by those acquainted with the genuine societal reforms unfolding in Saudi Arabia. This book offers a well-reasoned perspective on the sagacious governance of a statesman frequently criticized in the West yet regarded by many as a pivotal Arab leader capable of fostering peace in a region often misunderstood by Western nations.

---

4   "President Trump Participates in a U.S.-Saudi Investment Forum," The White House, May 13, 2025, https://www.youtube.com/watch?v=wj1QOz3iuCE.

Preface

The inaugural reflections presented here delve into the theories of the distinguished American intellectual, Samuel Huntington, particularly his idea of a "clash of civilizations." Central to our inquiry is this: In the vast expanse of international interactions, is there ample room for mutual comprehension? Are we, as global citizens, truly invested in recognizing others as our equals, in spite of our myriad differences?

Our paths have intertwined for many years, leading to countless exchanges on our perceptions of the world. Our professional journeys have taken us to distant lands, allowing encounters with diverse cultures, all of which have indelibly shaped our perspectives. While raw facts often stand unyielding, analysis can be mutable. To us, it appears that the cultural nuance is frequently absent in global dialogues. Ignorance, intolerance, and willful disparagement are descriptors we find apt for international pundits who lambast individuals or entities. While sometimes merited, at other times, their methodology raises eyebrows.

Should we assume that international relations are rooted in power dynamics where escalating quality equates to heightened competition, then such fervor implies our collective negligence in truly striving to understand "the other." Our conclusions, though based on facts, prejudices, and interpretations, might lack depth and surely omit cultural contexts. Utopian systems remain elusive, yet each can evolve, progress, and embed itself in a forward-moving trajectory that prioritizes respect over political, economic, or strategic agendas. Still, transformations are not instantaneous. Every substantial change demands foresight, planning, and meticulous execution. Building anything of worth takes time, and the underpinnings—those foundational elements—mustn't be overlooked, for they determine the resilience and enduring nature of what's built atop.

We consider our varied professional exposures invaluable. In the West, it is often posited that travels educate the young; but more crucially, they open one's eyes to global happenings, challenging preconceived notions and pushing for a deep dive into alien societies to truly grasp them. For us, this endeavor embodies genuine respect.

Before we cast judgments, we strive for understanding. Yet, the inherent unpredictability of diplomacy and politics complicates our disciplines. Our analysis leans on discernible patterns—specifically those consistent and enduring. Our insights also draw from a deep understanding of decision-making hierarchies, influential networks, and negotiation mechanics.

Our gaze then settles on the Kingdom of Saudi Arabia, particularly its Crown Prince, His Royal Highness (H.R.H.) Mohammed bin Salman bin Abdulaziz Al Saud, also known as MBS. Celebrated within his homeland, according to our concordant information, he draws significant skepticism in the West.

According to discussions with various denizens of the Kingdom, he seems to emerge as a reformist, a visionary, and an architect of the future. Yet, the Western lens often casts him as a cagey and inscrutable leader. A cursory scan of Western media outlets attests to the divisive opinions about him, with commendations being scant. Our intent here is not to rehash critiques made by others or to dwell on the past, but to bring forth a nuanced understanding.

The Crown Prince's overarching vision and the trajectory of governance he seeks to implement deserve a meticulous study. While critics abound, it is vital to objectively assess his tangible achievements both domestically and internationally while considering the difficulties of implementation. A case in point is the frequent oversight of his role in seeking sustainable peace within the Middle East, Africa, and Eastern Europe. Furthermore, his strides in reshaping the national global governance bear profound implications, inside and outside the purview of Saudi Arabia.

In 2016, the Crown Prince heralded the Vision 2030 program: an ambitious blueprint for a comprehensive transformation of the Kingdom of Saudi Arabia. This initiative maps out diverse objectives across economic, political, and societal terrains, with clear national ambitions and international aspirations. While the global perception often reduces Saudi Arabia to an opulent oil-rich nation, underpinned by its sovereign wealth fund,[1] the true essence of

---

1   The Public Investment Fund, commonly referred to as PIF, stands as one of the world's largest sovereign wealth funds. As of 2022, its assets under management surpassed an impressive total of $620 billion.

Vision 2030 lies in strategizing for a post-oil era. Indeed, oil is an invaluable asset for the Kingdom, yet the Crown Prince perceives an impending exigency: the need to wean the nation off this sole reliance. Such dependence, tethered to the volatile global oil market and the finite nature of the resource, is a precarious security risk. Thus, his vision encapsulates a pivot toward a privatized, diversified economy, bolstered by societal reforms targeting a modernized Saudi socioeconomic landscape.

In the Western hemisphere, the audacity and foresight of Vision 2030 often go unrecognized or misunderstood. Detractors raise eyebrows at the feasibility of the program and its financing, given the colossal investments it necessitates, both from domestic and international quarters.

Yet, our examination of this program adopts a unique lens. The Crown Prince's ability to introduce such a groundbreaking vision in a traditionally conservative nation represents nothing short of a bold gamble. His actions reveal an astute analytical prowess, evident when he astounded global spectators by brokering negotiations with formidable entities like China and Iran to stabilize diplomatic ties between Riyadh and Tehran through Beijing's mediation. Such successful diplomatic maneuvering, rooted in pragmatism, underscores his adaptability to the ever-evolving global landscape. As for Beijing, the West now identifies the Chinese capital as the main current threat to world order, an opinion shared by several American and British intelligence chiefs, which tends to recognize the fragmentation of the international community.[2]

Undoubtedly, the journey of nation-building is not a solitary endeavor. The Crown Prince is flanked by an ensemble of influential figures, each recognized for their adeptness in steering diverse realms—be it ministries, corporations, or religious bodies. Prominent among these allies are Prince Abdulaziz bin Salman Al Saud, brother to the Crown Prince and Kingdom's Minister of Energy, Prince Khalid bin Salman Al Saud, brother to the Crown Prince and the Kingdom's Defense Minister; His Excellency Mr. Yasir bin Othman Al-Rumayyan, steward of the Public Investment Fund

---

2   John Paul Rathbone, "Ukraine's Kursk offensive has triggered doubts among Russian elite, spy chiefs say," September 7, 2024, https://www.ft.com/content/56d16869-f9e1-4c82-8022-5f8d2044c5cd.

(PIF, the Saudi public sovereign fund) and head of Saudi Aramco's board; Sheikh Muhammad bin Abdul Karim Al-Issa, the erstwhile Justice Minister now helming the Muslim World League (MWL); His Excellency Mr. Turki bin Abdul Mohsen Al Al-Sheikh, an advisor at the Royal Court; Prince Abdulaziz bin Turki Al-Faisal Al Saud, tasked with Sports; Prince Badr bin Abdullah bin Mohammed bin Fahran Al Saud, overseeing Culture; Mrs. Sarah Al-Suhami, chairperson of Tadawul (the Saudi Arabian stock exchange); Prince Abdullah bin Bandar bin Abdulaziz Al Saud, managing the National Guard; Princess Reema bint Bandar Al Saud, Ambassador of Saudi Arabia to the United States; and Mr. Bader Al-Asaker, Head of the Private Office of HRH The Crown Prince. These illustrious figures, while instrumental, represent just a segment of the broader coalition buttressing the transformative aspirations of Vision 2030.

The Crown Prince's modus operandi is a delicate blend of caution and ambition. He does not rush things and works to make them evolve smoothly. While he fervently drives reforms, he strongly stands against radicalism. His strategy reflects a mature understanding of societal dynamics: ushering change too swiftly can unmoor a society from its foundational values. Thus, he eschews impulsiveness, refraining from an abrupt restructuring that could potentially unsettle the very fabric of Saudi society. Instead, he personifies the quintessential statesman: a visionary who not only conceives but meticulously orchestrates the future trajectory of Saudi Arabia. By delineating, advocating, and then meticulously enacting, he lays the groundwork for a post-oil Saudi Arabia, prepped to thrive in a contemporary milieu. While monumental, his initiatives are often understated in their acknowledgment, with many perhaps unaware of the true extent of his accomplishments.

Historically, his legacy will be etched as a master planner, an individual unafraid to redefine the conceivable. Come 2029, Saudi Arabia, under his auspices, is set to host the Asian Winter Games in Neom—a once-barren desert now earmarked for a groundbreaking megalopolis. This colossal endeavor is not merely an infrastructural marvel but stands as a testament to the Crown Prince's vision for Saudi Arabia. In 2030, Riyadh will host the World Expo (Riyadh 2030) an event of planetary proportions, while Saudi Arabia won the bid to organize the Fédération Internationale de Football Association (FIFA)[3] World Cup in 2034. And while the grandeur is palpable, it is far from mere ostentation. Every move, every decision, echoes a carefully crafted global strategy, devoid of excess but rich in intention.

—Frederic & Thierry

---

3   FIFA stands for Fédération Internationale de Football Association. In early November 2023, following Australia's withdrawal from the bidding process to host the 2034 FIFA World Cup, Saudi Arabia remained the sole candidate. In December 2024, FIFA officially awarded the hosting rights for the 2034 World Cup to Saudi Arabia.

Introduction

An old Arab adage suggests, *Time rules those who do not master it.* Time, in its unyielding nature, persists as the ultimate adjudicator for the Kingdom of Saudi Arabia. Beyond pride or resistance, it is the singular constant the nation seeks to harmonize with. For, in a nation steered by its kings, the descendants of Ibn Saud, who act with a vision for its people's longevity and prosperity, time becomes the crucible of progress. Progress, however, is never a given—it must be persistently nurtured. While foresight does not promise success, it exemplifies wisdom—the keystone in laying the foundation of a resilient legacy that withstands time's inexorable march.

In the vast tableau of global dynamics, we find ourselves amidst tumultuous shifts. The interplay among leading nations unravels the intricate weave of a global tapestry, rich in its myriad cultures. By "culture," we refer not just to traditions and customs but also the political, economic, military, and diplomatic ideologies—offshoots of collective heritages. Nothing remains set in stone; nations evolve, ideologies shift. In such a fluid landscape, visionary leadership, one that not only responds to the present but also paves the way for the future, becomes imperative. Yet, in this intriguing game of statecraft, complacency is the nemesis; every accomplishment must be earned.

Within an international community made up of 193 member states of the United Nations (UN), there are profound disparities. These disparities are political, economic, diplomatic, cultural, demographic, and military in nature. Throughout history, the world has always known dominant powers. Power struggles and shifting balances have consistently driven international relations. Empires have risen and fallen for a variety of reasons.

Today, in an increasingly globalized and interconnected environment, we are witnessing an extraordinary transformation in international relations. Over the past century, the global community has gone through major periods of turmoil and significant shifts in global power. After two world wars, the Western world rebuilt itself—though not without consequences. Colonial empires disappeared after the end of World War II. A multitude of new independent states emerged on the international stage. The Cold War, lasting four decades, symbolized the ideological confrontation between East and West, which ultimately ended in victory for the latter three decades ago. In the aftermath of this long struggle, the United States emerged as the overwhelmingly dominant global power. At the time, no one appeared capable of challenging its political, economic, military, or cultural leadership. Never before had a country exercised such supremacy in history. All signs pointed to a reign that would last. That was yesterday.

Since then, the world has changed dramatically. Many former certainties or beliefs have been swept away by the tides of history. When the Soviet Union collapsed, who would have predicted the resurgence of Russia just a decade later? And what about the economic rise of China in barely a quarter of a century? In the 1990s, the Western world saw it as an emerging economy. Today, China challenges American economic dominance—and it is not alone. Other countries, such as India, are asserting themselves and openly expressing their political and economic ambitions. This is reshaping global power dynamics. A major political and economic rivalry now opposes the United States and China. But more importantly, we must recognize that we now live in a multipolar and multicultural world. By "multipolar," we mean that Western domination[1] is increasingly challenged by growing international competition. The rivalry mentioned above seems likely to persist, but other regions of the world are also beginning to reject dominant paradigms in protest. As for the multicultural dimension, Western standards no longer impose themselves as they once did. International actors are asserting their unique characteristics and expressing them openly. They are demanding respect. They are increasingly resistant to relationships marked by domination or external interference. They speak out freely because they are independent and sovereign. All of them have that right. Yet many complain of interference orchestrated by foreign powers. Clearly, not all states compete in the same weight class. Each one defends its own interests. However, any dominant actor risks a serious misjudgment by

---

1   By Western domination, we mean a group of states including the United States, Canada, the member countries of the European Union, the United Kingdom, Japan, South Korea, and Australia. This is not an exhaustive list.

imagining it can coerce or subjugate others it considers weaker. We all make mistakes, but the most valuable lesson is not to repeat them—and above all, not to underestimate one's counterpart.

In such a fragmented world, dialogue remains essential. It is crucial to try to understand one another and accept our differences. One would think this appeal should be self-evident within the international community, yet that community appears increasingly divided. Moreover, states rarely act alone. They form political, economic, or military alliances. They pool their strengths and capabilities to defend shared interests and, when necessary, to counter competing or rival powers.

The Kingdom of Saudi Arabia operates within this global environment, aiming to play an increasingly influential role in the world's major political, economic, and other strategic affairs. It is ambitious and has equipped itself with the necessary means to fulfill those ambitions. It is building from within and extending outward. Above all, it understands the reality in which it operates. It does not intend to submit to anyone. It acts independently. It stands by its ideas and its positions. That is what the Kingdom of Saudi Arabia is striving to implement.

For a long time, the country's wealth was based on the exploitation and sale of a highly coveted natural resource: oil. Saudi Arabia holds vast reserves and has skillfully capitalized on them to modernize and establish itself as a key player in international relations. For decades, it has ranked among the world's top three oil producers alongside the United States and Russia, while global demand for oil has continued to rise. Today, worldwide production exceeds 100 million barrels per day, even as the international community grows increasingly concerned about the environmental consequences of over-consumption. As a result, efforts are being made to reduce the role of fossil fuels in the global energy mix. In short, there is growing support for a gradual decarbonization of the global economy.

At first glance, this might not bode well for Saudi Arabia. In reality, the Kingdom is already preparing for the future, having recognized the dangers of relying too heavily on a single commodity. While the oil sector remains its primary economic engine, the country is thinking beyond oil and actively advocating for a diversification of its economic model. For over a decade, it has become increasingly clear that excessive dependence on oil revenues poses

a risk to the long-term sustainability of the national economy. This was particularly evident when oil prices began to drop. The emergence of American shale
oil on the global market and the dramatic decline in global demand during
the COVID-19 pandemic exposed the fragility of economic models that rely
heavily on a single commodity with volatile prices. Although Saudi oil remains
in high demand, that does not shield the country from economic challenges
when global conditions are unfavorable. Yet, even during such difficult times,
Saudi Arabia has consistently remained a key interlocutor for the world's major
political powers.

In April 2016, as oil prices continued their decline that had begun
in 2014, US President Barack Obama traveled to Saudi Arabia just a few
months before the presidential election that would later be won by Donald
Trump. During his visit, the head of state delivered a speech that surprised
his audience when he announced his intention to reestablish dialogue with
Iran on the nuclear issue. Whether seen as a bold and principled diplomatic
move or a diplomatic misstep, the president defended his vision of diplomacy—despite knowing the adversarial nature of relations between Tehran and
Riyadh at the time. From the Saudi perspective, such a statement felt like a
show of disrespect, if not outright betrayal. One man openly expressed his
disapproval: His Royal Highness Mohammed bin Salman bin Abdulaziz Al
Saud, who was then serving as Minister of Defense and Chairman of the
Council of Economic and Development Affairs. He would later become
Crown Prince in June 2017 and Prime Minister in September of that same
year.

The realities of international relations meant that, despite the deterioration of ties between the two countries, shared strategic interests kept Washington and Riyadh connected—even as that connection teetered on the brink of
rupture. A few months later, the unlikely figure of Donald Trump, a political
newcomer, secured the Republican nomination and earned the privilege of
facing off against Democratic candidate Hillary Clinton, who had been the
clear favorite in polls and the media. Against all expectations, the well-known
businessman defied predictions and took up residence at 1600 Pennsylvania
Avenue in Washington, DC. After his inauguration in January 2017, Trump
waited several weeks before undertaking his first trip abroad. Symbolically,
his first international destination was Saudi Arabia—even before heading to

Brussels for a NATO[2] summit and then to Sicily for a G7 meeting. The choice of Saudi Arabia was no coincidence. For Donald Trump, it was essential to restore strong relations between the United States and Saudi Arabia. He made no secret of his desire to avoid reengagement with Iran and instead show unwavering firmness toward it. In his view, two key priorities in the Middle East stood out: rebuilding a solid alliance with Riyadh and securing strong political ties with Israel.

With hindsight, which event stood out as the main diplomatic achievement of Trump's term? This diplomacy culminated in the Abraham Accords in 2020, a peace agreement that aimed to normalize relations between Israel and several Arab nations: the United Arab Emirates and Bahrain, later joined by Morocco and Sudan. In essence, it was a momentous diplomatic achievement under Trump's administration, which took place only a few months prior to the November 2020 presidential election. However, burdened by the perceived mismanagement of the COVID-19 pandemic, the American electorate cast their faith in Joe Biden, who had been the vice president during the Obama administration. Regarding foreign policy, the seasoned senator from Delaware swiftly aligned with the strategies and vision of his former superior in the US executive hierarchy.

Riyadh was unmistakably disheartened by this direction. Opting to diverge from the capricious nature of its diplomatic rapport with the United States, the Kingdom set its gaze on alternative dialogue partners. In a move that stunned Western observers, China, in March 2023, proclaimed that it had orchestrated a diplomatic rendezvous in Beijing between Iran and Saudi Arabia. The achievement was not merely facilitating dialogue between two traditionally antagonistic nations, but rather the monumental revelation that Riyadh and Tehran harbored aspirations to swiftly normalize both diplomatic and economic ties. In the corridors of power across North America and Europe, there was a palpable sense of astonishment. Some even drew parallels with the cinematic narrative of *Good Bye, Lenin!*[3] pondering the inflection

---

2   NATO is the acronym for the North Atlantic Treaty Organization. Established in 1949, this international organization unites European and North American countries with the aim of ensuring the freedom and security of its member states through both political and military measures.

3   In this 2003 film directed by Wolfgang Becker, the narrative unfolds around an East

points of their missteps. How had they faltered where China had just executed
a spectacular and unforeseen diplomatic coup? Evidently, they had miscalcu-
lated the unyielding vision of a man set on propelling his nation into a new
global epoch: Crown Prince Mohammed bin Salman bin Abdulaziz Al Saud.

Yet, in 2023, the diplomatic world was caught off guard. Under the aegis
of China, historic adversaries Iran and Saudi Arabia convened in Beijing. Not
only did the meeting signify an unprecedented gesture reconciliation, but it
also spotlighted China's burgeoning influence in global diplomacy. The West,
accustomed to its diplomatic primacy, was left grappling with questions of its
missteps and miscalculations. Where had they faltered, and where China succeeded? At the epicenter of these seismic shifts stood Crown Prince Mohammed bin Salman bin Abdulaziz Al Saud.

Emanating from a lineage that was the bedrock of the Saudi monarchy,
son of King Salman bin Abdulaziz Al Saud, and grandson of King Abdulaziz
bin Abdul Rahman Al Saud, also known in the Western world as Ibn Saud,
Mohammed bin Salman's ascendancy in global attention began in 2015.
Appointed as the Minister of Defense, his age and relative inexperience juxtaposed starkly against the backdrop of a tumultuous Middle East.

However, rather than being a fleeting decision, his appointment proved to
be an indicator of Saudi Arabia's intent. His responsibilities quickly expanded
beyond defense, and by April 2015, he was steering the Kingdom's Economical
and Development Affairs Council. His role grew to encompass key strategic
sectors, heralding an era where he would play a pivotal role in shaping Saudi
Arabia's present and future. Undeniably, Prince Mohammed bin Salman's trajectory has been nothing short of astounding. In a complex geopolitical stage,
rife with volatility, he emerged not just as a national leader but as a figure
whose decisions would reverberate across the international community.

The Vision 2030 program introduced by Crown Prince Mohammed bin
Salman in 2016 was nothing short of ambitious. The plan's heart beat with

---

German Berlin family during the seventies and eighties. The mother, a devoted communist
activist, experiences a heart attack just days before the fall of the Berlin Wall, slipping into
a coma. When she awakens months later in a reunified Germany with the communist era
now a part of history, her son and family, in an attempt to shield her from further health
complications, embark on a mission to conceal the truth. They weave a delicate facade,
convincing her that nothing has changed since the moment of her heart attack.

the rhythm of diversification, attempting to steer Saudi Arabia away from its deep-seated reliance on oil. But this vision was introduced at an inopportune moment, when the oil market was far from bullish. The plummeting oil prices threatened the feasibility of this grand vision, leading many international analysts to cast aspersions on the initiative. They believed Saudi Arabia, with its declining revenues from oil, would find it difficult to finance this transition.

Yet the Crown Prince, undeterred by these concerns and driven by unwavering conviction, aimed to bring not just economic but also societal transformation to the Kingdom. The country's international image had been of a deeply conservative nation, resistant to change. But here was the Crown Prince, charging forward with a clear intent to modernize, not just in terms of economy but also in societal norms, setting the nation on a new trajectory.

His rapid ascent to power, marked by his appointment as the Chairman of the Council of Political and Security Affairs in 2017 and subsequently as the Crown Prince, only served to magnify his influence. However, this swift climb was accompanied by skepticism. Doubts loomed large over his youth and inexperience. Would it be an impediment or an asset?

In the face of a daunting economic landscape, the newly enthroned Crown Prince remained unwavering in his commitment to steer his nation toward modernity. His vision was not merely confined to economic rejuvenation; it encapsulated a broader ambition to revamp a society known globally for its conservative mores. His objectives were crystal clear: to instigate meaningful change and align his country with the contemporary zeitgeist. This encompassed navigating the intricacies of governance amidst the whirlwind of swift alterations in global dynamics.

From an external vantage point, the proliferation of the Crown Prince's national duties invariably sparked a plethora of inquiries. Would his relative youthfulness be a detriment? However, the international community soon grasped the depth of his resolve to champion what he deemed essential and propitious for his nation. In the realm of global affairs, his audacious choices often caught many off guard, leading to reactions that ranged from acceptance to bafflement.

The events of March 2020 provided a telling answer. Amidst the COVID-19 crisis, with the world reeling under its implications, the oil market suffered. The demand-supply mismatch drove prices down, and the problem of storage loomed ominously. Saudi Arabia successfully overcame the challenge, with oil being its primary source of revenue.

And then, in a move that astounded the global community, the Crown Prince turned aggressive, ramping up oil production, even when the world was grappling with an oversupply.[4] The immediate consequence was a tussle with Russia over oil strategy, and an already beleaguered market was flooded with more oil.

The effects were almost immediate and cataclysmic. Oil prices, in an unprecedented move, dipped into the negative. A situation where sellers were, in theory, paying buyers to take the oil off their hands. The fallout of this strategy was felt far and wide. In the United States, the oil industry, which had been a significant supporter of President Trump, faced shutdowns and massive layoffs. The political repercussions for Trump, who was already managing a health crisis, were significant. His advocacy for low oil prices had backfired spectacularly.

In the midst of this, the Crown Prince's strategy came into sharp focus. Rather than being an impulsive decision, it appeared to be a meticulously orchestrated move to assert Saudi Arabia's influence and importance on the global stage.

By influencing the market dynamics and compelling other players to react, the Crown Prince was sending out a powerful message: Saudi Arabia, under his leadership, would not be a passive player, bending to the whims of global powers. It was a strategy that many initially failed to grasp. But with time, it became clear that the Crown Prince, with his decisions and maneuvers, was scripting a narrative of a resurgent and assertive Saudi Arabia, determined to claim its rightful place in global geopolitics.

In prior discussions, reference was made to the Abraham Accords, to which Saudi Arabia was not a direct party. This warrants further explanation, particularly in light of the Crown Prince's assertive global vision. Several damaging episodes, notably the death of journalist Jamal Khashoggi, drew widespread criticism and was followed by a trial where figures who were involved were held accountable for their actions.

In 2019, the United States suggested that Saudi Arabia assume guardianship of the Islamic Holy Places in Jerusalem, a duty then held by the Hashemite

---

4   This oil battle is described at length in chapter 9.

Kingdom of Jordan under King Abdullah II. The world has witnessed for decades how Saudi Arabia protects the Holy sites of Mecca and Medina.

However, King Abdullah II resisted this proposal that made sense, given the complex domestic dynamics of Jordan. Predominantly made up of individuals of Palestinian origin[5] and grappling with significant unemployment, the Jordanian public would likely have perceived the abdication of this sacred duty as a betrayal of King Hussein's legacy. Notwithstanding various enhancements to the US proposal, including the mooted Jerusalem-Riyadh rail link[6] funded jointly by the international community and Saudi Arabia, the initiative fell through.

Although the prospect of overseeing Jerusalem's Islamic holy sites appealed to the Crown Prince, he respected the Jordanian King's desire. It is notable that, given the trajectory of Saudi-Israeli ties, Israel wouldn't have opposed the Crown Prince's stewardship over these sites.[7] The Crown Prince's laudable efforts in fortifying Mecca's and assuring the safety of pilgrims during *hajj*, i.e., the pilgrimage, are acknowledged and valued.

To understand the Crown Prince's stance, one must delve into the religious significance of Jerusalem in Islam. The city, revered alongside Mecca and Medina, holds immense historical and spiritual gravitas. Mecca, the "Mother of the Cities," the birthplace of Prophet Muhammad, is the epicenter of Islamic spirituality. Medina, or the "illuminated city," is the Prophet's resting place. Jerusalem, known to Muslims as the "Holy House" and "Holy City" afterward, has deep significance for all three Abrahamic faiths. For Muslims, it is the commencement point of Prophet Muhammad's nocturnal journey and was the initial qibla (the direction of prayer). The symbolic nexus connects to the "noble sanctuary" that overlooks the ancient Temple of King Solomon in which lie

---

5   The recurring escalations of tension between Israel and the Palestinian Authority are an exceedingly delicate matter for Jordan. Although it is difficult to estimate precisely the proportion of the national population of Palestinian descent, various sources estimate it between 60 percent and 75 percent.

6   Israel has expressed its support for the American proposal to designate Saudi Arabia and its Crown Prince as custodians of the Muslim holy sites in Jerusalem. The preexisting railway line that connects the cities of Jerusalem and Medina inspired this proposal.

7   Recent events, following the events of October 7, 2023, in Israel, are analyzed in chapters 17 and 18.

the Dome of the Rock and the Al-Aqsa Mosque.[8] On the outskirts of Medina, the Quba Mosque stands, facing two directions—one toward Mecca and the other toward Jerusalem. Every devout pilgrim is expected to visit the mosque, as Jerusalem was the primary direction for prayer for a span of eighteen months.

Jerusalem's storied past, replete with interreligious tensions,[9] underscores the Crown Prince's chagrin at not assuming the guardianship role over such sacred Muslim sites. The city's multifaceted historical, ethnic, and religious tapestry remains pivotal to many geopolitical dynamics in the Middle East. Though Islam emerged after Judaism and Christianity, it acknowledges and respects other faiths.[10] Islam, for instance, extols Judaism's contributions toward the moral evolution of humanity, emphasizing one's covenant with God, liberation narratives such as the Exodus, and the overarching promise.[11] These doctrines enshrine the core idea: every individual should be receptive to divine calls, acknowledging God's capability to emancipate all from subjugation, and upholding his decrees to foster a world bound by divine covenants.[12]

The Crown Prince stands poised to assume a definitive leadership role in the region, championing both sustainable peace and security. Given Saudi Arabia's significant religious and cultural influence in the Muslim world, his authority is firmly anchored. This authority is further fortified by his strategic diplomatic choices and positioning.

In a 2022 interview with the renowned American publication *The Atlantic*,

---

8   "La Mecque et Médine," *Les Essentiels*, https://essentiels.bnf.fr/fr/image/ff4fa9bf -a1bc-4da5-9c52-f910546ad499-mecque-et-medine, consulted on August 2, 2023.

9   Authors' note: It is often overlooked that the issues surrounding Jerusalem are tripartite, as they involve the followers and practitioners of the three major monotheistic religions. In the late eleventh century of the Gregorian era, Christians initiated the First Crusade, a series of military expeditions that continued into the late thirteenth century, aimed at challenging Muslim dominance in Jerusalem. These events created conflicts between Christians and Muslims and featured prominent historical figures such as Saladin (1138–1193), the first ruler of the Ayyubid dynasty; Richard the Lionheart (1157–1199), the King of England; and Saint Louis (1214–1270), more commonly known as Louis IX, the King of France.

10   Reference made to Sura 2, verse 285 (2:285) of the Quran, which explicitly confirms this recognition.

11   Djelloul Seddiki delivered a lecture titled "Sur l'expansion de l'Islam" at the Institut Élie Wiesel in Paris on April 10, 2019.

12   Ibid.

the Crown Prince delved deep into his vision for Saudi society and the pivotal transformations underway.[13] His insights and directives are set to indelibly influence theological and intellectual paradigms. Distinctively, he has tackled challenging dogmatic questions and intellectual debates—subjects many leaders and scholars have avoided, fearing *fitna*.[14] His approach to reform, characterized by its finesse and judicious selection of terminology, would have been deemed unthinkable merely a decade ago.

Signifying his determination, the Crown Prince eschews terms like "moderate" or "renewed" when referencing his vision of Islam. Instead, he opts for "authentic," epitomized by the Arabic expression *al-Assil,* symbolizing a return to the foundational tenets of Islam. Drawing from Sura 2, verse 256 of the Quran, which proclaims "there is no compulsion in religion," he emphasizes a long-overlooked freedom. His intent is clear: to transcend a past marked by constraints and redirect Saudi society away from historical burdens that predominantly served erstwhile ruling dynasties.[15] Opening the avenues for *ijtihad*[16]—an in-depth interpretation based on the Quran and the Prophet's teachings—becomes pivotal. Essentially, the focus is on interpretations that align with Quranic doctrines, the *sirra,* and benefit the wider community, the *ummah.*

The Crown Prince's discourse with *The Atlantic* was distinguished by its candidness. In contrast to the typical guarded rhetoric of state leaders on sensitive subjects, he displayed refreshing transparency. He navigated the weight of

---

13   "Full transcript of Crown Prince interview on reforms, religious, future of Saudi Arabia and relations with US," March 3, 2022, https://saudigazette.com.sa/article/617738. Authors' note: this lengthy interview is a fundamental part of the Crown Prince's vision and public policies. It highlights the depth of the reforms undertaken, which remain largely undervalued and even misunderstood outside the Kingdom's borders. We therefore affirm that the Crown Prince's work as a builder is historic. He is promoting what had never been done before, what no one had dared to initiate. This demonstrates his unfailing determination to lead Saudi Arabia into a new era in which he justifies his decisions with a more authentic interpretation of the precepts of the Quran.

14   Discord.

15   The Umayyads from 661 to 750, the Abbasids from 750 to 1258, and then the Ottomans from 1258 to 1921.

16   *Ijtihad* refers to the process of thinking of Islamic scholars, including Ulama, muftis, and other scholars, engaging in critical thinking and interpretation of the foundational texts of Islam. Through this process, they derive legal principles and provide guidance to all Muslims regarding the nature and permissibility of specific actions.

history, charted the course for the future, and underscored the urgent need for societal evolution to align with contemporary Saudi aspirations. Envisioning an economic road map spanning three decades, he emphasizes investment, tourism, and cultural enrichment to cater to the diverse facets of the Saudi populace. His dialogue is less about embracing novel rhetoric and more about updating religious understandings. The Crown Prince envisions a faith liberated from antiquated doctrines, one where believers are emancipated from undue reverence for individuals and realigned with the core relationship with the Prophet and his four wise immediate successors.

This is no ordinary media appearance. The Crown Prince's message transparently showcases an extensive intellectual journey, one he meticulously oversees. Concurrently, the establishment of research institutions and specialized workshops strives to crystallize his enlightened perspective on religion and the sciences, especially concerning hadith studies.[17] An assembly of distinguished scholars spearheads these initiatives. The potential global influence of this comprehensive intellectual and religious work is immense, especially given today's volatile global scenario. Should he succeed in amplifying this vision—a vision resonating with a significant silent majority—it promises to align closely with the Quran's teachings and the Sunna[18] of the Prophet. At its core, the Crown Prince's vision champions an authentic Islam. Yet, we believe that this perspective remains largely misinterpreted by the West. We stand at a potential historical juncture, with the Crown Prince's influence becoming increasingly evident. We're witnessing something momentous.

Several shifts in global politics are noteworthy. In December 2022, Chinese President Xi Jinping visited Riyadh, meeting with Arabian Gulf state leaders. He declared an intent to transact oil and gas purchases in yuan[19]—a move that had been speculated for some time. Clearly, Beijing aims to undermine the US dollar's dominance in global trade. This move is strategic, considering

---

17 Hadith refers to the oral communications of the Prophet and, more generally, to all the traditions relating to the words and deeds of the Prophet and companions.

18 The Sunna refers to the tradition and practices of the Prophet. It refers to what the Prophet's contemporaries followed and passed on to subsequent generations.

19 Maha El Dahan, Aziz El Yaakoubi, "China's Xi calls for oil trade in yuan at Gulf summit in Riyadh," Reuters, December 10, 2022, https://www.reuters.com/world/saudi-arabia-gathers-chinas-xi-with-arab-leaders-new-era-ties-2022-12-09/.

the current tension between the United States and Saudi Arabia on issues like human rights, energy, and Russia. The Crown Prince contemplates President Xi's proposition, recognizing its potential repercussions on US economic strategies.

Boasting vast oil reserves and strategically positioned at the confluence of three continents, Saudi Arabia possesses significant global influence—an advantage not lost on the Crown Prince. While the West might misconstrue his intentions, he has an unwavering goal: to modernize the Saudi economy, instigate lasting domestic reforms, and champion regional peace amidst persistent turmoil. The war in Gaza is just the latest avatar, not to mention the bloody conflict in Sudan and some others in the region. The closer ties with nations like China and Iran reflect more than mere diplomatic shifts—they signal a strategic recalibration in addressing conflicts that Western interventions have yet to resolve.

The Crown Prince's communicative style is definitive and clear. Recognizing Saudi Arabia's international clout, he endeavors to amplify this leverage. His standpoint is clear: while he remains open to dialogue, he will not kowtow to external pressures. Saudi Arabia's geopolitical stance could redefine the power dynamics between the United States and China. Many global policymakers might underestimate the Kingdom's leverage, but the astute leader knows otherwise. As the world watches intently, the Crown Prince holds pivotal cards, poised to redefine his burgeoning leadership.

1

From Tribes to the Modern Kingdom: The Formation of Saudi Arabia

Encompassing an area close to 2,200,000 square kilometers, Saudi Arabia stands as a regional giant within the Arabian Peninsula, occupying the majority of its expanse.[1] As of 2024, the country boasts nearly 36 million inhabitants, of which nearly a third are foreigners. Yet, how many truly know its national history and the unique characteristics that make it one of the world's key geopolitical centers? Most people primarily associate Saudi Arabia with its economic wealth, derived from the exploitation of its abundant petroleum resources. The Kingdom also holds a unique position in the Arab-Muslim world, forever remaining the birthplace of the Prophet Muhammad, who founded Islam after receiving revelations from the Angel Gabriel in the cave of Hira, located a few kilometers from present-day Mecca in the Hijaz region. This monotheistic religion is now practiced by over 1.5 billion followers worldwide. The holy cities of Mecca and Medina host millions of pilgrims annually, fulfilling one of the five pillars[2] of Islam.

Despite its profound symbolic significance for many Muslims, Saudi Arabia remains relatively unknown to outsiders, who often overlook its rich and complex history that predates the Islamic period. Several ancient Kingdoms coexisted[3] within the Arabian Peninsula. Even Ancient Rome established military garrisons on various islands in the Red Sea. The Nabatean Kingdom, whose capital was the famous city of Petra in present-day Jordan, bequeathed

---

1   The Arabian Peninsula covers an area of almost 3,100,000 square kilometers. In addition to Saudi Arabia, it includes six other countries: Bahrain, the United Arab Emirates, Kuwait, Oman, Qatar and Yemen.

2   The five pillars of Islam are the declaration of faith (*shahada*), prayer (*salah*), alms-giving (*zakat*), fasting during the month of Ramadan (*sawm*), and the pilgrimage (*hajj*).

3   Among the best-known Kingdoms are those of Sheba, Awsān, and Kinda.

remarkable archaeological sites, some of which are located in northern Saudi Arabia and are now part of UNESCO's (United Nations Educational, Scientific and Cultural Organization) World Heritage, such as the site of AlUla, the ancient capital of the Kingdom of Lihyan, situated on the "Incense Trade Route," was a genuine commercial crossroads during antiquity. Archaeologists have uncovered inscriptions in various languages, such as Nabatean, Lihyanite, and Dadanite, which confirm not only a very ancient human presence but also a meeting point for diverse peoples of the region. A few dozen kilometers away, the site of Mada'in Saleh evokes Petra with its monumental rock-carved tombs. This oasis was also on the trade route linking the Nabatean capital to the Hijaz mountains along the Red Sea coast, encompassing contemporary cities like Tabuk, Mecca, Medina, and Jeddah.

Since antiquity, the Arabian Peninsula has been a geographic area conducive to exchanges. Caravanners traversed it, using routes skirting the Red Sea to supply themselves with incense and myrrh from the southern part of the region, which also benefited from the bustling commercial activity of the Indian Ocean. These interactions fostered the growth of various societal activities, including the establishment of legal systems and the flourishing of cultural practices. Tribes met to establish societal rules, resolve disputes through judgments, and practice the art of poetry in the purest form of the Arabic language, Fusha. All these elements had a lasting influence on local populations, benefiting from the dissemination and advancements in the arts and sciences, as well as the spread of Islam. Humans have traveled since ancient times. As Islam spread rapidly over a vast geographical area, including the Middle East, Central Asia, North Africa, and Southern and Eastern Europe (Al-Andalus), several major Arab cities like Baghdad and Damascus gained a prestigious reputation in the known world, thanks to their contributions to arts and sciences. Fields such as medicine, mathematics, astronomy, geography, navigation, and literature saw significant advancements, with Arab civilization bringing forth an unparalleled array of inventions and innovations, perfectly aligned with the original teachings of Islam that advocated for an education combining authenticity and progress.

The predominantly desert terrain of the Arabian Peninsula gave rise to numerous tribes, each cultivating its own unique traditions, some of which endure to this day. These traditions form the very DNA of Saudi society, with the oldest tracing their origins back to antiquity.[4] This diverse dimension is also reflected in the practice of Islam, which is not uniform across the Arabian lands. Some of the contemporary challenges faced by Saudi political leaders stem from this rich historical and cultural heritage, with traditions continuing to play a significant role within the tribes and clans that compose modern Saudi society. Behind the simplistic images of the Kingdom's economic opulence lies a reality where the royal family, descendants of the founder of the modern and unified Kingdom, King Abdulaziz ibn Abdul Rahman Al Saud, also known as Ibn Saud, maintains an unbreakable bond with the desert tradition. The royal family holds the guiding belief that "to lead men, a man must be educated in his own country, among his people, growing up amidst their traditions and understanding the psychology of its inhabitants."[5] This profound principle undoubtedly influenced King Salman in his decision to appoint his son Mohammed as the future monarch. To fully comprehend twenty-first century Saudi Arabia, one must acknowledge the pivotal milestones in the construction of a political society that has been intimately linked to religion for centuries. Often underestimated are the modernizing efforts, both contemplated and executed, by Ibn Saud and his successors since 1953, which we will revisit later.

For centuries, the Arabian Peninsula comprised numerous emirates centered around oases. The tribes, some nomadic and others sedentary, were often pagan. Many Jewish and Christian travelers frequented the region predominantly for commercial purposes, while Muslims converged on the holy cities of Mecca and Medina to undertake their pilgrimage. This region, a genuine cultural and religious crossroads, embraced Islam but also endured the Mongol invasion in the thirteenth century. During this period, the Mamluk sultans, who at the time ruled Egypt and Syria, fighting both Christian crusaders and pagan Mongols, assumed the title of "Servants of the Two Holy Mosques."[6] Ottoman influence became dominant from the late fifteenth century, lasting four centuries. The sultans ruled over the Hijaz region but not the heart of

4   Christian Chesnot, Georges Malbrunot, *MBS confidentiel. Enquête sur le nouveau maître du Moyen-Orient*, éditions Michel Lafon, 2024, p. 109.

5   Ibid., pp. 36–37.

6   Fatiha Dazi-Héni, *L'Arabie saoudite en 100 questions*, Éditions Tallandier, 2020, p. 24

Arabia, particularly the Najd region,[7] where "sedentary emirs and tribal con-federations"[8] retained control over their territories. In this poor and inaccessible desert region of Arabia, an agreement was reached in the eighteenth century between the political authorities of the time and those of the religious sphere. Emir Al Saud was recognized as the political leader of the community,[9] while religious authority was entrusted to a preacher intent on imposing a "true" Islam on the local population, enforcing stringent lifestyle rules that Ibn Saud's descendants have since struggled to moderate. A significant reformative turn occurred in 2016 under King Salman's impetus, limiting the role of the *muttawa*, the authority responsible for enforcing strict lifestyle rules. The Crown Prince aligns with this dynamic promoted by his father and advocates for a vision of authentic Islam, thereby distinguishing himself from the so-called "true" Islam that prevailed following the agreement sealed three centuries ago.

Between the eighteenth century and the prolonged unification process of the modern Kingdom under King Ibn Saud from 1902 to 1932, the Arabian Peninsula experienced various conflicts with the Ottoman occupier. Numerous tribes contested and revolted against Ottoman authority. This period of political instability continued due to internal disagreements within the emirates, all eager to escape Ottoman rule even after the empire's dissolution in 1922, the abolition of the sultanate, and the proclamation of the Turkish Republic in 1923. This context highlights the monumental efforts of Ibn Saud to unify the region into what would become the Kingdom of Saudi Arabia and illustrates the enduring influence of tradition. This historical reality has been keenly considered by the reigning kings since 1932.

Since its unification, Saudi Arabia has experienced remarkable economic growth, primarily fueled by the discovery and exploitation of oil, which has positioned it as a pivotal player in global geopolitics concerning this crucial resource. This natural asset has also cemented its influence on the international

---

7   It corresponds to the central region of the Arabian Peninsula, where the city of Riyadh, the Kingdom's current capital, has developed.

8   Fatiha Dazi-Héni, *L'Arabie saoudite en 100 questions*, Éditions Tallandier, 2020, p. 26.

9   The national history is commonly framed around three distinct phases of the Al Saud state. The first, formally dated 1727, gradually crystallized through a convergence of local authority and religious legitimacy. The second spanned from 1824 to 1891. The third began with the proclamation of the unified Kingdom on September 22, 1932.

political and geopolitical arenas, notably through its significant role in the Organization of the Petroleum Exporting Countries (OPEC), of which Saudi Arabia was a founding member on September 14, 1960, alongside Iran, Iraq, Kuwait, and Venezuela. Nonetheless, from the 1970s through the 1990s, a series of domestic and international developments presented significant challenges for Saudi monarchs to navigate.

The political history of contemporary Saudi Arabia has been marked by several tumultuous periods, particularly the assassination of King Faisal in 1975 by one of his nephews. This monarch, who sought to modernize the Kingdom, encountered severe opposition from the most conservative religious authorities who rejected his initiatives. Subsequently, the Islamic Revolution in Iran in 1979 profoundly influenced religious life in Saudi Arabia, prompting the establishment in 1980 of the Committee for the Promotion of Virtue and the Prevention of Vice. This rigorous, religious police force, known as the *muttawa*, was charged with the strict enforcement of sharia, significantly tightening control over the population's public and private life. Another event in 1979 deeply affected Saudi Arabia and the broader Arab-Muslim world: the seizure of the Grand Mosque in Mecca on November 20 by Salafist extremists who denounced the modernizing policies of the late King Faisal. They called themselves Ikhwān, referencing a tribal militia that the future King Ibn Saud had victoriously subdued in 1929.[10] During the same year, the Pahlavi dynasty was overthrown in Iran and replaced by the ayatollah regime.

In 1979, the Iranian Revolution marked a pivotal turning point in the modern history of the Middle East. The overthrow of the Shah and the rise of an extremist religious regime under Ayatollah Khomeini gave birth to a new model of governance rooted in a revolutionary Shia ideology. This regime sought not only to transform Iran internally but also to export its ideology regionally, leading to the establishment and support of various proxies such as Hezbollah in Lebanon and the Houthis in Yemen. These groups were instrumental in projecting Iranian influence and reshaping regional dynamics.

The ideological ripple effects of the Iranian Revolution were not confined to Shia movements. Sunni extremism also surged in reaction to the perceived success of religious revolution in Iran. Just months after the revolution, the

---

10   Fatiha Dazi-Héni, *L'Arabie saoudite en 100 questions*, Éditions Tallandier, 2020, p. 67.

Juhayman al-Otaybi-led seizure of the Grand Mosque in Mecca in November 1979 demonstrated that Sunni extremists were also inspired by the notion that religious fervor could overthrow ruling regimes and take control of sacred Islamic institutions.

The Grand Mosque Seizure, also known as the Mecca Incident or the Juhayman Affair, was a violent armed attack and siege of the Grand Mosque in Mecca carried out by an extremist group on the 1st of Muharram, 1400 AH[11] (November 20, 1979). Over two hundred armed men stormed the holy mosque—one of the most sacred sites in Islam—claiming the appearance of the Mahdi, a messianic figure in Islamic eschatology. This occurred during the reign of King Khalid bin Abdulaziz and shocked the entire Muslim world. The assault took place at the dawn of the new Hijri century and led to bloodshed within the mosque's courtyard, causing the deaths of civilian worshippers, security personnel, and the attackers themselves. The incident was widely condemned by Muslims around the world, who rejected and opposed the attackers' actions.

Among Sunni Muslims, there is a widely accepted belief—based on a hadith narrated by Abu Dawud[12]—that God will send a renewer (*mujaddid*) for the faith at the head of every century. The hadith states: "Indeed, Allah will send to this ummah at the head of every hundred years someone who will renew its religion." This is considered authentic. Additionally, Muslims believe in the coming of the Mahdi, a descendant of the Prophet Muhammad whose name is said to be Muhammad al-Mahdi, according to certain narrations. To Juhayman al-Otaybi, the leader of the Grand Mosque attack, the equation was complete: A new Hijri century was beginning, and his brother-in-law and companion was named "Muhammad bin Abdullah." Therefore, the Mahdi must take refuge in the Holy Mosque, and the prophecy would be fulfilled.

This ideological framing gave Juhayman's group a sense of religious urgency and legitimacy in their minds, though their actions were widely rejected by mainstream scholars and the Muslim community at large.

Meanwhile, the broader Islamic revival was intensifying. The Muslim

---

11   AH stands for Anno Hegirae, or Hijri year.

12   Abu Dawud (817–889) was a renowned hadith collector and the author of "Sunan Abu Dawud," one of the six canonical hadith collections referenced by Sunni Muslims.

Brotherhood had grown influential in Egypt, Islamic movements were forming across Saudi Arabia and the Arab world, and Islamist activism was rising in Syria. Regionally, the Camp David Accords had just been signed, marking what seemed to be the beginning of Arab recognition of Israel and the end of the era of wars. Simultaneously, the Iranian Revolution had just succeeded, offering Islamist groups a practical example of religious takeover and governance. These events deeply alarmed Arab and Western governments, who feared the rise of similar Islamic republics outside their control.

It is also noteworthy that the Grand Mosque seizure occurred just sixteen days after the beginning of the US Embassy hostage crisis in Tehran—both events signaling a new era of religiously driven confrontation and upheaval.

Over the subsequent decades, Sunni extremist groups like Al-Qaeda and later ISIS emerged as significant threats. Although they managed to destabilize parts of Iraq, Syria, and beyond, they failed to establish an enduring rule in the stable and economically advancing Gulf countries. This resilience was partly due to strong state institutions, intelligence operations, and the prioritization of national development and stability by Gulf governments.

The Arab Spring of 2011 further underscored the region's vulnerability to extremist exploitation. The brief rise to power of the Muslim Brotherhood in Egypt revealed the continuing appeal of political Islam. However, the swift collapse of their government also showed the limits of their legitimacy and organizational readiness to govern. These developments further confirmed that many societies in the region valued stability and growth over ideological experiments.

Interestingly, alliances emerged that crossed traditional sectarian lines. The Iranian regime, despite its Shia roots, supported Sunni groups like Hamas, which has historical ties to the Muslim Brotherhood. This highlighted that such alliances were often motivated by shared political goals and opposition to common enemies, rather than religious alignment. It also emphasized the strategic nature of extremist cooperation across sectarian boundaries.

In brief, the period since 1979 has been defined by the rise of extremist ideologies across both Shia and Sunni lines, shaped by revolutionary ambition, regional rivalries, and power vacuums. Yet, amidst these challenges, the Gulf states have largely maintained stability and continued their focus on development. This enduring tension between extremism and order remains a central feature of Middle Eastern geopolitics today.

These events influenced King Fahd, who in 1986 declared the Saudi monarchs "Custodians of the Two Holy Mosques," a title that grants the King and the Kingdom a unique role within the Arab-Muslim world. In August 1990, the Iraqi invasion of Kuwait alarmed Saudi authorities, prompting them to seek US protection to prevent any Iraqi invasion of their national territory. A few days later, US armed forces arrived in Saudi Arabia. The royal family prudently consulted the *ulema* beforehand to legitimize the arrival of foreign troops, resulting in a fatwa (i.e., a legal ruling on a point of Islamic law, the sharia) supporting this decision. However, this decision did not find favor with all of the Kingdom's religious leaders, resulting in a division within the religious community. This schism saw some supporting the royal family while others distanced themselves, thereby engendering a climate of politico-religious crisis in the country.

These elements underscore the political and religious history of the Kingdom, as well as the tribal mosaic and myriad customs and traditions maintained by the clans. For the monarchy, this complexity necessitates considering a multitude of factors to ensure effective governance and prevent internal crises. The stringent conditions enforced by the unwavering control of the religious police have sparked public discontent—a sentiment recognized by the kings, who subsequently attempted to moderate these rules. However, they encountered vehement opposition from the most extremist *ulema*, who resisted any form of societal progress or modernization. This religious radicalism is at odds with the aspirations of the national populace and contradicts the economic realities of the Kingdom, which, in striving to sustain its national model and reduce oil dependency, must implement a comprehensive program of internal reforms, including the relaxation of restrictive living conditions.

In 1998, King Abdullah initiated several significant reforms to advance women's rights, notably amending Saudi labor law to no longer formally prohibit gender mixing. He enabled women to participate in municipal elections and appointed some to the Kingdom's Consultative Council. While these decisions did not confer extensive responsibilities, they nevertheless represented a substantial shift in limiting the *muttawa*'s power. In 2016, King Salman limited the religious police's powers, significantly impacting their effective role, marking a major societal transformation in light of the historically maintained relationship between political leadership and religious institution. Since assuming governmental duties, the Crown Prince has expanded on the policies promoted by his father to advance all the modernization reforms introduced in 2016 through his Vision 2030 program. This initiative marks the commencement of a new era in the ongoing evolution of the nation's history.

2

Ascendancy of Crown Prince Mohammed bin Salman: From Royal Lineage to Visionary Leadership

Since the unification of the Kingdom, the succession to the throne has traditionally occurred within a single generation, passing between the sons of King Ibn Saud.[1] However, few of these sons remain alive, the youngest having been born in the late 1940s. The transfer of power has at times involved differences within the ruling family. When Crown Prince Salman bin Abdulaziz Al Saud ascended to the throne following the death of his brother, King Abdullah bin Abdulaziz Al Saud, in 2015, a new figure quickly emerged in the Saudi corridors of power: his son, Prince Mohammed bin Salman bin Abdulaziz Al Saud, who assumed significant responsibilities before reaching the age of thirty. At a pivotal moment in its history, Saudi Arabia required a visionary figure to steer the Kingdom toward a future marked by modernization, stability, and prosperity.

The new king initiated a series of reforms aimed at profoundly transforming the Kingdom's economic model and the rules governing the lives of Saudis. To implement these changes, he entrusted various missions to his son, Mohammed. One of the first major decisions involved curbing the powers of the religious police, the *muttawa*, setting off a chain of reforms encapsulated in the Vision 2030 program. This modernization drive necessitated the relaxation of living conditions in Saudi Arabia.

Before ascending to the highest office in the Kingdom, King Salman held positions that endowed him with an unparalleled understanding of Saudi society, having served as the governor of the Riyadh Province for forty-eight

---

1   See chapter 5, "The Ascendance of a Statesman Amidst Global Scrutiny."

years, from 1963 to 2011.[2] His tenure ended when his brother, King Abdullah, appointed him Minister of Defense, a role he held until his coronation on January 23, 2015. On June 18, 2012, King Abdullah had also named him Crown Prince. During his long tenure as governor of Riyadh Province, he witnessed the transformation of the state capital from a town of 150,000 residents to a megacity nearing a population of eight million by the early 2020s.[3] Nowadays, nearly 85 percent of the national population resides in urban areas.[4]

King Salman created a diversity in appointments of government positions involving an expanded segment of the society based on qualification and experience. Additionally, he garnered significant popularity through the various charitable foundations he once headed. He established strong relationships with the clergy, earning their deep respect, which enabled him to undertake unprecedented reforms once he became king. Throughout his life, he has skillfully balanced the competing demands of legitimacy within the royal family and in the eyes of the national populace.

From his first marriage to Princess Sultana bint Turki Al Sudairi, six children were born—five sons and one daughter—between 1955 and 1974.[5] These children pursued their education at prestigious universities in the Anglo-Saxon tradition. Among them, Prince Sultan bin Salman distinguished himself as the first astronaut from an Arab country. Prince Salman's subsequent marriage to Princess Sarah bint Faisal Al Subai'ai resulted in one son. His third marriage, to Princess Fahda bint Falah bin Sultan Al Hithalayn, produced six sons, the eldest of whom is Prince Mohammed bin Salman, born on August 31, 1985.[6] Growing up as the son of the governor of Riyadh Province, Prince Mohammed was deeply influenced by his father's leadership, despite the absence of any early indication that he would ascend as Crown Prince within a family comprising several thousand members.

Prince Mohammed's fascination with history took root early in his adolescence. He simultaneously cultivated a passion for the business world, driven

---

2   Before becoming governor, Prince Salman used to be vice-governor of the same province from March 1954.

3   Fatiha Dazi-Héni, *L'Arabie saoudite en 100 questions*, Éditions Tallandier, 2020, p. 96.

4   Ibid., p.128.

5   See Appendix 1, "Saudi Arabia's Royal Family Tree."

6   Ibid.

by a determination to secure his country's future. This sense of responsibility not only endeared him to his father, Prince Salman, but also propelled him to strive for noble objectives. Known for his diligence, Prince Mohammed viewed his father as a paragon. Opting to stay closer to home, contrary to his brothers who pursued their education abroad, he undertook legal studies in Riyadh. His choice to refine his education within Saudi Arabia was motivated by a desire to thoroughly understand the Saudi society and its tribal system, deepening his respect for traditional customs and protocol. Alongside this, he developed a firm conviction regarding the necessity of modernizing the national society and economic system to propel Saudi Arabia into a new era of development.

When his father became king, Prince Mohammed's life changed dramatically as he quickly assumed leadership responsibilities, which have continued to expand since then. Following in his father's footsteps, he swiftly embraced modernization reforms, most notably the Vision 2030 program. Despite being perceived as the Kingdom's de facto leader, especially since his designation as Crown Prince on June 21, 2017, he had already held various positions that familiarized him with the mechanisms of power. At twenty-nine, he became Minister of Defense on January 23, 2015, then Deputy Crown Prince, Second Deputy Prime Minister, and Chairman of the Council for Economic and Development Affairs on April 29, 2015. On June 21, 2017, King Salman appointed him Chairman of the Council for Political and Security Affairs and designated him Crown Prince, a revolutionary decision considering the traditional succession within the sons of King Ibn Saud. On September 27, 2022, he became the Prime Minister of the Kingdom. Despite his rapid ascent, it is essential to note that he guides public policies with the approval of King Salman, who remains the Kingdom's highest authority.

Known for his passion for new technologies in addition to video games, the Crown Prince embodies the image of a modern leader. His tenure as a statesman has equipped him with the insights necessary to pinpoint strategic focus areas essential for achieving the objectives outlined in Vision 2030. This vision requires a departure from certain traditional governance practices, aiming to propel Saudi Arabia into a new era marked by economic, societal, and religious reforms. Given the Kingdom's demographic changes and evolving international relations, diversifying income sources has become imperative. Reliance solely on oil revenues is no longer sustainable, as evidenced by the economic strains during oil price drops in the 2010s and the COVID-19 pandemic.

Economic disparities continue to be a significant issue within the national population. As of 2016, the average salary in the public sector stood at 9,500 Saudi riyals, compared to 5,500 in the private sector.[7,8] The Crown Prince is actively working to mitigate these disparities by creating numerous job opportunities and encouraging the integration of women into the workforce. Although many are university graduates, only a minority are employed. By fostering employment opportunities for women, the Crown Prince aims to enhance their autonomy. Since 2016, their proportion in the active population has steadily increased, now constituting 34 percent with a target of reaching 40 percent by 2030.[9] Concurrently, the unemployment rate has seen a significant decline, dropping from 12.3 percent at the time Vision 2030 was announced to 7.7 percent in 2023.[10] These encouraging results underscore the need for sustained efforts to maintain and build upon this progress.

Saudi Arabia has undertaken significant economic reforms as part of Vision 2030, including the implementation of Value-Added Tax (VAT) as of January 1, 2018, and adjustments to energy and water subsidies. While these measures are essential for long-term fiscal sustainability and economic diversification, they have also led to an increase in the cost of living for many households. To mitigate the impact on low and middle-income families, the government launched the Citizen's Account Program in December 2017. This program was introduced under the Fiscal Balance Program to ensure that vulnerable segments of society are protected from the direct and indirect effects of economic reforms. The Citizen's Account provides monthly financial support directly to eligible citizens. It aims to promote fair access to government benefits, encourage responsible consumption, and reduce wasteful use of resources. To improve accessibility, the program introduced a mobile application in

---

7   Fatiha Dazi-Héni, *L'Arabie saoudite en 100 questions*, Éditions Tallandier, 2020, p. 163.

8   Equivalent to 2,533 USD and 1,467 USD with an average exchange rate of 3,75 Saudi rials for 1 USD in 2016.

9   See Appendix 2, "Summary and Progress of Vision 2030."

10   Ibid.

2019, allowing users to track payments, update information, and check eligibility.[11] In July 2022, the program received an additional injection of eight billion riyals[12] (just over two billion US dollars), as directed by King Salman and based on the recommendation of Crown Prince Mohammed bin Salman, to counter the global rise in prices. This reaffirms the government's commitment to social equity and economic stability while advancing national development goals. The program reflects a broader strategy of targeted support for efficient resource use—replacing universal subsidies with direct cash transfers to those who need them most. It ensures fairness, sustainability, and the optimal use of national resources for current and future generations.

The Crown Prince is tirelessly continuing his reform efforts. In the field of education—as we will see later—he champions excellence. However, achieving this goal first required significant changes in teaching methods. Traditionally, these methods were centered around memorization. Now, there is an emphasis on deeper knowledge and critical analysis. Textbooks are also being revised to reflect a historical narrative less influenced by the strong religious imprint of the past. In this regard, history books have been purged of anti-Jewish or anti-Christian references that they once contained. This change aligns with the Crown Prince's message of openness and tolerance. This example is part of a broader logic, such as Saudi Arabia's intention to normalize diplomatic relations with the State of Israel (prior to the events of October 7, 2023, and the ongoing armed conflict, which led to the suspension of the normalization process), with the Kingdom supporting a two-state solution.

The Crown Prince continually relies on the advice of his father, who encourages him to always deepen his understanding of his environment. For any head of state, this is a crucial step in identifying the challenges and needs that must be addressed to establish a sustainable model—whether political, economic, or societal. On the international front, the Crown Prince is exploring various options to capitalize on one of Saudi Arabia's key advantages, as outlined in Vision 2030: its geographic location. He aims to transform the country into a global trade hub, which would in turn benefit the national

---

11   "About Citizen Account," website visited on May 15, 2025, https://portal.ca.gov.sa/about.

12   Ibid.

economy—through job creation, increased attractiveness to foreign investors, and more. In November 2023, he turned his attention to the India–Middle East–Europe Economic Corridor (IMEC)—a trade route initiative launched by India at the G20 Summit in New Delhi.[13] This infrastructure project is seen as a competitor to China's Belt and Road Initiative.

During a landmark conference in Riyadh in October 2017, which was attended by prominent global business leaders, the Crown Prince articulated his resolute determination to "going back to what we were: a moderate Islam that is open to all religions and to the world and to all traditions and people."[14] He further underscored his commitment to "obliterate the remnants of extremism very soon."[15] Although some may have been skeptical of these proclamations, the Crown Prince has consistently reiterated this stance, asserting that his generation fell victim to the events of 1979.[16] This conviction drives his determination to carry out a bold and unprecedented modernization policy—one he has been building for nearly a decade, sometimes at the cost of making enemies both within Saudi Arabia and abroad. Nonetheless, he has the most vital support in the Kingdom: that of King Salman. While the rules of succession have shifted—marking a transition from appointing one of the few surviving sons of King Ibn Saud to choosing a grandson—both the King and the Crown Prince are aligned on the strategic direction for the country's future. Though they have not broken with the tribal traditions they hold dear, they have significantly curtailed the once-powerful influence of the Kingdom's most conservative clerics—an enormous societal shift and likely a necessary one to reshape the country's image on the international stage.

---

13   Christian Chesnot, Georges Malbrunot, *MBS confidentiel. Enquête sur le nouveau maître du Moyen-Orient*, éditions Michel Lafon, 2024, p. 242.

14   Eliot C. McLaughlin, "Saudi crown prince promises 'a more moderate Islam,'" 25 October 2017, https://edition.cnn.com/2017/10/24/middleeast/saudi-arabia-prince-more-moderate-islam/index.html.

15   Ibid.

16   See chapter 1, "From Tribes to the Modern Kingdom: The Formation of Saudi Arabia."

3

A Tumultuous and Evolving
Global Landscape

In his examination of international relations, the eminent French philosopher Raymond Aron draws attention to two pivotal figures: the soldier and the diplomat. The former engages in battle, while the latter endeavors to circumvent violence. They stand as embodiments of war and peace, respectively. At the heart of these representations is the notion that interpersonal relationships are inherently bound by power dynamics. In all facets of human interaction, individuals, perhaps subconsciously, seek to exert their influence over others, aiming for dominance. This dominance is pursued through various means, be they persuasion, negotiation, or sheer force. Is this not the essence of debate? In such confrontations of ideology, the underlying intent leans toward supremacy; individuals engage in debate not merely to participate, but to triumph. And while debates can end in stalemates, participants often aspire to deliver an argument that seals their victory.

Philosophers have extensively deliberated on the dichotomy of man in his natural state versus his existence within societal rules. Absent any governing laws or means to enforce them, human relationships would incessantly devolve into intimidation, coercion, and other manipulative tactics aimed at asserting one's will. This holds true on a grander scale, reflecting the relations of nations. The global stage is akin to an arena where 193 UN-recognized countries coexist. Yet, the reality is complex. Even though these sovereign states form a single international community, their influence and strength differ significantly. Some nations wield significant power owing to their economic prowess, political clout, or military might. Equality remains an illusion. Despite international law dictating the terms of state relationships, a stark divide exists between the dominant nations and the rest. Often, it seems as if these dominant players unilaterally assert their will, overshadowing any state unable to counteract their influence. Every nation must safeguard its interests, upholding commonly accepted norms that are occasionally undermined, often to the detriment of overarching global objectives. The disparity is glaring: the most vulnerable nations frequently find themselves outmatched by the more powerful ones.

Recognizing its inherent strengths, Saudi Arabia has embarked on a decisive path to shape its political, economic, and societal trajectory. It aspires to ensure its prosperity while striving to champion a cause deemed paramount for both its welfare and that of the global community: the pursuit of peace. The nation takes definitive positions on issues, underscoring its commitment to fostering peaceful resolutions.

In this volatile, strained, and unpredictable international climate, the efforts of global organizations in tension alleviation and prevention are indispensable. Nonetheless, their success often hinges on the backing of nations steadfast in their support and driven by an unwavering belief in collective well-being and mutual respect. The prevailing global sentiment remains one of skepticism. While the dynamics of international relations have historically been dictated by power balances, technological advancements are accentuating these dynamics, presenting profound challenges to global equilibrium. Modern weaponry, digital innovations, and innovations from scientific laboratories (such as the creation of new viruses) harbor immense destructive capabilities. The escalation of certain hostilities and strains is increasingly alarming. The possibility of a catastrophic recourse to nuclear, biological, or other devastating arsenals remains ever-present. Hence, it becomes imperative for global players to remain vigilant of ongoing and potential crises. No stone can be left unturned. Even the slightest hint of conflict deserves scrutiny, for its potential to escalate and proliferate is ever-present.

Following the Cold War—a four-decade standoff after World War II characterized by ideological clashes between two major blocs—the world transitioned into an era marked by the emergence of a singular, overwhelmingly dominant global power.

The United States, for a time, stood unparalleled on the global stage. Its supremacy across political, economic, military, diplomatic, and cultural spheres was unmatched. The trajectory of America's future seemed to shine with unmitigated brilliance and built on a solid foundation. But this was not the case.

The sands of the global arena were indeed shifting, even if imperceptibly at first. To many, the overwhelming American dominance made any potential competition seem implausible. The disparity between the United States and the rest of the world appeared so vast that it was perceived as an enduring status quo. The collapse of the Soviet Union had left a vast expanse of disarray, with territories embroiled in their newly acquired independence, secured after hard-fought battles. Emerging from these ashes, Russia appeared fragmented, weakened, and on a path of prolonged recovery.

Yet, merely a decade on, Russia showcased renewed global aspirations, emboldened by its regained strength. Simultaneously, in Asia, the two demographic titans, India and China, held unprecedented growth potential, largely due to their massive domestic markets. While the 1990s saw these nations undergo impressive economic strides, few anticipated them evolving into economic juggernauts. However, in a span of under thirty years, China not only contested American economic dominance but also aimed to assert itself as the premier global economic powerhouse. During the Clinton[1] administration in the United States, China was regarded as an ascending economic force. Fast-forward to the present, and China emerges as a formidable rival, unabashedly declaring its ambitions to assume global economic and political supremacy.

The landscape of international competition has grown more intricate. This trend was evident from the early 2000s, marked by Russia's resurgence on the world stage and, more broadly, the ascent of the BRICS nations—a group that Saudi Arabia joined on January 1, 2024.[2, 3] These nations continue to articulate their economic growth aspirations, an endeavor paralleled by their burgeoning political influence globally. The chasms that once existed are closing,

---

1   William J. Clinton was the 42nd president of the United States. He held office from January 20, 1993 to January 20, 2001.

2   BRICS is a diplomatic conference bringing together Brazil, Russia, India, China, and South Africa. Effective January 1, 2024, the alliance comprises Saudi Arabia, the United Arab Emirates (UAE), Iran, Ethiopia, and Egypt. Argentina, originally slated to join, reversed its decision after the election of President Javier Milei. His stance, rooted in a belief that the group does not uphold principles of free trade and democracy, led to Argentina's withdrawal from membership.

3   As we finish this book, Saudi Arabia would have not yet completed its integration into the BRICS as some analysts seem to assert, its status within the organization remaining vague.

with China especially positioning itself as the primary contender to the United States, both politically and economically. Such shifts naturally breed tensions. Dominant powers are seldom receptive to challenges to their hegemony. As rivalries level, they precipitate conflicts, thrusting nations into competitive scrambles over a multitude of vested interests.

Presently, Sino-American diplomatic relations are fraught with complexity and occasional aloofness, largely due to their divergent and often conflicting objectives. The global stage is hardly conducive to dual leadership. Inevitably, one will strive to overshadow the other or, at the very least, posture as the dominant entity.

Amidst this scenario, Washington and Beijing find themselves on opposing sides of myriad issues. Their rivalry manifests in diverse forms. For instance, as China advances its ambitious Silk Road infrastructure initiative, the United States redoubles its efforts to fortify bonds with its time-honored allies, but also with new partners such as Vietnam, countering China's growing ambitions. Nations engage in strategic power plays, aiming to assert dominance. Trade restrictions, the space race, showcasing technological advancements, the Taiwan impasse, and other pivotal matters all serve as arenas for these two giants to measure their respective strengths. This contest for supremacy is escalating daily, with episodes of intensity that have undoubtedly caught the global community's attention.

The simmering tensions on the global stage often evoke chilling uncertainties and high-stakes drama reminiscent of the Cold War's most volatile moments. The dynamics of leadership and dominance, especially in international relations, are fraught with complexities. Unlike Stockholm syndrome, where hostages develop a psychological alliance with their captors, nations under the yoke of a dominant force rarely harbor any form of affection or loyalty toward their oppressors.

Historical wounds, particularly from colonial periods, leave deep scars. Former colonies still bear the burdensome memories of domination, exploitation, and subjugation. The specter of colonialism, marked by decades or even centuries of oppression and degradation, continues to cast a long shadow on contemporary international relations. Every nation and its people yearn for the respect and recognition they duly deserve. To deny them this basic dignity is to invite backlash, resistance, and deep-rooted animosity.

The terrorist attacks on September 11, 2001, undoubtedly represented a pivotal juncture in global history. With thousands of innocent dead civilians and many more injured, the United States, in its quest for justice, pinpointed a terrorist organization based in Afghanistan as the orchestrators. What ensued was an unprecedented military campaign operated by a group of countries against a non-state adversary. While America's pursuit of the perpetrators is entirely justifiable, the subsequent prolonged intervention, which lasted nearly two decades, left Afghanistan in a quagmire of instability and turmoil. Military intervention has done little to restore peace to a nation already battered by endless wars.

Furthermore, the contentious war in Iraq, predicated on misleading pretexts, only exacerbated regional vulnerabilities. The overthrow of Saddam Hussein did not usher in the anticipated stability since then. The aftermath has seen civilian populations bearing brunt, with many attributing the incessant unrest to foreign interventions.

Compounding the situation, numerous incidents involving foreign military forces have reinforced anti-American and anti-Western sentiments in regions already grappling with upheaval. Such resentment is further accentuated by the larger backdrop of historical grievances.

Amidst the evolving US-China rivalry, we have been able to observe that America's dwindling popularity in parts of Asia has paved the way for an ascendant China. But China's strategy differs significantly. Instead of military might, Beijing wields its economic prowess, primarily through investments. The ambitious Silk Road initiative, promising significant investments, is a testament to China's distinct approach. By focusing on expansive infrastructure projects and trade policies without delving into the internal affairs of its partners, China not only safeguards its economic interests but also circumvents potential hostilities. Consequently, it continues to amass influence, often at the expense of the United States.

The heightened economic and political rivalries on the global stage have unquestionably shaped Russia's stance toward the West. For nearly twenty years, President Vladimir Putin has consistently articulated his vision of a multipolar world. In this worldview, multiple dominant global powers compete for influence, marking a clear departure from the erstwhile unchallenged Western supremacy. This belief might have colored Putin's interactions with his critics and guided his decisions on Ukraine. One might wonder if he would have made similar moves two decades earlier when the United States and Europe were the predominant political and economic powerhouses. The timing of Russia's intervention in Ukraine is crucial, coinciding with a period where the West's dominance is under scrutiny. Institutions like NATO and the European Union (EU), alongside their allies, have vehemently opposed Russia's military actions, levying sanctions, especially on its hydrocarbon exports, which now face embargoes.

In contrast, several nations remain reserved, offering only generic sympathies to the Ukrainian populace. Within the BRICS nations, both China and India tread carefully, refraining from outright condemnation of Russia. Brazil has expressed an interest in diplomatic mediation, with President Luiz Inácio Lula da Silva's outreach sparking a notable Western response. Following discussions with Russian Foreign Minister Sergey Lavrov, President Lula da Silva's stand led the United States to assert that Brazil was echoing Russian and Chinese narratives.[4] Such a declaration came as a disappointment to certain quarters that had anticipated more conventional policies from him after his election. Lula da Silva's rejection of arms supplies to Ukraine and his proposal for a peace-negotiating consortium, involving Brazil and China, elicited both shock and bafflement in Washington. Nevertheless, Lula da Silva's diplomatic stance should be interpreted within the evolving dynamics of global relations, as he aims to elevate Brazil's diplomatic standing. Brazil's actions exemplify a broader trend: nations are seizing the opportunity to amplify their influence in the shifting geopolitical landscape.

Saudi Arabia is another actor seeking to redefine its role, envisioning itself as a peace advocate. The nation believes that long-term resolutions to Middle Eastern conflicts require dedicated local intermediaries committed to sustainable solutions. Emphasizing diplomacy over conflict, the Kingdom recognizes that peace is the linchpin of prosperous economic futures. Prolonged crises negatively impact national economies, and instability deters potential investors seeking regions with robust security assurances.

---

4   "US accuses Brazil of 'parroting Russian and Chinese propaganda,'" *Euronews*, April 18, 2023, https://www.euronews.com/2023/04/18/us-accuses-brazil-of-parroting-russian -and-chinese-propaganda.

Hence, Saudi leadership is extending an olive branch to those who are earnest about contributing to Middle Eastern peace and who possess an intimate understanding of the challenges within volatile regions. However, meaningful intervention in such crises hinges not just on the desire to foster peace but on acquiring the credibility to be heeded. Equally vital is a nuanced understanding of the underlying issues and the identification of areas where negotiated resolutions can have a lasting impact.

The current global landscape is one in which a multitude of nations are signaling their aspirations to become pivotal actors in world diplomacy. This trend is neither abrupt nor unpredictable; rather, it affirms the ambitions of some and reflects the evolving contours of international relations. Within this context, Saudi Arabia, guided by its Crown Prince, is striving not only for long-term relevance but also to be acknowledged as a credible advocate for peace.

In March 2023, global observers were caught off guard by a significant development. In a tripartite gathering held in Beijing, China achieved what many had considered inconceivable: facilitating dialogue between Saudi Arabia and Iran, two nations historically entrenched in rivalry. How did Beijing manage to broker dialogue between these two, especially when Western counterparts had scarcely envisioned such an outcome?

By choosing a path of dialogue and collaboration, Riyadh and Tehran exhibited discernment, recognizing that forging a normalized diplomatic relationship would have extensive beneficial implications for their region. For China, this diplomatic maneuver was a revelation to the West, which seldom acknowledged Beijing's capacity to mediate in such geopolitical matters. In orchestrating this dialogue, China demonstrated a diplomatic finesse, securing the trust of two dominant political entities in an arena where Western initiatives have often been stymied.

China's motives are not mysterious. Given its ambitious Belt and Road Initiative, fostering harmony between Saudi Arabia and Iran aligns with Beijing's interests. Equally pressing is China's dependence on the oil and gas these nations supply. More broadly, this diplomatic feat bolsters China's stature in a region where Western influence is perceivably waning.

Washington's vexation with Riyadh is palpable and comprehensible. How could an erstwhile ally heed the beckoning of a competing global player? The answer is stark in its realism: in the flux of international dynamics, enduring alliances should resonate with contemporary realities. Saudi Arabia felt a sense of betrayal stemming from an unreliable partner across multiple fronts: the abrupt American withdrawal from Afghanistan, public accusations leveled against the Crown Prince in the Khashoggi affair, and the US engagement in negotiations with Iran concerning the nuclear dispute. Yet, Saudi Arabia's trajectory seems misaligned with American expectations. Intent on charting its own path, the Kingdom seeks partners that resonate with its vision and objectives.

In this context, the rapprochement between Beijing and Riyadh is hardly surprising, given that Saudi Arabia has repeatedly expressed its disappointment with the Western world. As previously mentioned, this situation is of great concern to US authorities, who view any loss of influence in the Middle East to the benefit of China with deep unease. All this takes place in a particularly tense global context, especially in the United States, as the presidential election looms just a year and a half away. Although foreign policy traditionally isn't at the heart of electoral campaigns, Joe Biden knows he is expected to deliver on this issue, as he is criticized for the decline of American influence in the Levant. There is little doubt about what will follow regarding his political future. Aspiring to run for a second presidential term, he is forced to withdraw his reelection bid in July 2024.[5] Kamala Harris then becomes the official Democratic Party candidate, facing off against Donald Trump, who aims to restore America's capacity to sway the Middle East with his characteristic verve.

Meanwhile, Saudi authorities have sent a clear message to the international community: They will pursue the strategic choices they deem most beneficial to achieving their national and international goals. This vision stems from a long-considered strategy now championed and advanced by one man: His Royal Highness Crown Prince Mohammed bin Salman bin Abdulaziz Al Saud.

---

5   President Joe Biden announced his decision not to seek reelection on July 21, 2024, under pressure from the Democratic Party, which feared a difficult campaign and the prospect of defeat on November 5, 2024. His vice president, Kamala Harris, officially accepted the Democratic nomination on August 23 during the party's convention held in Chicago.

4

Regional Dynamics in a Volatile Landscape

The Middle East, a vast expanse stretching across diverse terrains and cultures, has long been an epicenter of multifaceted crises, many with regional implications. Often perceived as a tinderbox of simmering tensions, its complexities arise from the myriad causes of strife and their intricate interplay. It is not merely the presence of a new disturbance that garners attention; it is the potential for its rapid escalation and the challenge of containment. Spanning territories like Türkiye, the Caucasus, the Arabian Peninsula, the Eastern Mediterranean, Iraq, and Iran, a mere cursory examination reveals the deep nature, heterogeneity, and depth of the security concerns prevalent.

To decode these crises, it is paramount to delve into their historical underpinnings—often labyrinthine and profound. Numerous nations grapple with a multitude of internal challenges. This volatile backdrop hardly fosters an atmosphere conducive to conflict resolution. The entanglement of external entities further muddies the waters, often stemming from a fundamental misapprehension of the core issues at stake. In this vast region, home to hundreds of millions, the emergence of any new crisis stokes apprehensions about potential escalation and raises concerns over the ability to manage the situation effectively.

Zooming out to the global stage, we witness wars engulfing regions like Ukraine, a yet elusive social harmony in Afghanistan, and the perennially turbulent Indo-Pakistani relations. These scenarios underscore the imperative for nations like Saudi Arabia to be instrumental in fostering peace. Any regional instability poses a significant impediment to national economic trajectories. From a humanistic lens, is it not a universal aspiration to reside in a peaceful enclave, devoid of the omnipresent dread of imminent conflict? Tragically, in certain nations, generations have grown up in the shadow of perpetual war.

These challenges are not constrained within national boundaries. They manifest in multifarious forms—terrorism, territorial disputes, ethnic or religious conflicts, and tribal warfare, among others. Türkiye, with its unique position bridging Europe and Asia, epitomizes this nexus of divergent strategic interests. While it grapples with its internal quandary, notably its skirmishes with Kurdish separatists, its external affiliations are no less intricate—navigating its NATO membership while courting officially EU accession. Its Black Sea coastline is a stark geographical reminder of its proximity to Ukraine, embroiled in a prolonged conflict with Russia. Türkiye's adjacency to Armenia, a nation holding grievances from historic Ottoman transgressions culminating in genocide, further adds to the geopolitical complexity. The entrenched conflict between Armenia and Azerbaijan (the war led to the Armenian laying down of arms in September 2023), especially over contested territories like Nagorno-Karabakh, and Armenia's claim on Nakhichevan, accentuate regional key issues. Armenia's tightrope walk with its neighbors only magnifies the challenges.

Lastly, a spotlight on the Kurdish issue in Türkiye underscores the unique plight of the Kurds—a distinct ethnic group yearning for a homeland.[1] While Iraqi Kurdistan enjoys a semblance of autonomy, full-fledged independence remains an elusive dream. The Kurdish populace, thirty million people, is dispersed across four nations: Türkiye, Syria, Iraq, and Iran. In Iraq, the central government in Baghdad remains apprehensive about granting independence to the oil-rich Kurdish region.

Iraq's journey toward societal harmony has been tumultuous since the foreign intervention of 2003, spanning nearly two decades. A lingering sense of insecurity remains the government's paramount concern where corruption remains a plague, a sentiment mirrored in Syria, which battles its own insurgent forces. The Arab Spring swept into Syria, with public outcries aimed at challenging the established order. However, foreign meddling, aiming for a regime change, thrust Syria into a protracted civil war in 2011, which festers to this day. Both Iraq and Syria, while contending with internal upheavals, also grapple with insurgent territories commandeered by terrorist factions. Their concerted effort to reclaim these lands remains an ongoing struggle.

---

1   This configuration results from the Treaty of Lausanne of July 24, 1923, which replaced the Treaty of Sevres signed on August 10, 1920. It provided for new state borders in the Middle East following the breakup of the Ottoman Empire.

In the Mediterranean basin, nations like Lebanon, Israel, and the Palestinian territories stand on a precipice due to a plethora of different reasons. Israel and the Palestinian Authority have navigated periods of intense tension, punctuated by several intifadas. Periodic skirmishes underscore the volatility of this long-standing conflict. Lebanon, once a theater of war against Israel, is now enmeshed in domestic political and economic turmoil, casting a pall over its future prospects. This mosaic of cultures and faiths in the Mediterranean paints a tableau of regional and interstate tensions, underlining the profound challenges at hand.[2]

Iran's stance is a study in complexities. Internationally isolated, its political structure[3] has withstood pressures since its establishment in 1979. Its interactions with Saudi Arabia are tinged with animosity, driven by both nations' ambitions to emerge as regional political, economic, and religious hegemons. Saudi Arabia, with pronounced Western, particularly American, backing, finds itself at odds with Iran. 1979 was a watershed year, marking a rift between the United States and Iran. The Islamic Revolution signaled the end of Mohammad Reza Shah Pahlavi's reign, and the subsequent hostage crisis at the US embassy in Tehran severed their bilateral ties. Consequently, the United States embarked on a sanctions regime, aiming to destabilize Iran's economic and political infrastructure.

Iran's geopolitical significance is further magnified when considering its history. During the 1980s, against the backdrop of the Cold War, Iran was embroiled in an eight-year-long war with Iraq, which is said to have claimed one million lives on both sides. Post-conflict, the Iraqi President Saddam Hussein's efforts to restructure his debts were rebuffed, leading him to believe that he had been unduly burdened in safeguarding Western and regional interests against Iran. Feeling aggrieved, he retaliated by annexing Kuwait, catalyzing the first Gulf War, shortly after the Cold War's cessation. For Iran, the prolonged war drained its fiscal resources. The financial burden intensified in the 1990s when the United States imposed an oil embargo in 1995, soon followed by comprehensive trade sanctions against Tehran.

---

2   The current situation post-October 7 in the Middle East will be looked at in chapters 18 and 19.

3   *Wilayat al-faqih* imposed by Ayatollah Khomeini, describes the imposition of guardianship by a member of the Muslim clergy over the community.

Over the years, regardless of the ruling administration, the United States. has exerted consistent pressure on Iran, the modern descendant of ancient Persia. Relevant sanctions have impeded Iran's economic momentum, though not entirely crippling it. In response to the adversarial posturing and to safe-guard its interests, Iran embarked on both civil and military nuclear ventures. This nuclear ambition unnerved the West (and Israel), triggering an intensi-fication of the existing sanctions. Ironically, this restrictive policy indirectly favored Saudi Arabia. In the grand chessboard of geopolitics, any strategy or tactic that weakens a competitor is often welcomed. The sanctions impaired Iran's full utilization of its prime economic assets, notably hydrocarbons. This created opportunities for other global producers, Saudi Arabia being a prime beneficiary.

However, a strategic pivot was observed during President Obama's tenure. In his second term, he charted a fresh diplomatic direction toward the Iranian nuclear conundrum. By advocating dialogue and offering the possibility of rekindling US-Iran ties based on Tehran's goodwill, he brought a breath of fresh diplomatic air. Yet, during a visit to Saudi Arabia in April 2016, this proposed approach was met with reservations. The foundational agreement between King Ibn Saud and President Franklin D. Roosevelt aboard the USS *Quincy* in 1945 emphasized mutual benefits and strategic cooperation. For over seventy years, notwithstanding occasional strains, the United States and Saudi Arabia have maintained their allegiance. Obama's diplomatic overtures, however, cast a shadow of uncertainty. Pundits and analysts wondered if this was the beginning of the end for US-Saudi ties. While that might be an exag-gerated prognosis, it was undeniable that the new US diplomatic leanings did leave Saudi Arabia feeling somewhat sidelined.

A few months later, Donald Trump emerged victorious in the presidential election and swiftly heralded a profound transformation in foreign policy. His approach was a stark departure from President Obama's, with its rigidity occa-sionally perplexing even traditional Western allies. Trump's "America First" doctrine resonated throughout his decisions. His first official overseas trip post-inauguration in May 2017 was to Saudi Arabia, underscoring a deliberate recalibration of ties. For Trump, Saudi Arabia represented a staunch ally in exerting consistent pressure on Iran. His ultimate aspiration was to destabilize the Iranian leadership through economic asphyxiation. True to form, in 2018, he pulled the United States out of the Vienna Agreement[4] crafted to address the nuclear issue. Trump's "Make America Great Again" slogan was manifest in his unilateral approach to safeguarding US interests, even if it meant the United States found itself increasingly isolated on the global stage. In the wake of profound astonishment in Iran, Tehran endeavored to placate the other signatories of the Vienna Agreement, while these nations decried America's stance.

Concurrently, American and Saudi strategic interests aligned once more, with Iran persistently seen as a shared adversary. Israel, due to its distinct security concerns, lauded the American withdrawal from the multiparty negotiations. These developments set the stage for Donald Trump's diplomatic masterstroke just weeks before his electoral defeat in November 2020. The Abraham Accords were inked on August 13, 2020, with Israel and the United Arab Emirates (UAE), and on September 15, 2020, with Israel and Bahrain.

Additionally, in the frameworks of the Abraham Accords, Morocco participated in the process, signing on December 22, 2020, in Rabat, and Sudan joined with a signature on January 6, 2021, in Khartoum. For Trump, this was a move to crystallize a broad geopolitical strategy aimed at sidelining Iran. Strategic aims overshadowed any genuine push for peace, serving only to deepen the divide with Tehran.

With the ascension of Democrat Joe Biden, the Middle Eastern geopolitical tableau transformed once more. Biden, stepping into the legacy of the administration he had once served as vice president, signaled his openness for dialogue with Iran. Yet, this vision of American diplomacy found little favor in Saudi Arabia, which bristled at the White House's overtures regarding OPEC

---

4   The Vienna Agreement on the Iranian nuclear issue (or Joint Comprehensive Plan of Action according to the EU and the International Atomic Energy Agency) refers to the document signed on July 14, 2015, bringing together Iran, the permanent members of the United Nations Security Council (the United States, China, Russia, France, and the United Kingdom), Germany, and the EU. The aim of the discussions was to control the development of Iran's nuclear program. In return, the other parties to the talks undertook to gradually lift economic sanctions. The finalization of the agreement was widely welcomed around the world, notably by United Nations Secretary-General Ban Ki-moon. The world was hoping for an easing of tensions with Iran and an end to the potential nuclear threat from that country. The US withdrawal from the agreement triggered bewilderment and astonishment, especially on the part of Tehran and the other parties involved. They were left questioning the potential repercussions of this decision, especially in light of former US President Donald Trump's call to intensify economic sanctions against the country.

oil production. The dynamic between Washington and Riyadh entered a period of frostiness. It was a jolt to the United States when, in March 2023, news broke of a tripartite pact brokered by China with Saudi Arabia and Iran.

This brief overview, though not exhaustive, of Middle Eastern crises in the global context underscores the challenge of acting as a mediator in such multifaceted situations. A comprehensive grasp of these issues transcends a mere analytical or situational understanding—it necessitates cultural nuance. The West's recurring hesitations on regional matters have left local actors weary, dismayed by the enduring, unresolved crises, such as the commencement of the second Iraq War in 2003. Strategy remains at the core of diplomacy, shaping political decisions driven by geopolitical, geostrategic, and diverse motives. Moreover, recognizing the milieu in which stakeholders operate is paramount. As international relations evolve, so do the aspirations and perceptions of national leadership. Leaders buoyed by strong beliefs and aware of their nations' strengths might seek alternative paths for their nations' benefit. The Crown Prince epitomizes this shift in orientation. As already exposed, the newfound alignment with China and Iran shouldn't be misconstrued as a slight to the West but seen as a testament to Saudi Arabia's sovereignty in determining its path.

Saudi Arabia's diplomatic vision has undergone a transformation, now placing peace at the forefront for the regional prosperity and economic resurgence of the Middle East. This perspective is not geographically insular. Peace epitomizes the security, stability, and tranquility vital for any nation's economic progression. While these elements might not guarantee success, they certainly do not deter it. Investments are scarce in conflict-riddled nations, given the elevated risks inherent to such volatile environments.

Saudi Arabia is forging its own path forward. Central to its soft power[5]

---

[5] Hard power and soft power are theories of international relations. They originated with Joseph Nye, who is an eminent political scientist and author of numerous internationally acclaimed books and articles. He served as Assistant Secretary of Defense for International Security Issues under President Clinton from 1994 to 1995. Nye argues that hard power is characterized by the traditional means of exerting pressure within political and military power relations. Soft power is based on a more subtle and flexible power of influence. It can take the form of economic or cultural policies. With Robert Keohane, Nye founded neoliberal institutionalism, a theoretical vision of international relations in which the power of institutions is paramount in the international system. Nye is one of the great names in international relations theory and one of the most prestigious figures in liberal thought.

is the pursuit of peace. Superficially, this aligns with the aspirations of its Western counterparts. However, when it comes to dissecting the nuances, the methods and understanding of the issues sharply diverge, such as the Western disapprobation or disappointment in regard to the partnerships sealed by Riyadh with countries that share neither its democratic values nor its vision of human rights.

The Kingdom is shifting to actionable diplomacy, seeking to establish the credibility required to engage with influential actors. Its alliance with China and Iran transcends mere strategic intent. It signals a pivot toward new dialogues, especially when traditional partners have faltered in crisis resolution efforts. This recalibration garners skepticism from the West, mainly because it carries implications—the West's plausible diminishing sway in the Middle East to a burgeoning global contender, which includes China.

Saudi Arabia possesses the diplomatic resources to substantiate its peace aspirations, notably by forging new ties with Iran. From historical animosity emerges a triumph of pragmatism, igniting momentum anchored in the hope for a sustained détente. Through these actions, Riyadh, Tehran, and Beijing are staking their claims as champions of peace,[6] particularly if this rapprochement endures. For China, this is a venture into uncharted waters, as it traditionally has not spearheaded global tension resolutions outside its affiliated international bodies. Iran, on the other hand, seems to showcase its leadership's pragmatism, keen on reshaping its global persona to the world's eyes. It is crucial for Iran to project itself as a nation eager for peace. While it does not alleviate its strained Western ties, a harmonious rapport with Saudi Arabia could potentially recalibrate the West's perspective of Tehran, ushering in optimism for enduring peace—a dream long-held by generations in a region historically embroiled in conflict.

Saudi Arabia is heralding a fresh diplomatic epoch. It is attuning to global realities, aspiring for an impactful role on the world stage. At the helm of this ambition is the Crown Prince. His foreign policy vision might invite critique from the West, hinting at a possible miscomprehension on their part. Yet, his overture toward Iran, evidenced by his acquiescence to China's proposition,

---

6   Before the events of October 7, 2023, in Israel and Iran's open support to Hamas since then.

exemplifies a bold move. It underscores a proactive global approach charac-terized by judicious, resolute decisions aligned with national priorities. While he's mindful of the ripples it may create among Western allies, he remains undeterred. Instead, he beckons them to reconceive his global perspective—one that commands respect, especially in a region where he possesses profound insights into its key issues.

5

The Ascendance of a Statesman Amidst Global Scrutiny

When Mohammed bin Salman was first thrust into the upper echelons of power, the burden of state responsibilities that fell upon him was considerable and has only increased since. At that time, he had yet to receive the official title by which he is now globally recognized. Shortly after his father King Salman ascended the throne of Saudi Arabia in 2015, the young prince was appointed Deputy Crown Prince and Second Deputy Prime Minister. The name Mohammed bin Salman bin Abdulaziz Al Saud swiftly entered the lexicon of international policymakers and media outlets alike. His youth aroused curiosity, yet he remained relatively reserved, careful not to overstep the established hierarchies of power, despite being the son of the newly enthroned monarch.

For reasons often misunderstood beyond the Kingdom's borders, the man now regarded as the King's favored heir rose through the ranks with astonishing speed, outpacing those who had long been presumed successors to the throne: first Prince Muqrin bin Abdulaziz Al Saud, and later Prince Mohammed bin Nayef Al Saud. In a remarkably short period, he emerged as the Kingdom's second-most-powerful figure. This meteoric ascent provoked a host of questions. How had he managed to consolidate power so decisively? By what mechanisms were other designated heirs sidelined?

To grasp this evolution, one must understand the principles governing royal succession in the Saudi system, principles that are, in fact, well-defined when viewed through the lens of legal tradition. The King ultimately holds final authority. His decisions are not contested. Mohammed bin Salman's elevation was thus the result of choices formally endorsed by his father. Nevertheless, the inner workings of Saudi decision-making remain largely opaque to Western observers. This opacity has given rise to conflicting narratives, some of which have misrepresented the Crown Prince, even as the international community has increasingly acknowledged him as a pivotal figure in global affairs.

Yet international attention has at times shifted away from his strategic vision and toward more contentious episodes, most notably, the 2017 detention of royal family members and prominent business figures under the banner of an anti-corruption campaign. That initiative, jointly spearheaded by King Salman and the Crown Prince, resulted in the recovery of substantial assets. In numerous cases, these were returned to the state following negotiations conducted during the detainees' confinement at the Ritz-Carlton in Riyadh.

The founder of the reigning dynasty, King Ibn Saud, fathered many sons and defined a fraternal model of succession, whereby the throne passed laterally among his sons.[1] This system, however, carried an inherent generational constraint: vast age gaps between the heirs and the eventual depletion of viable successors from among the founder's sons. With only a few of them still alive—and now in advanced old age—King Salman concluded that the time had come to transition from horizontal succession to a vertical model, passing the mantle to the next generation.

Given his position, one can hardly fault King Salman for seeking to avert a generational bottleneck: The eventual death of the last living son of Ibn Saud with no prearranged line of succession could have plunged the Kingdom into fraternal and dynastic discord. In naming his son, rather than a surviving brother or half brother, as Crown Prince, King Salman introduced a structural reform to preserve the stability of the monarchy. Though this decision necessarily departed from the tradition established by his father—and was unlikely to please all stakeholders—it nonetheless served a higher aim: to ensure the continuity of governance and to prevent internecine strife from erupting within the palace walls.

In recent decades, the Kingdom of Saudi Arabia has witnessed a series of dramatic episodes within its royal family, particularly among the direct descendants of King Ibn Saud. The traditional agnatic seniority system of succession—based on fraternal transfer of power—has increasingly revealed its limitations, prompting King Salman to seek a recalibration aimed at preserving

---

1   The current King Salman is the most recent of six siblings to reign since the death of King Ibn Saud in 1953. The Kings Saud reigned from 1953 to 1964, Faisal from 1964 to 1975 (assassinated), Khaled from 1975 to 1982, Fahd from 1982 to 2005, Abdullah from 2005 to 2015, and Salman since January 2015.

political equilibrium. Yet, this internal shift remains widely misunderstood outside the Kingdom.

In 2015, while serving as Deputy Crown Prince and Second Deputy Prime Minister, the current Crown Prince gave an interview to *The New York Times* in which he described the country as "a tribal form of monarchy, with many tribes and subtribes and regions connecting to the top."[2] This formulation sheds light on the extraordinary complexity of Saudi governance, underscoring that executive authority is exercised within a framework deeply rooted in custom and tradition. Governance in the Kingdom is not a matter of personal will; it is bounded by the weight of inherited norms. At the apex of this intricate structure stands the King, an uncontested figure of authority entrusted with the Kingdom's political direction.

The designation of the Crown Prince is formally enshrined in the Basic Law of Governance (Al-nizām al-asāsī li-l-hukm), promulgated in 1992, which grants the monarch exclusive authority over the succession process. In practice, however, the procedure is far more nuanced. The sovereign's prerogative must ultimately ratify a consensus emerging from the constellation of tribal and familial branches that comprise the ruling House of Saud. Article 5, paragraph (b) of the Basic Law stipulates that rule is to pass among the sons and grandsons of King Ibn Saud.[3] On the surface, this appears to provide a clear framework for succession. In reality, it has engendered fierce internal competition among numerous contenders for the throne.

In 2007, King Abdullah established the Allegiance Council (Hay'at al-Bay'ah) to institutionalize the succession process. Initially composed of thirty-five members—including the sixteen surviving sons of King Ibn Saud and nineteen grandsons—the council was tasked with overseeing appointments according to predetermined criteria, including mental and physical fitness and a minimum age threshold. Yet the King was under no obligation to abide by its recommendations and retained the discretionary authority to name a Crown Prince independently.

---

2   Thomas Friedman, "Letter from Saudi Arabia," *New York Times*, November 25, 2015, https://www.nytimes.com/2015/11/25/opinion/letter-from-saudi-arabia.html.

3   Nabil Mouline, "Pouvoir et transition générationnelle en Arabie Saoudite," *Critique internationale*, 2010/1 (n°46), 125–46.

This arrangement was tested for the first time in 2011, following the death of Crown Prince Sultan bin Abdulaziz Al Saud. The council convened and selected Prince Nayef bin Abdulaziz Al Saud as successor. His death in June 2012 necessitated another round of consultation, resulting in the elevation of Prince Salman, who ascended to the throne in 2015.

Upon his enthronement, King Salman's decisions to reshuffle the line of succession raised significant questions. The first Crown Prince appointed under his reign was Prince Muqrin bin Abdulaziz Al Saud, the thirty-fifth and youngest son of King Ibn Saud and half brother of the late King Abdullah. Prince Muqrin was soon relieved of his duties, and the title of Crown Prince passed to Prince Mohammed bin Nayef. Simultaneously, a new position was created: Deputy Crown Prince, conferred upon Prince Mohammed bin Salman.

Prince Muqrin's resignation was unexpected. To many observers, it appeared a calculated move by King Salman to sideline him for strategic reasons. Muqrin had been designated by King Abdullah partly to counterbalance the influence of the powerful Sudairi faction, a bloc descending from Hassa Al Sudairi, one of Ibn Saud's most prominent wives. Upon ascending the throne, King Salman made clear his intent to usher in a new generation of rulers, effectively signaling the end of the fraternal succession model and indirectly conveying his intentions toward Prince Muqrin.

Mohammed bin Nayef, Muqrin's successor as Crown Prince, held the prestigious post of Minister of the Interior and was regarded by US intelligence services as a dependable ally. This portfolio made him one of the most influential figures in the royal hierarchy. Yet his fortunes changed abruptly in 2017, when he was swept up in the Kingdom's high-profile anti-corruption purge, orchestrated by King Salman and his son, then-Deputy Crown Prince Mohammed bin Salman. Stripped of his title, Mohammed bin Nayef was formally removed from the line of succession, and King Salman confirmed his own son as first in line to the Saudi throne.

Voices were soon raised denouncing what many came to describe as a "purge." Indeed, it took a considerable degree of audacity to target such a wide array of princely dignitaries and former ministers in so sweeping a manner. Though carried out under the auspices of royal authority, the Ritz-Carlton affair left a deep impression, not least because of the sheer number of high-profile individuals detained and compelled to return vast sums in exchange for their release. In the West, the operation's modus operandi provoked indignation. It was portrayed as an arbitrary campaign designed to eliminate all forms of competition surrounding the newly appointed Crown Prince, Mohammed bin Salman. Yet, some clarification is warranted.

The anti-corruption drive was not merely a convenient pretext for a spectacular crackdown within the royal family and the Kingdom's most powerful economic circles. In truth, numerous dignitaries had long enjoyed excessively lenient and indulgent business conditions, enabling them to amass immense fortunes, often at the direct expense of the nation's public finances. King Salman and his son Mohammed, acutely aware of the Kingdom's economic vulnerability—particularly in the wake of plummeting oil prices that cast doubt over the very feasibility of financing the Vision 2030 program—undertook to confront the entrenched dysfunctions that were undermining Saudi Arabia's economic health.

In Europe and North America, the episode was largely perceived as a calculated move to neutralize would-be rivals to the throne. Yet in point of fact, King Salman held full prerogative to elevate his son to prominence. As for the methods employed, they were far from novel; rather, they echoed the traditional power dynamics that have long characterized palace intrigue. Within a royal family as extensive as that of the House of Saud, the adelphic succession system had become not merely a structural impediment to the orderly transfer of power among brothers, but also a source of behaviors that threatened both political stability and economic integrity.

These realities were, without doubt, weighed by King Salman, who was deeply concerned about the uncertain future facing the Kingdom. His vision found resonance in Mohammed, who shared his apprehensions. The result was the conception of an anti-corruption initiative that, though widely misunderstood in the West, was in fact part of a broader effort to lay the groundwork for sweeping reforms. Domestically, the episode did little to tarnish the popularity of either King Salman or his designated successor. Years later, Western media would cite Gallup polling attesting to the enduring support both figures enjoyed among the Saudi public.[4]

---

4   Steven A. Cook, "Saudi Arabia Is Extremely Popular in the Middle East," *Foreign Policy*, May 11, 2023, https://foreignpolicy.com/2023/05/11/saudi-arabia-mbs-popularity -middle-east-gallup-poll-arab-barometer/.

Yet a single, inescapable conclusion asserted itself: the Crown Prince's reputation within the international community had suffered a palpable decline. A change of course became imperative in light of the criticisms leveled against him. What followed was a concerted effort to rehabilitate his image, a campaign of persuasion aimed at restoring a more favorable perception, an undertaking that would necessarily require time. Without such rehabilitation, how could the Kingdom hope to attract foreign investors? Vision 2030 promised the economic and societal modernization of Saudi Arabia and presented the nation as a land of opportunity. But in the West, who truly believed it?

The Crown Prince's achievements—though real—remained largely underestimated. He came to appreciate the strategic value of lobbying efforts, of granting interviews to international media, of answering even the most uncomfortable questions directly, of traveling widely and being seen in the company of influential global figures, especially the entrepreneurs of Silicon Valley. This strategic reconfiguration of his public persona did nothing to impede the steady advance of his ambitions. On the contrary, his determination to cease making headlines for the wrong reasons only strengthened his resolve to assert Saudi Arabia's rightful place on the global stage. The Kingdom, in his eyes, was not to be diminished nor disrespected; least of all on the most sensitive matters and the all-too-frequent sources of misunderstanding.

6

Understanding Others

The discourse on human rights remains a perennial topic of intense debate, especially within Western realms that ardently champion the democratic principles intertwined with them. France immortalized these rights in its seminal 1789 Declaration of the Rights of Man and of the Citizen. Such ideals were intrinsic to the revolutionary fervor that consequently precipitated the monarchy's demise. However, a cursory glance at history reveals that in the wake of this mass upheaval, France soon found itself mired in a protracted period of internal turbulence, culminating in numerous public executions during the 1790s. A semblance of stability only resurfaced with the ascendancy of a dominant general who then pursued relentless expansions to amplify the grandeur of what eventually became his empire—Napoleon Bonaparte. This empire was short-lived, collapsing in 1815 after Napoleon's defeat at Waterloo.

The French experience underscores the sensitive challenges of recalibrating individual rights and liberties during revolutionary epochs. While the intent was laudable, it emerged at a precarious juncture when society was seemingly unprepared for such a profound political and societal metamorphosis, compelling them to navigate uncharted waters. Though the revolutionaries aspired to reaffirm humanity's esteemed position within the nation's fabric, the era's tumultuous climate paradoxically endangered individual safety, with one's allegiance to the Revolution often becoming a matter of life and death. While France has indelibly shaped the global human rights narrative, it is poignant to reflect on the protracted and sometimes violent journey that culminated in the acquisition of these rights by its citizenry.

Across the Atlantic, the United States proclaimed its emancipation from British dominion by placing paramount emphasis on individual liberty in the preamble to its Constitution. However, the bitter irony remains that when the Founding Fathers heralded national independence, the grotesque institution of slavery evaded their libertarian vision. Nearly a century would elapse before President Abraham Lincoln's advocacy for abolition would begin to address this egregious oversight, a crusade that cost him his life, prior to the adoption of the Thirteenth Amendment to the Constitution on December 18, 1865, which formally established the abolition of slavery. Tragically, this advancement hardly ameliorated the tribulations of African Americans, who then grappled with the specter of racial segregation. Another protracted century was required for these societal scars to begin their process of healing.

Both the French and American historical narratives offer indispensable insights. While significant societal advancements are often rooted in foundational documents, they invariably underscore the myriad imperfections that arise when prevailing conditions or external variables hinder the complete realization of ideals conceived and championed in the legal realm. In France, the tumult following the Revolution necessitated an authoritarian figure to reestablish societal equilibrium. Similarly, in the United States, despite a constitutional emphasis on individual rights, the shadows of slavery and racial segregation bore testament to a societal reality that starkly deviated from its foundational charter.

No governance model stands as a panacea. Irrespective of its democratic or authoritarian nature, no political structure offers a guarantee of perpetuity. After the Cold War, several intellectuals posited the ascendancy of liberal and democratic paradigms over their authoritarian counterparts,[1] a viewpoint shaped predominantly by the zeitgeist. According to the UN Secretary-General António Guterres, the number of democratic regimes worldwide is steadily declining. When viewed through a Western lens, authoritarian regimes often bear the stigma of curtailing individual freedoms.

The Universal Declaration of Human Rights, ratified in 1948, epitomized the inaugural international decree promising universal safeguards for every individual's cardinal rights. As delineated by the UN, these rights are intrinsic to our human existence, transcending national, ethnic, religious, and other demarcations. They span from the quintessential—such as the right to life—to

---

1   Francis Fukuyama, *The End of History and the Last Man* (New York, Free Press, 1992) 418.

those that enhance the quality of existence, encompassing rights to food, education, work, health, and freedom.[2]

At its core, this legal blueprint is both commendable and human-centric. Yet, it grapples with the nuances of state sovereignty. Jurisprudential scholars might argue that ratified international treaties, once operational, must be unconditionally adhered to. However, the pragmatism of global affairs frequently deviates from this ideal. The discourse surrounding human rights epitomizes this dichotomy—it is not merely about attaining universal acknowledgment. External factors ensure that nations perceive the matter through distinct prisms, often precipitating disputes in the arena of international diplomacy.

Democratic regimes recurrently censure human rights transgressions, especially within territories that historically fell under colonial dominion. This remains a contentious issue in today's unpredictable geopolitical landscape. Some emerging or ascendant political and economic juggernauts now contest Western primacy, questioning the West's evangelism of democratic values and human rights. These nations posit that the era of unilateral Western dictate is waning. Countries that challenge Western communication on the topic do not necessarily reject democratic values, but they openly now express their dissatisfaction with judgments they perceive negatively.

Take Saudi Arabia, for instance, which often finds itself at the receiving end of Western reproach. But does this imply a blanket endorsement of human rights violations by the nation? Contrarily, the Crown Prince has embarked on a journey to liberalize societal norms, emblematic of his modernization vision for the Kingdom. The depth and breadth of these reforms often elude Western comprehension.

It is perplexing to witness criticism directed at a political regime that has consciously chosen legal rules less limiting of individual rights and freedoms. This discourse becomes even more confounding when emerging from jurisdictions that cast aspersions upon others while failing to exemplify ideal standards themselves—particularly concerning matters such as the death penalty.

In our evolving global landscape, where power dynamics are perhaps

---

2   "What are human rights?" https://www.ohchr.org/en/what-are-human-rights, website consulted on July 31, 2023.

noticeably pivoting away from Western hegemony, this relentless reiteration of criticism agitates those capable of influencing the geopolitical chessboard. Human rights, once a universal aspiration, now teeter on the precipice of becoming a weaponized political tool. Ignoring its implications can have strategic and potentially detrimental repercussions.

Saudi Arabia, for instance, has embarked on societal reforms, necessitating extensive dialogues with elite groups historically wedded to the nation's conservative societal values. The Crown Prince has been at the vanguard of this transformation. When Western observers level criticism at human rights practices in Saudi Arabia, the Crown Prince perceives it as a discourse that undermines the genuine reforms underway. This sentiment has incited a recalibration of his strategic international alignment. He views these critiques not merely as academic observations but as profound affronts to both his leadership and Saudi Arabia's sovereignty. This perspective has, in part, influenced his increasingly nuanced relationship with Western nations, most notably the United States.

Yet, undeniable societal metamorphoses have transpired within Saudi Arabia, mirroring the liberalizing ethos encapsulated in the Vision 2030 program. While these changes are part of a broader tapestry of transformation, they demand a nuanced understanding and balance. Contrary to prevailing assumptions, the Crown Prince does not wield unchecked authority in determining Saudi Arabia's governance trajectory. As subsequent chapters will elucidate, his decisions are neither capricious nor solely reactive to Western pressures, but rather a pursuit of modernizing the Saudi societal fabric. Human rights, in their current global discourse, seem mired in obfuscation. While they can serve as potent tools for condemnation, placing nations in defensive postures, it is pivotal to differentiate between regimes that perpetuate systemic atrocities and those genuinely striving to enhance their citizenry's quality of life. Saudi Arabia distinctly belongs to the category of nations genuinely striving for progress regarding the societal reforms we will describe later. Those well-acquainted with the intricacies of the Kingdom will corroborate this assertion. External critiques, rather than being constructive, have oftentimes been a source of consternation for Saudi decision-makers. The reason? The commendable strides they've taken in the realm of human rights go unrecognized. The incessant and sometimes piercing critiques from Western powers, in their failure to acknowledge progress, inadvertently create a chasm of misunderstanding and breed resentment.

There's a palpable parallel between the quagmire of human rights discourse and the nebulous nature of ESG (environmental, social, and governance) criteria.[3] The methodology behind these criteria is, at best, opaque. This haziness has led to inconsistent assessments—some entities face sanctions while others, in analogous circumstances, remain untouched. One must wonder: do truly objective evaluation criteria, devoid of political undertones, even exist? An illustrative instance arose in October 2020 when the prominent US investment fund Candriam declared its intent to ostracize Russia, China, and Saudi Arabia due to subpar ESG ratings.[4] Given the temporal proximity to the US presidential election, it is challenging not to perceive this move as politically motivated. At its core, human rights were undoubtedly a factor in this investment decision. However, in focusing on Saudi Arabia, it is pivotal to acknowledge the Kingdom's extensive reforms concerning individual rights and freedoms, well before 2020. Can't we, then, recognize and appreciate the progress that has been made?

This query underscores the inherent challenges in the dialogue between Saudi Arabia and the West on the contentious subject of human rights. Saudi Arabia perceives the static nature of criticism as an affront, especially when set against the backdrop of its tangible developments. Such discord only accentuates misunderstandings. The narrative from the West, especially when it emanates from powers witnessing their global influence wane, becomes harder for the Kingdom to digest. Concurrently, the Crown Prince and the Saudi establishment abstain from leveling critiques at Western nations, anticipating a spirit of mutual respect in future engagements.

---

3   These criteria are used to assess the sustainability and ethical aspects of investments in a company or economic sector. Contrary to some misconceptions, these criteria didn't originate from the UN. They were initially conceptualized by authors drawing from religious morality. However, in 1992, the UN, inspired by these ideas, laid the groundwork for what later became known as responsible finance through the Statement of Commitment by Financial Institutions on Sustainable Development, which is part of the UN Environment Program (UNEP). It took two decades for responsible finance to become mainstream, meaning that the financial sector began to actively incorporate the principles of sustainable development into its investment policies and strategies.

4   Natasha Doff, Selcuk Gokoluk, "Top Fund's Blacklist Shows ESG Coming for Emerging Markets," Bloomberg, October 16, 2020, https://www.bloomberg.com/news/articles/2020-10-16/top-fund-s-blacklist-shows-esg-is-coming-for-emerging-markets.

Amidst this milieu, the Crown Prince remains unwavering in his commitment to areas of reform, especially those he's personally championed. Vision 2030 elucidates this path: the fulcrum of success will pivot on comprehensive modernization. The intent to enhance the living conditions in Saudi Arabia is a testament to a broader ambition—to usher the Kingdom onto the global stage. After all, how can one envisage attracting tourists and investors in a restrictive environment? The Crown Prince's decisions align with this vision, but he remains steadfast in emphasizing the Kingdom's autonomy and sovereignty. The challenges faced are not just pivotal internally; they shape Saudi Arabia's geopolitical stance on the grand chessboard.[5] It is evident in the Kingdom's inclination toward nations that refrain from unjust accusations.

---

5   This expression refers to the title of a book published in 1997 by Zbigniew Brzeziński (*The Grand Chessboard: American Primacy and Its Geostrategic Imperatives*). Brzeziński was an American political scientist of Polish origin who served as National Security Advisor from 1977 to 1981 under President Jimmy Carter.

7

The Emergence of a New Role

Each individual and nation retains the freedom to determine its own destiny. In a world that grows more competitive by the day, a nation cannot make its aspirations heard on the international stage unless those aspirations are rooted in legitimacy, credibility, and the strength to realize them. Possessing the means to execute a policy does not always equate to economic might. Nations hoping to carve out or amplify their roles within the global community must leverage a blend of hard and soft power. While some might lean toward the use of force, others might choose the subtler route of persuasion—each entity has its unique approach.

To command respect and credibility, a nation's intent must be deeply grounded in legitimacy. It is unrealistic for any nation to suddenly announce ambitions of becoming a prominent regional or global force based purely on an isolated decision of leadership. Such aspirations require meticulous planning and preparation. It is also vital to possess the resources to see policies through fruition. Recognizing this, and with an eye toward the future, Saudi Arabia aims to heighten its influence in areas where it can offer notable contributions. The nation places considerable faith in the vision of its Crown Prince.

Historically, Saudi Arabia's voice on the global stage was synonymous with its vast oil reserves. The twentieth century saw the rapid rise of a resource that became integral to the global economy and international politics: oil. Blessed with vast reserves, Saudi Arabia has for decades exploited this resource, making the country an economic powerhouse. Its commanding presence in the global oil market allows it to exert significant influence, with even the slightest hint of disruption in oil production, sales, or transportation raising global alarms—especially as the worldwide demand for oil soars. While oil has endowed the Kingdom with immense influence, it does not provide a complete solution to the nation's long-term economic challenges. Relying heavily on oil, to the extent that it dominates their economic landscape, is risky. Such dependency becomes perilous when fortunes are tied solely to the volatile oil market and its fluctuating prices. A surge in prices benefits national economic interests, but a downward trend can have severe repercussions, particularly if sustained.

Oil has undoubtedly propelled Saudi Arabia into a position of global prominence. The major geopolitical shifts after World War II—including decolonization, the Cold War, and the soaring demand for oil—further augmented Saudi Arabia's influence. This was particularly evident when it collaborated with fellow oil producers to safeguard their collective economic interests amidst the ever-shifting sands of international dynamics.

OPEC was established in 1960, initially consisting of Saudi Arabia, Iran, Iraq, Venezuela, and Kuwait. This cartel expanded over time and soon occupied a dominant role in international relations, bolstered by the vast reserves of its member nations and the nationalization strategies[1] that curtailed foreign interference. In an era of decolonization, it seemed only logical for sovereign nations to harness and benefit from the wealth within their borders.

Saudi Arabia astutely capitalized on two pivotal factors: Firstly, its vast oil reserves and its membership in an organization of increasing influence positioned the country advantageously within a rapidly changing global landscape. Secondly, the unparalleled quality of its oil, which could be accessed at shallow depths, made it unbeatably cost-effective to extract and produce. The profitability threshold for a barrel of Saudi oil is remarkably low, becoming lucrative for sellers with even modest price points.

Such favorable conditions inevitably drew the attention of international buyers, for whom Saudi Arabia emerged as an indispensable oil ally. This relationship was underpinned by the dual promise of abundant supplies and consistently competitive prices. The Kingdom strategically leveraged this demand, propelling its oil sector to rank among the world's top producers. Recognizing the paramount role of petroleum in the global economy and against the backdrop of major international disruptions, Saudi Arabia's economic horizon appeared promising. However, to ensure long-term prosperity, it was

---

1   www.aramco.com; authors' note: In the case of Saudi Arabia, the process of nationalization occurred in multiple phases during the early 1970s. It was finalized in 1980, with the changes retroactively applied to 1976. In 1988, the Arabian American Oil Company changed its name to the Saudi Arabian Oil Company (Saudi Aramco).

imperative for the country to solidify its stature as a primary force in the oil industry, particularly during the heightened attention of the 1960s and 1970s, after the creation of the OPEC cartel in September 1960 and nationalization of several oil companies that became major players in the global market.

This era stands out due to its geopolitical undertones. The Cold War was at its zenith, with events like the Cuban missile crisis, the erection of the Berlin Wall, and the space race epitomizing the tension between the East and West. While the United States and the Soviet Union often maintained their distance, their strategic maneuvers constantly intersected. If one power intervened directly, such as the United States in Vietnam, the other would bolster the opposition with funding and human and military resources. Meanwhile, many Western nations enjoyed robust economic growth, driven largely by post–World War II reconstruction—a phase eloquently termed "Trente Glorieuses" by French economist Jean Fourastié. Central to these economic revivals was an escalating demand for oil.

The year 1973 witnessed a geopolitical upheaval that sent shock waves throughout the world. The "October War" (also known as the Ramadan War or the Yom Kippur War) erupted with Israel on one side and Egypt and Syria on the other. While Israel garnered Washington's backing, Damascus and Cairo drew support from a coalition of Arab nations, including Saudi Arabia, nations with Islamic affiliations, and others propelled by communist ideologies led by Moscow.[2]

This three-week conflict is indelibly linked with the first oil shock. In its aftermath, OPEC opted for a drastic increase in oil prices—quadrupling them in a brief span—while simultaneously slashing production. The resultant surge in energy costs forced nations to reevaluate their energy dependencies, sparking a collective push toward diversification. France pivoted toward civil nuclear energy. Italy and the United Kingdom (UK) looked into the option of using natural gas. Meanwhile, Germany diversified its electricity sources to encompass natural gas, nuclear energy, and coal.

The October War profoundly reshaped the perspectives of oil purchasers,

---

2   Egypt and Syria were reinforced by contingents from Morocco, Algeria, Tunisia, Jordan, Iraq, Saudi Arabia, Kuwait, Cuba, North Korea, Sudan, Libya, Pakistan, and Uganda. They also received support from the Soviet Union and East Germany.

who felt an urgent need to diversify their energy sources to mitigate the ramifications of potential oil price crises. This conflict significantly strained relations between Saudi Arabia and the United States. Washington's support for Israel provoked Riyadh, leading the latter to enforce an oil embargo against the United States. At this juncture, Saudi Arabia was responsible for nearly one-fifth of global crude oil production.

The war afforded OPEC an unparalleled platform, showcasing its formidable influence over both oil production and pricing. During this period, under the leadership of King Faisal, Saudi Arabia ascended as a pivotal actor in the global oil arena. International buyers began to perceive Riyadh not merely as a purveyor of a treasured commodity, but as a potent political entity—a force to be reckoned with.

In a separate turn of events, 1979 saw another oil shock ripple through the global community, stemming from the fall of the Shah of Iran and the subsequent Islamic Revolution in Tehran. Oil prices soared, doubling in a short span. The trajectory was further exacerbated by the Soviet Union's invasion of Afghanistan, and the subsequent outbreak of hostilities between Iraq and Iran—both OPEC members and major oil producers.

By 1986, the world witnessed an unexpected twist when oil trading prices took a steep dive. This price slump wasn't a consequence of financial speculation, but rather a calculated geopolitical strategy. The Soviet economy, already teetering, faced the devastating Chernobyl nuclear disaster in April, highlighting its acute need for external financial aid. Recognizing that oil exports were a lifeline for Moscow, the United States discerned an opportunity to weaken its rival by strategically targeting this sector.

Through negotiations with Saudi Arabia, Washington and Riyadh reached a consensus that manipulating global crude oil output was in their mutual interest. Their tactic was straightforward: inundate the global market with oil. By fostering a scenario where supply drastically exceeded demand, oil prices tanked, hastening the Soviet Union's economic decline. The United States. relished this outcome, viewing it as a significant victory. Meanwhile, Saudi Arabia, in conjunction with OPEC, aspired to reignite global demand and accrue substantial profits. Their gambit succeeded, further solidifying Saudi Arabia's stature as a formidable influencer in international geopolitics.

Close cooperation between the United States and Saudi Arabia on oil extraction, production, and sales started on May 29, 1933. Since then, oil has served as a linchpin for the global economy, international finance, and many of today's pivotal political and diplomatic challenges. From the 1990s onward, worldwide oil consumption has seen a twofold increase. The landscape of the oil market has transformed significantly, with non-OPEC entities emerging as dominant producers. The cartel's proportion of global production has seen a steady decline due to increased supply from non-OPEC sources and production interruptions among certain OPEC members. Today, OPEC oil constitutes roughly one-third of global production, marking a noticeable dilution of its influence.

In the realm of political governance, a commonly held belief is that effective governance necessitates foresight. Recognizing its diminishing global influence, Saudi Arabia, spurred by its Crown Prince, has acknowledged the imperative of diversifying its economic blueprint to lessen its reliance on oil revenue. Its primary revenue source has simultaneously come under scrutiny, especially from the scientific community that attributes climate change, in part, to the voracious consumption of fossil fuels. The resultant emissions from their combustion not only pollute but also contribute significantly to greenhouse gas volumes. The Intergovernmental Panel on Climate Change (IPCC) annually releases its research and findings on the climate's trajectory. Their analyses are consistently sobering, bordering on distressing. These sentiments find resonance in the words of United Nations Secretary-General António Guterres, who laments the ecological degradation while simultaneously expressing concerns over the unabated surge in oil consumption over the past five decades.

On July 27, 2023, he amplified the urgency, cautioning, "The era of global warming has ended, the era of global boiling has arrived."[3] This poignant declaration, replete with forewarnings, alerts humanity to an impending climatic disaster. Guterres beckons all to fathom the gravity of this crisis and the monumental challenges on the horizon.

Ever since the Earth Summit in Rio de Janeiro in 1992, there have been incessant calls for the world to curtail its dependency on polluting resources.

---

3   "Hottest July ever signals 'era of global boiling has arrived' says UN chief," United Nations News, July 27, 2023, https://news.un.org/en/story/2023/07/1139162.

The annual UN climate summits convene global policymakers to deliberate on forthcoming strategies to combat climate change. While commitments are often professed, tangible outcomes seldom align with the established objectives.

Humanity stands at a crossroads marked by significant apprehensions about its future. On one side, prevailing climate change projections depict a harrowing acceleration of environmental degradation. The planet confronts an ominous outlook characterized by increasingly frequent, potent, and devastating natural disasters. Alongside this, the escalating temperatures may imperil the existence of numerous flora and fauna. It is imperative for the world to recognize this looming threat and curb its reliance on contaminating resources, with oil standing paramount.

For oil producers, especially those whose enterprise foundations are steeped in petroleum extraction, the hour beckons a strategic pivot. The horizon may not necessarily herald a post-oil epoch imminently, but it necessitates reimagining revenue streams. This ethos is embodied in the strategic foresight of the Saudi Crown Prince, culminating in the conceptualization of the Vision 2030 initiative.

The Crown Prince aspires to recalibrate the nation's economic trajectory by championing ambitious sectorial diversification. His ambition is to attract global talent to Saudi Arabia and promote the nation's future leaders across diverse sectors, invigorating national economic vitality. While petroleum remains a lucrative revenue source, its finiteness cannot be overlooked. Even with Saudi Arabia's staggering proven reserves—approaching 260 billion barrels[4]—this wealth does not eclipse the broader vision: championing a sustainable, lucrative economic model that amplifies Riyadh's global footprint and influence.

The Crown Prince envisions Saudi Arabia as a beacon and protagonist of enduring peace. To realize this aspiration, he must galvanize the international community's trust in his nation's dedication to this cause. Initiatives such as the rekindled dialogue with Iran manifest promising overtures for regional

---

4   "Oil reserves—Country rankings," The Global Economy, https://www.theglobale conomy.com/rankings/oil_reserves/, 2021, Authors' note: Only Venezuela has more proven reserves than Saudi Arabia, with just over 300 billion barrels of exploitable oil. Only six countries hold more than 100 billion barrels of proven reserves: Venezuela, Saudi Arabia, Iran, Canada, Iraq, and Kuwait.

harmony. Leading by example augments legitimacy. Beyond such strategic endeavors, Saudi Arabia wields an unparalleled geopolitical advantage: its strategic location.

The hallmark of visionary leadership is not confined to meticulously crafted strategies and foresight alone. Leaders also astutely leverage external dynamics to their advantage. In the regional context, Saudi Arabia, with its expansive geography and populace, stands peerless against neighbors like Bahrain, the UAE, Qatar, Oman, and even Yemen—with the caveat of Yemen's comparable population size. Although its population might fall short of those of Iraq and Iran, Saudi Arabia's geostrategic placement is an unparalleled asset, situated at the nexus of numerous trade and cultural corridors. Riyadh seamlessly interfaces with Europe, Africa, and the vast expanse of Asia. Numerous Asian nations maintain vibrant trade relations with Saudi Arabia, underscored by China's ambitions to rejuvenate the Silk Road. The Saudi realm possesses an optimal geolocation, keenly positioning it not just for economic prosperity but also to extend the international clout envisioned by its Crown Prince.

Legitimacy is not a commodity to be purchased—it must be genuinely earned. In this spirit, Saudi Arabia is resolute in championing an internal policy focused on economic, social, and cultural growth. Attracting global talent and excellence is analogous to the art of persuasion. The nation synchronously aspires to present itself as a pragmatic regional powerhouse, committed both to ensuring its economic longevity and to championing just and important causes on the world stage. In this endeavor, setting a tangible precedent is pivotal. The Crown Prince champions multiple facets he deems essential in sculpting the nation's global persona—aiming for a modern stance and an openness to dialogue while maintaining agility to harness emerging opportunities.

Any discerning analysis of Middle Eastern geopolitics reveals that the region's sociopolitical volatility often reduces its appeal. While peace is not a panacea for every economic challenge, its establishment undeniably instills confidence in potential foreign partners, thus making investment prospects more alluring. Achieving this requires addressing the specters of warfare, terrorism-induced instability, and intra-regional discord. The Crown Prince perceives peace not just as an economic boon but also as a potent enhancer of reputation for entities actively invested in the peacemaking process.

Earning international acclaim is a culmination of consistent actions, further solidified by persuading global counterparts of the merit in a nation's engagements. The Crown Prince is circumspect—he is not set on a radical overhaul of Saudi Arabia's reputation, either domestically or internationally, as this could be fraught with risks. Thus, he leans toward evolution rather than revolution. Societal habits do not shift overnight, and abrupt changes can be disconcerting, especially if the populace is not prepared for such shifts. Imposing a new mindset upon a society based solely on elite decision-making is not pragmatic.

In orchestrating domestic reforms, the Crown Prince treads with discernment. The Western press often scrutinizes his ambitions, especially when he ventures into transformative social initiatives in a nation known for its entrenched traditions. Implementing radical societal shifts could potentially disorient citizens, a scenario fraught with peril. In the quest for modernization, patience and pacing are crucial—incremental progress is key.

A similar philosophy underpins the cultivation of a nation's international reputation. It requires sustained effort and commitment. One does not amass recognition or influence by mere proclamation. To shift away from an oversimplified identity linked predominantly to oil, Saudi Arabia must demonstrate that its choices—in political, economic, diplomatic, and cultural realms—yield outcomes that resonate with, and are validated by, the global community. Without rigorous dedication and effort, it is impossible to set a global standard that garners recognition. This principle underpins the evolution of Saudi Arabia's image. Through the introduction of his Vision 2030 program, the Crown Prince has established the blueprint for the transformative economic and societal framework he envisions for the nation. This domestic progression, coupled with strategic initiatives on the global stage, is poised to amplify Saudi Arabia's stature worldwide.

8

Transitioning to the Post-Oil Era

Sheikh Zaki Yamani, the former Saudi Minister of Oil, once wisely stated, "The Stone Age did not end for lack of stone, and the Oil Age will end long before the world runs out of oil."[1] This astute observation by a leading authority on oil underscored a forthcoming shift with exceptional foresight. At the time of his pronouncement, few could fathom the prospect of abandoning such an invaluable and lucrative commodity as oil.

The allure of "black gold" has been undeniable. Those who have successfully harnessed and profited from it have amassed immense wealth. A simple examination of extraction rates and consumption patterns makes it clear: oil is depleting faster than new reserves are being discovered. Yet, the more we acknowledge its finite nature, the more voraciously we consume it. Notably, its intensive consumption is identified as a significant factor exacerbating climate change. Predictions of oil's impending obsolescence abound. Still, the challenge lies in identifying environmentally benign energy alternatives that can fulfill the colossal energy demands satisfied by oil. As global energy consumption surges, the pivotal issue becomes not the inevitability of a post-oil epoch but identifying sustainable energy alternatives that reduce our reliance on fossil fuels.

While it is a noble aspiration for humankind to mitigate the alarming levels of pollution alarming climatologists, the global economic landscape does not support a swift decline in oil production. By 2025, global demand is projected to surpass a staggering 104 million barrels daily. The paradox is clear: as the clarion call to diminish our reliance on oil grows louder, its demand and consumption reach new heights.

---

1   Terry Macalister, "Look east: Doors open to majors," *The Guardian*, November 15, 2000, https://www.theguardian.com/business/2000/nov/15/12.

Oil remains a revered commodity, primarily because it offers convenience and monumental profits. Despite advances in research and the development of cleaner energy sources, these greener solutions have yet to make a significant dent in meeting global energy requirements. Nevertheless, a time will inevitably come when we must bid adieu to oil, willingly or otherwise. Should the wells of "'black gold" run dry, how would humanity adapt? Such a prospect invites moral contemplation that transcends mere economic or strategic considerations, prompting us to ponder the legacy we intend for subsequent generations.

The core issue with oil, and fossil fuels in general, is the sheer volume of consumption and the consequent pollution from combustion. A glaring discrepancy exists between the global discourse championing an urgent energy transition and the actual patterns of energy consumption. While international policymakers set quantifiable targets at annual UN climate conferences, we must confront an uncomfortable truth. Despite the ambitions of agreements like the Conference of the Parties (COP) such as the COP 21[2] in Paris in 2015, many objectives remain unmet. This shortcoming is a growing concern for the Secretary-General of the United Nations, who frequently warns of a bleak future unless significant shifts in energy consumption habits ensue. Moreover, we ought to approach statistics indicating a decline in fossil fuel's global energy share with a healthy dose of skepticism. Following the conclusion of COP 28 in Dubai in December 2023, the United Nations embraced the agreement, marking the "beginning of the end" of the fossil fuel era.[3]

The percentage representation often fails to capture the sheer volume of consumption, a figure that continually grows in tandem with global energy demand. Notably, prominent figures like the Secretary-General of the United Nations and experts from the IPCC recognize this reality. They consistently advocate for heightened global awareness and decisive action. By emphasizing the perils of climate change, they also highlight its link to human consumption

---

2   "The increase in the global average temperature to well below 2°C above pre-industrial levels" and pursue efforts "to limit the temperature increase to 1.5°C above pre-industrial levels."

3   "COP28 Agreement Signals "Beginning of the End" of the Fossil Fuel Era," UNFCC, December 13, 2023, https://unfccc.int/news/cop28-agreement-signals-beginning-of-the-end-of-the-fossil-fuel-era.

patterns. At its core, the debate grapples with the complex challenge of harmonizing humanity's future with the pressing demands of our contemporary economic landscape.

In this discourse, oil commands a central position. Even minor international disturbances incite swift reverberations in financial markets. Fluctuations in oil prices often mirror the prevailing geopolitical climate. Such palpable trepidation is unique to this "black gold." No other resource elicits comparable emotional resonance. The mere speculation of disruptions in oil markets can set off a cascading chain of reactions. Any whisper or insinuation about reduced supply or potential shortages stirs deep anxieties concerning ramifications for entire nations.

Indeed, oil or its derivative deficit can swiftly incapacitate a country, with profound implications even for national defense. In the absence of oil, systems become susceptible, given the critical dependence of military sectors—land, naval, and air—on vast volumes of petroleum products. No other resource invokes such heightened security and strategic concerns. Yet, rationality dictates a pressing pivot toward alternative energy avenues, both for environmental sanctity and humanity's sake.

Nations like the United States, China, India, and those of the EU, among others, champion energy policies rooted in environmentally congenial solutions. However, the staggering global demand ensures that mere intent falls short. Perhaps the real transformation will be heralded by visionary leaders ardently committed to a post-oil future. The world yearns for champions, advocates, and stalwarts with an unwavering resolve to chart a future enriched with sustainable energy initiatives. Wouldn't it be poignant if the vanguard were an oil-rich nation itself?

Under the Vision 2030 initiative, the Crown Prince of Saudi Arabia opined, "All success stories start with a vision, and successful visions are based on strong pillars."[4] He identified three foundational tenets upon which Saudi Arabia aspires to grow: its pivotal role in the Arab-Muslim realm, its formidable investment prowess, and its unique geographical nexus connecting three continents. These undeniable strengths position the nation favorably for

---

4   Vision 2030, 2016, p. 6, https://www.vision2030.gov.sa/media/rc0b5oy1/saudi _vision203.pdf.

bankrolling research, development, and pioneering projects. Energy certainly emerges as one of the Kingdom's paramount challenges, starting with diminishing its fiscal reliance on oil. While this sector has been instrumental in Saudi Arabia's economic ascendancy, it also shackles the nation to the volatile whims of financial markets. A decline in oil prices has previously threatened the nation's economic stability, casting doubts among analysts, journalists, and observers about the viability of the Vision 2030 blueprint, given its ambitious scope and the economic milieu of the time. To this end, diversifying economic realities and bolstering alternative revenue-generating sectors appeared crucial. However, true visionaries have the audacity to dream, strategize, and execute. Foremost, they stand as builders. Vision 2030 transcends mere architectural drafts of prospective projects.

The Crown Prince's foresight into the post-oil epoch is illuminated by his early initiatives. Despite ascending to a senior position in the Kingdom merely a year prior, by 2016 he had already set the wheels in motion. Appointed as the Minister of Defense in January 2015, he was swiftly tasked with leading Saudi Arabia's Economical and Development Affairs Council shortly thereafter. In essence, irrespective of the weight of his official duties, he plunged headfirst into envisioning the nation's future trajectory. Such was the ambition and contemporary nature of the program that it begged the question: Was Saudi Arabia ready for the transformation envisioned by its architect?

The Crown Prince's commitment to swiftly transition into the post-oil age is underpinned by tangible objectives. By 2030, he aims to augment the nation's non-oil revenues sixfold.[5] This underscores the government's resolve to diversify the economic paradigm, offering more stability than relying solely on oil, a commodity vulnerable to international market fluctuations. This intent is also mirrored in Vision 2030's strategy to amplify the export of non-oil goods and services, contributing to the nation's gross domestic product (GDP).[6] As

5   Ibid., p. 67. Authors' note: The target set is to increase from 163 billion rials (44 billion USD) to 1,000 billion (250 billion USD) in less than fifteen years.

6   Ibid., p. 61. Authors' note: The program aims to promote exports of non-oil goods and services. At the time of publication of Vision 2030, they accounted for 16 percent of GDP generated by exports. The Crown Prince wants them to account for 50 percent of the value of GDP generated by exports.

of this writing, oil-centric goods and services constitute 84 percent of export revenues, spotlighting the Kingdom's substantial reliance on its oil industry.

Yet, it remains alluring to capitalize on a resource yielding significant dividends. Saudi Arabia, within the global oil landscape, is no outlier. It modulates its production in harmony with market dynamics to safeguard its national interests. As one of the mere trio of nations (which includes the United States and Russia) capable of producing over ten million barrels daily, it stood as the preeminent exporter in 2022, dispatching over seven million barrels daily,[7] primarily to pivotal Asian markets, including China, Japan, and South Korea.

Preparing for a post-oil future does not entail that Saudi Arabia anticipates relinquishing oil profits. Even as the nation espouses sustainable development, the importance of oil is not poised to vanish from the global discourse—unless supplanted by a newer, universally sought-after resource. While there's a concerted effort to bolster other sectors, oil will remain the economic linchpin for the Kingdom for a while. Vision 2030 adopts a pragmatic approach toward this impending reality.

Once again, the Crown Prince is not promoting a revolutionary program as he sets long-term goals, initially spanning the period from 2016 to 2030. While this timeline might appear compressed, it remains attainable, provided the Kingdom harnesses the requisite resources and remains propelled by a spirit of collective ambition. The benchmarks are challenging, yet vital to catalyze a national shift. It is a testament to the road map crafted by its chief architect. The program leans heavily on evoking national pride. It is pivotal for Saudi citizens to champion this vision, recognizing its inherent value. At the same time, the Crown Prince envisages a gradual rollout, ensuring the transition remains palatable for the populace.

One of the often-underestimated facets of governance is the need to tailor reforms to the sociocultural fabric of the nation. The Crown Prince's reforms, groundbreaking in the context of Saudi Arabia, demand this precise calibration. It necessitates an adaptive phase, ensuring reforms are not

---

7   "Production et exportations de pétrole brut de l'Arabie saoudite en 2022," March 23, 2023, https://www.tresor.economie.gouv.fr/Articles/2023/03/23/production-et-exportations -de-petrole-brut-de-l-arabie-saoudite-en-2022.

only understood but also internalized. The social changes under his leadership exemplify this approach, representing a deliberate, step-by-step progression toward modernity. Historically, Saudi society adhered to a conservative communal life ethos. It was imperative not to alienate or confuse by introducing excessively progressive reforms. The judicious strategy lies in endorsing incremental changes, ensuring they resonate with the populace and are devoid of widespread misapprehensions. The ambitious and innovative reforms initiated by the Crown Prince for the Kingdom necessitate alignment with the values of the national society. It is crucial for these reforms to be comprehended and seamlessly integrated by the Saudi people. Striking a balance is essential, avoiding reforms that might be overly progressive and risk being misunderstood by the very individuals they are intended for, thereby increasing the potential for shock or confusion.

This philosophy extends to the economic transition envisioned for the post-oil era. Given oil's dominance in the national economic blueprint, an abrupt pivot would have been imprudent. Vision 2030 serves as an intermediary stage, laying the groundwork for Saudi Arabia's post-2030 aspirations. Diminishing the economic reliance on oil aligns with global environmental concerns and strategically positions the nation to not solely depend on a singular, albeit lucrative, revenue source influenced heavily by extrinsic variables. Economic diversification is not just advisable—it is paramount. Although Saudi Arabia commands its oil production, its fiscal destiny is intrinsically tied to global financial market health. Such dependence is perilous in the absence of other vibrant economic sectors capable of countering downturns in oil. The Crown Prince, thus, champions an essential economic reorientation. Pivoting away from oil-centric dependence will undeniably mandate the inception of novel industries. Such an endeavor demands time for both implementation and fruition.

The post-oil vision also intersects with Saudi Arabia's stated global objectives, showcasing a commitment to the broader human experience. Beyond seeking global acknowledgment in peace advocacy, Riyadh aspires to establish itself as a touchstone in addressing paramount global challenges, notably climate change. Vision 2030's emphasis on environmental issues is driven by its progenitor's conviction and an ambition to position Saudi Arabia within a collaborative global effort. Historically, Saudi Arabia's oil consumption has raised eyebrows. In 2018, it ranked as the world's fifth-largest oil consumer.[8] Strikingly, its consumption overshadowed nations with significant populations like Russia and Brazil. While challenging climatic conditions and vast energy consumption partly justify this, the disproportionate reliance on oil highlights the necessity for change.

Historically, given the implications of burning oil, Saudi Arabia wasn't perceived as a nation deeply invested in environmental concerns or global issues threatening humanity. However, the vision articulated by the Crown Prince reflects a significant shift, advocating for the transformation of consumption habits. While Riyadh's continued exportation of oil is motivated by economic imperatives, there's an inherent responsibility for the nation to champion alternatives that minimize environmental impact.

Despite the skepticism of a few, the reality of climate change is undeniable. The consecutive record temperatures observed annually are not mere coincidences, nor are they solely natural phenomena. Human actions undeniably contribute to these daunting repercussions. As we hear of impending threats to the survival of diverse species, including humans, the alarm bells ring louder. Leaders endowed with the capability to influence outcomes must seize the opportunity. The rapid thawing of polar ice caps and glacial retreats across mountain ranges serve as harbingers of the unsettling rise in global temperatures. Their accelerated depletion leads to rising sea levels, potentially rendering vast regions uninhabitable.

The United Nations forecasts that these changes will disrupt the lives of hundreds of millions, ushering many into the growing fold of climate refugees. The escalating frequency and severity of climate disasters underline the urgency. Climatologists predict that cataclysms akin to Hurricane Katrina in 2005 may become less an anomaly and more a recurring nightmare. Much of this unfolding reality appears regrettably irreversible.

---

8   "Ranking of the top ten oil-consuming countries in the world in 2018 (in millions of tonnes)," en.statista.com, 2023. Authors' note: Only the United States (1,016 million tons), China (628), India (237) and Japan (173) consumed more oil than Saudi Arabia (154). In other words, national consumption exceeded that of Russia (146) and Brazil (141). All the countries on the list have a national population that exceeds one hundred million, or even one billion in the cases of China and India, which remains an anomaly given the estimated national population of thirty-six million in 2023.

Yet, humanity bears the onus of mitigating further harm and actively countering environmental degradation. Saudi Arabia, recognizing this duty, is embarking on a journey to decarbonize its economy. The push for energy diversification is not merely an economic strategy—it signifies the leadership's commitment to championing an ethical, proactive stance on pressing environmental concerns. This alignment with sustainable development seamlessly integrates with the Crown Prince's overarching vision: modernizing both Saudi society and its economy.

9

Vision 2030: The Evolution of a Nation

The guiding ethos of the Crown Prince of the Kingdom of Saudi Arabia is to evolve with the times. With precision and care, he champions transformative societal change. Such undertakings are not without their risks. The task is to usher in these reforms while striking a delicate balance between understanding and acceptance. A society cannot be modernized without repercussions if it is not ready. As such, reforms must be introduced progressively, even those pertaining to economic restructuring. Effective communication is pivotal to the success of these transitions.

In the West, there's a palpable skepticism concerning the reforms in Saudi Arabia. Questions abound. Has the status of women genuinely shifted? Undoubtedly. Saudi women now move about freely, no longer requiring prior authorization from their husbands or male guardians. They work, they drive, they smoke, and they are no longer subjected to enforced segregation from men in shopping malls. Their freedom of movement is now unparalleled compared to the past, when the feared morality police exercised stringent surveillance over their actions. Some women have abandoned the full-face covering that once concealed their entire head, opting instead to cover only their hair, while others have embraced Western styles that leave their heads entirely uncovered. Similarly, is the influence of religion in the national fabric diminishing? Some even doubt the sincerity behind the term "modernization," viewing certain decisions as mere pacification attempts for the populace, giving them an illusion of a progressive wind sweeping the Kingdom. In 2016, in a bold move that predated the official unveiling of Vision 2030, the Deputy Crown Prince curtailed the powers of the religious police, a body responsible for enforcing stringent Islamic laws. This showcased a profound resolve to usher in societal change. Yet, in 2019, the Western media spotlighted a new law safeguarding Saudi values and principles. This stoked concerns about a possible regression to a stricter moral code, particularly concerning dress codes deemed contrary to "general taste."[1] So, what's the actual narrative?

It is evident that genuine societal strides have been made in Saudi Arabia. To ensure these do not lead to social discord, a nuanced approach is crucial. Women's rights and opportunities have seen significant advancement. The youth, —in our reflection, the population under thirty—have found their voice. Activities once banned are now commonplace. The nation is undoubtedly undergoing a transformation. It is more evolutionary than revolutionary. These reforms are calibrated, taking into consideration both modern aspirations and the deeply rooted conservative values, especially those tied to religious beliefs. The Crown Prince's aim is to harmonize, balancing the needs of both the progressives and the traditionalists. This showcases a governance model rooted in judiciousness and moderation. Though it is hard to gauge all of his decisions, especially concerning women's rights, he is methodical, ensuring each advancement is not met with overpowering dissent, which could destabilize a nation where traditions are deeply interwoven into the societal fabric. Perhaps, in the not-too-distant future, reforms may address the issue of alcoholic beverages, currently forbidden but conspicuously present in private gatherings across the Kingdom's urban landscapes.[2]

The Crown Prince is treading with both caution and intent. As he shapes the future, he seeks not only to decide but also to be understood and supported, embodying the traits of a visionary leader. The real challenge is not necessarily in persuading the majority but in navigating the resistance from a minority fervently attached to time-honored traditions. He listens to staunch traditionalists and then offers a reimagined perspective, aiming to sway them toward a modified religious approach that augments Saudi Arabia's global stature and appeal.

The Crown Prince ardently upholds his vision, which he characterizes

---

1   AFP, "En Arabie saoudite, une nouvelle loi fait craindre un retour à un strict ordre moral," *Le Point*, June 19, 2019, https://www.lepoint.fr/monde/en-arabie-saoudite-une -nouvelle-loi-fait-craindre-un-retour-a-un-strict-ordre-moral-19-06-2019-2319752_24 .php.

2   In January 2024, a first outlet was granted permission to sell alcohol in Saudi Arabia only to non-Muslim diplomats and under certain conditions. To date, this Riyadh-based store remains the only one authorized in the Kingdom.

as socially liberal. Yet, he is deliberate and measured in his approach, driven by concerns of security and potential misinterpretations that could resonate beyond the Kingdom's confines. The sensitivity arises from the fact that many Muslims, even moderates, might find it challenging to reconcile the presence of non-Muslim worshippers at Islam's most revered sites. Saudi Arabia is the custodian of the most sacred locations in Sunni Islam and the pilgrimage destination for the fifth pillar of Islam, the *hajj*.

Mindful of the profound influence of words and rhetoric, the Crown Prince refrains from articulating a more moderate interpretation of Islam. He believes that such articulations could inadvertently "'make terrorists and extremists happy' because they could assert that 'we in Saudi Arabia and other Muslim countries are changing Islam into something new, which is not true.'"[3]

Saudi Arabia's unique stature, anchored in the holy cities of Mecca and Medina, lends it an inherent international prominence within the Arab-Muslim realm. Every reform enacted is meticulously observed and analyzed beyond its borders. It is imperative for the Crown Prince to remain attuned to this broader context, avoiding choices that could jolt the worldwide Islamic community. His circumspect approach is not just indicative of national governance but recognizes the broader spiritual implications that transcend national delineations. As the designated future king of a territory that hosts pilgrims from across the globe, his caution is strategic. While he might aspire to be heralded as a transformative visionary within the Islamic world, he is unlikely to radically challenge established norms at the risk of widespread misunderstanding or backlash. Every novel proposition requires thoughtful phases of implementation. Raw ambition must always be tempered by the potential fallout that could derail its objectives.

In another vein, advocating for more adaptable reforms augments Saudi Arabia's appeal on the global stage. Vision 2030, as an ambitious blueprint, embodies a palpable momentum toward excellence and progress. Its overarching goal is to maximize the potential for success of the new economic paradigm in place. Transitioning to a post-oil era demands massive investments from

---

3   James M. Dorsey, "Is Religious Reform Coming to Saudi Arabia?" *Algemeiner*, July 24, 2023, https://www.algemeiner.com/2023/07/24/is-religious-reform-coming-to-saudi-arabia/.

both domestic and international stakeholders. However, attracting expertise and championing excellence is just one aspect. There's an equally pressing need to draw foreigners to the Kingdom. The allure of societal modernization is pivotal in this endeavor. Monetary incentives alone might prove inadequate, especially when considering a nation where living conditions starkly contrast with what potential expatriates are accustomed to. This rationale is evident even in conflict zones. While some might be enticed by lucrative offers, many prioritize their safety, declining any engagement regardless of the financial lure. Not all motivations are tethered to material gains.

For years, the Western perspective on Saudi Arabia painted it as a nation where societal norms, deeply rooted in a conservative interpretation of Islam, mandated strict adherence to sharia. Such an environment, perceived as an enigma by those of other religious persuasions, often seemed at odds with Western lifestyles.

In fostering a more relaxed societal framework, the Crown Prince is reshaping global perceptions of Saudi life, signaling an era of unprecedented openness. Saudi Arabia, while proud of its rich traditions, is not an isolated entity. It thrives in symbiosis with the global economy, not only to bolster its revenues but also to cater to its diverse needs. While the Kingdom stands tall as an independent and sovereign nation, the Crown Prince acknowledges that its blueprint for progress is intertwined with international collaboration. Elevating Saudi Arabia's global stature aligns with his strategic plan, but realizing these lofty economic aspirations hinges on engaging international partners to invest in, educate, and mentor the nation's budding talents.

Embracing privatization and integrating with the global economy entails adhering to rigorous international standards. This involves collaborative ventures with those who can offer invaluable expertise and insights. The competence of a well-trained workforce will be the linchpin for the competitiveness of Saudi's public and private sectors, which will, in turn, define its economic trajectory. The challenge is creating an allure for Saudi Arabia, balancing the aspirations of its citizens with the expectations of international stakeholders, all while safeguarding the rich cultural tapestry that instills national pride.

True economic evolution is not merely aspirational—it demands meticulous planning, foresight, and a deep understanding of potential challenges. Adopting a pragmatic governance approach means grappling with both opportunities and obstacles. The initial societal reforms weren't sporadic; they were strategically timed ahead of the Vision 2030 announcement. This reflects the Crown Prince's holistic vision for the Kingdom's metamorphosis. This all-encompassing strategy recognizes the interdependence of diverse elements. It is untenable to envisage Saudi's economic rejuvenation without simultaneously preparing its societal fabric to engage with the global community. A stark disparity between societal norms and the progressive economic ideals being championed would be discordant to external observers, potentially diminishing Saudi Arabia's global appeal.

From an external vantage point, the Crown Prince's ambition transcends mere entrepreneurship or innovation; he is, in essence, an architect of transformation. In the West, there's a tendency to underestimate the enormity of the transformation underway, overshadowed by criticisms that betray a limited grasp of the ground realities. Vision 2030 is not just a fleeting strategy; it is a long-term commitment, ensuring Saudis are equipped to navigate and collaborate within the global arena. Fostering this spirit of mutual respect and understanding requires shattering outdated stereotypes and misconceptions about Saudi Arabia. True allure is not just about showcasing opportunities to foreign investors (the United States, the UAE, UK, China, India, France, Singapore, Japan, Kuwait, and Malaysia remain the main investors);[4] it is about presenting an authentic, comprehensive vision of a nation in flux. To date, there is no guarantee that this global modernization dynamic will achieve its objectives, but the intentions are real.

Vision 2030 envisions a profound transformation of Saudi Arabia's economic paradigm. The plan strongly endorses the growth of a diversified private sector, placing significant emphasis on small and medium-sized enterprises. In essence, the Crown Prince is fostering a spirit of entrepreneurship. This is a remarkable pivot for a nation that had predominantly revolved around Saudi Aramco, the state-owned colossus. Historically, its immense economic footprint had established it as one of the nation's key assets. Its initial public offering in 2019 was momentous. At the time, its valuation stood at an

---

4	"Foreign direct investment (FDI) in Saudi Arabia," Lloyds Bank, https://www.lloyds banktrade.com/en/market-potential/saudi-arabia/investment, website checked on January 21, 2024.

impressive $1.7 trillion, positioning it as the world's most valuable company, significantly outstripping its closest competitors. However, this preeminence of Saudi Aramco concealed an underlying narrative. Beyond this behemoth, what epitomized economic achievement in Saudi Arabia? Falling into the same predicament as Venezuela, another global oil heavyweight, would have been a misstep.

For years, Venezuela has been enmeshed in an enduring economic and societal quagmire, largely due to a lack of foresight, despite possessing the world's largest proven oil reserves—a monumental economic boon. A series of misguided governance decisions eventually exposed the limitations of their economic framework. The nation's financial fabric was interwoven with the fortunes of PDVSA,[5] Venezuela's counterpart to Saudi Aramco. During times of surging oil prices, the South American nation basked in prosperity. However, the economic structure crumbled when oil prices nosedived and did not rebound enough to stabilize the national budget. Venezuela's Achilles' heel was its scant sectoral diversification and the absence of a robust private entrepreneurial spirit. The model's inherent fragility was its excessive dependence on the unpredictable fortunes of the oil sector.

The Crown Prince astutely recognized the imperative of cultivating diverse revenue streams. Saudi Arabia, too, felt the pinch during the challenging oil years, notably since 2014 when prices started their downward trajectory. Few anticipated this trend would persist. The downturn was marked by two particularly severe phases, with oil prices tumbling to under thirty dollars per barrel. For many oil producers, these rates were unsustainable, translating to operational losses. The prolonged impact of this economic downturn posed serious concerns about the feasibility and funding of Vision 2030. Had the state coffers been insufficient, foreign investors would have been the next port of call. However, in the absence of the societal reforms and with a fragile economy providing minimal assurances beyond a potential oil market revival, what would have been the investor's incentive? It was clear: diversifying the economic sectors was not just advantageous—it was indispensable.

In 2020, the world was blindsided by the onset of the COVID-19 pandemic. Within mere weeks, the virus had proliferated globally, claiming the lives of

---

5   PDVSA for Petróleos de Venezuela SA.

millions. To stem its advance, countries worldwide implemented lockdowns, grinding global economic activity to a halt. One immediate repercussion was the precipitous decline in global oil demand. As consumption plummeted, supply channels remained overwhelmingly bloated. Surpluses of the so-called "black gold" began to accumulate with no takers in sight. To exacerbate matters, storage capacities neared their limits. A looming question presented itself: What would become of these accumulating, soon-to-be-unmarketable stocks? This culminated in an unprecedented event in April 2020 when West Texas Intermediate (WTI)[6] crude oil, in a historic plunge, was traded at a negative thirty-seven dollars per barrel!

Amidst this chaos, then US President Donald Trump reached out to the world's two other primary oil producers, Saudi Arabia and Russia, to jointly navigate a path out of this economic quagmire that threatened the US economic landscape. The strategic acumen of the Crown Prince in oil diplomacy, though initially enigmatic, would soon come into sharper focus. But to understand this, a brief historical backdrop is essential.

A few years prior, the United States had introduced shale oil to the global market. Revised regulations also permitted American producers to export domestically produced oil. These shifts played a critical role in the onset of declining oil prices in 2014. The United States aimed to reduce crude prices, positioning its own oil as an enticing, competitive choice in global markets. As American oil production surged, the supply began to outstrip demand, leading to plummeting prices. Initially, this trajectory seemed detrimental to economies like Saudi Arabia's. The US tactic appeared clear: pressuring Saudi Arabia or Russia into reducing production to potentially elevate prices. But the anticipated response was elusive. Prices continued their descent, seemingly favoring the United States—until the COVID-19 crisis radically altered the landscape. The global contraction in oil demand drove prices to dire lows, ensnaring US producers in a market reality they hadn't foreseen.

The timing was particularly inopportune for President Trump, who was gearing up for his 2020 reelection campaign. Then, in March 2020, amidst a brewing discord between Saudi Arabia and Russia over production strategies,

---

6   WTI stands for West Texas Intermediate. This oil is extracted in Texas and is a major benchmark for American oil.

the Crown Prince astounded global stakeholders. Contrary to expectations and despite the adverse economic implications for Saudi Arabia, he resolved to saturate the already overburdened market. This aggressive maneuver contributed to the unparalleled situation in April where, bizarrely, sellers were essentially compensating buyers to relieve them of their surplus stocks.

Reflecting upon these events with the benefit of hindsight reveals the Crown Prince's audacity and tenacity. He managed to escalate an existing oil crisis, triggered initially by the global demand shock due to COVID-19. This compelled President Trump to urgently seek cooperation between Saudi Arabia and Russia to formulate a strategy to revitalize prices. However, in the grand chessboard of international relations, desperation often equates to vulnerability. The fact that Trump was prompted to make such a move wasn't due to a myriad of choices; rather, the Crown Prince had cornered him into making that very decision.

This episode of tumultuous market fluctuations serve as a stark reminder to Saudi Arabia's leaders of the inherent vulnerabilities in depending solely on oil revenues. The 2016 crisis, an outcome of US strategic interventions influencing trading prices, and the unforeseen external shock in 2020 that paralyzed the global economy underscore the exigency for Saudi Arabia to diversify its sources of economic strength. The Kingdom's reliance on oil, while historically lucrative, is manifestly fraught with peril. For a genuine economic metamorphosis to occur, it needs to be supplemented by evolving societal norms. However, the drive for economic and societal change, though initiated with fervor, has often been met with skepticism in the West. Doubts persist. Many in the international community view the reforms as less a genuine commitment to societal transformation and more a calculated charade aimed at a more nuanced control of the populace. While this perspective may seem convenient, it belies a nuanced understanding of the Saudi political and societal fabric.

Undertaking societal reforms in Saudi Arabia was no mean feat. It entailed navigating a complex landscape, where the buy-in of influential stakeholders was paramount. The success of the reforms will need to be carefully assessed by 2030. As for the pivot toward economic diversification, an integral component involved enticing international talent to mentor and nurture Saudi Arabia's emerging generation of leaders and professionals. To entice such expertise, it was indispensable to promise living conditions congruent with their global experiences and expectations. Through championing Saudi Arabia's economic and societal modernization, the Crown Prince is not merely embarking on domestic reforms but is attempting to actively usher the nation onto the global stage. To merely focus on the endgame and overlook the myriad challenges and considerations that had to be meticulously navigated before his reformative vision could be predominantly embraced and implemented is to miss the true essence of this transformational journey.

10

Saudization and the Resurgence of National Pride

Introduced by the Ministry of Labor and Social Development in 2011, Saudization—also known as Nitaqat—is a policy compelling Saudi companies and businesses to employ a specified number of nationals within their workforce. This initiative aligns with the broader goals of Vision 2030, which places a priority on tackling unemployment. As the Crown Prince endeavors to diminish the overbearing influence of Saudi Aramco on the national economy, bolstering the private sector has become imperative. Under Nitaqat, private entities are categorized based on the proportion of Saudi nationals they employ. "Platinum" denotes those with the highest national employment ratio, while "Red" signifies the least. The policy accounts for company-specific factors and proposes incentives for top performers and punitive measures for those lagging.

While Saudi Arabia's national employment strategy might seem unique, several nations have embraced similar policies. As Saudi Arabia looks to the future, it is likely that reforms will be introduced to enhance the nation's appeal to foreign enterprises. Considerations might include relaxing stringent legal provisions, such as the current mandate requiring businesses to establish their registered office within the Saudi jurisdiction, which potentially deters some prospective investors.

Saudi Arabia's pivot toward prioritizing domestic employment springs from a combination of demographic shifts and economic considerations. The burgeoning young population and the consequent surge in working-age individuals underscored a pressing need, especially given the relatively nascent private sector in the Kingdom. Despite oil revenue influxes, the nation faced a looming challenge: ensuring ample employment opportunities for its citizens. It became evident that a strategy anchored solely by Saudi Aramco's dominance was unsustainable, particularly with the uncertainty surrounding long-term oil price stability vital for national budget equilibrium.

This dual challenge precipitated the inception of Nitaqat, a sentiment echoed and championed by the Crown Prince in Vision 2030. Beyond its overt employment objectives, this policy subtly nurtures a renewed sense of national pride. This facet is paramount in grasping the Crown Prince's vision. By championing sustainable employment for Saudi nationals, he fortifies their unwavering allegiance. This, in turn, empowers the populace, fostering pride in being part of an evolving, efficient economic framework.

The success of Vision 2030 is contingent upon its resonance with the people. When policies prioritize Saudi nationals, enhancing their professional prospects, it engenders a pervasive sentiment of being valued by the leadership. Furthermore, the state's considerable investments in ensuring a promising economic trajectory underscores the commitment to the populace. When viewed through this prism, Vision 2030 becomes more than just a plan; it is a testament to a nation's commitment to its citizens. This social contract benefits individuals by providing employment stability and the associated financial security. Remarkably, this is set against a backdrop where Saudi nationals are not burdened with personal income tax, and the corporate tax structure remains highly favorable.

From the perspective of the state, ensuring full employment of nationals and fostering prosperity acts as a bulwark against potential protest movements and diminishing support for the ruling elite. Given this context, it is hard to fathom any substantial opposition to Nitaqat.

However, the reality of unemployment looms large in Saudi Arabia. According to the Vision 2030 program, the unemployment rate stood at 11.6 percent in 2016, with an ambitious goal to bring it down to 7 percent by 2030,[1] this initiative being achieved in 2025. Profound disparities persist

---

1   Vision 2030, 2016, p. 39, https://www.vision2030.gov.sa/media/rc0b5oy1/saudi _vision203.pdf. Authors' note: When the Vision 2030 program was introduced in April 2016, the primary international oil benchmarks were trading at less than thirty dollars per barrel, a level that was unsatisfactory for the Saudi economy. This challenging economic environment contributed to an increase in the unemployment rate. The employment targets set by the program might have appeared ambitious, especially considering the country's economic hardships, as the future of the global oil market was uncertain.

between the nation's privileged elite and its impoverished citizens. The societal landscape in Saudi Arabia has experienced seismic shifts, necessitating a reimagined employment model. The country's demographic trajectory is striking: from 4 million in 1960, the population swelled to 6 million by 1970, surged to 16 million by 1990, and stands at a staggering 36 million today.[2] Over six decades, the population has seen a near ninefold increase. The fertility rate has experienced a simultaneous decline, plummeting from over seven children per woman in the 1980s to just below three post-2009.[3] Compounding this demographic shift is the increased national life expectancy, which went from fifty-two years in 1970 to a notable seventy-seven years in 2023.[4] The Crown Prince envisions pushing this number to eighty by 2030.

Collating these demographic trends paints a clear picture: the working-age population has experienced exponential growth. Relying on the revenues from Saudi Aramco became untenable, especially when oil market prices were not conducive to balancing the national budget. This prompted a strategic shift in the state's employment policy, culminating in the Saudization model, which would later be enshrined in the Vision 2030 initiative.

Addressing employment is not merely a fleeting concern; it is a strategic imperative across short-, medium-, and long-term horizons. The logical step forward was to bolster the private sector, instilling it with regulatory frameworks that favored the employment of Saudi nationals. The nation wasn't insulated from the ramifications of the 2008 global financial crisis. Symbolized by the collapse of Lehman Brothers, the infamous subprime crisis sent shock waves through the global financial ecosystem, with the oil sector caught in its crosshairs. Speculation around oil led to volatility, with Brent crude oil prices peaking at nearly $140 a barrel in June 2008, only to plummet to $45 by the end of the year. Between December 2006 and June 2008, oil prices witnessed an unprecedented rise of $80 per barrel. Financial institutions, in their quest for short-term gains, speculated heavily on this essential commodity, reaping substantial profits. However, when the subprime bubble eventually burst, its

---

2   Saudi Arabia, https://datacommons.org/place/country/SAU, site consulted on July 29, 2023 (original source: www.datacatalog.world.org).

3   Ibid.

4   Ibid.

impact was cataclysmic, engulfing everything in its path—with the oil sector bearing a significant brunt of the fallout.

The period from 2007 to mid-2008 marked an epoch of astounding revenue for Saudi Arabia. As the nation accumulated historic profits, the juxtaposition between its profits and the production cost of its oil was stark. However, the financial crisis starkly illustrated the volatile nature of global events and their capacity to abruptly disrupt prevailing trends. The plummeting oil prices during this period destabilized the fiscal stability of numerous public and private oil conglomerates. While the oil market demonstrated resilience by rebounding, the 2008 crisis was an alarming harbinger for Saudi authorities. It forced introspection: Should the nation persist in its heavy economic reliance on oil? With global demand steadily increasing, would this be sustainable? And if adverse oil market conditions persisted indefinitely, how would Saudi Arabia cater to its burgeoning workforce, already precariously poised with scant job opportunities?

As early as 2011, Saudi leaders began working on anticipating the future and mitigating the effects of a downturn in oil revenues. It became necessary to design regulatory frameworks and mechanisms aimed at facilitating Saudi nationals' access to the labor market. The contribution of the program developed by the Crown Prince lies in its pursuit of balance. To achieve the stated goals, the plan cannot rely merely on rhetoric. It proves coherent insofar as it promotes entrepreneurship while acknowledging the surrounding realities that must be addressed. It safeguards Saudi employment while also encouraging openness to the world—offering opportunities for investors to pursue their interests in Saudi Arabia and to rely on a national workforce, one that will be educated and trained to meet high standards. In essence, Saudization existed before the Crown Prince came to power. However, he restructured and incorporated it into his broader vision, aimed at attracting foreign companies to establish a presence in the Kingdom.

Embedded within this economic paradigm, Nitaqat epitomizes the Crown Prince's developmental vision. The ethos of "Let's put Saudis in Saudization" serves as a clarion call, urging nationals to resonate with this narrative and wholeheartedly embrace it. The legal frameworks in place are tailored to empower Saudi job seekers, mandating companies to maintain a stipulated quota of nationals. These strategic maneuvers are pivotal in transitioning to a post-oil epoch while securing employment opportunities.

But this vision transcends mere economic pragmatism; it resonates as a tribute to national pride. For Saudis, the journey is not solely about abiding by the established regulations. It is a palpable sense that the state, in its wisdom, is meticulously crafting a road map for collective prosperity. The audacious objectives of Vision 2030 demand unanimous endorsement, transcending mere rhetoric. The Crown Prince's vision stands poised to thrive because Saudis not only support it but also take immense pride in it. They envisage their model as a hallmark of success and sustainability. The Crown Prince, to many Saudis, is not just a figurehead but an emblem of hope, charting the nation's future across political, economic, and societal spectrums. He embodies aspiration, stirring collective ambition, urging Saudis to not merely dream, but to actualize their vision, thereby sculpting the nation's future on the world stage.

By 2030, Saudi Arabia aspires to raise the percentage of foreign direct investment (FDI) from 3.8 percent to 5.7 percent of its GDP.[5] Successfully achieving this would position the nation as an increasingly attractive jurisdiction for investment. While the establishment of small and medium-sized enterprises is crucial, it alone cannot address the national employment challenge. Integrating foreign companies that generate employment opportunities becomes essential, as the governing authorities actively pursue international partnerships.

Saudi Arabia's diplomatic strategies on the global stage carry significant weight. As the Kingdom safeguards its economic interests, it projects a sense of national pride, which may be interpreted differently in Western contexts.

Many critics question the feasibility of Vision 2030 due to its ambitious scope and immense financial requirements. Skepticism surrounds the nation's financial capacity and the proposed myriad social and economic reforms. There's a prevailing sentiment that the brand of nationalism endorsed by the Crown Prince may face challenges, especially if the economic policies do not yield the anticipated outcomes. In essence, the link between Saudi nationalism and its economic success seems intertwined: the more robust the economic performance, the more profound the national pride.

---

5   Vision 2030, 2016, p. 5, https://www.vision2030.gov.sa/media/rc0b5oy1/saudi_vision 203.pdf.

However, our perspective is more optimistic. According to our research and discussions held with several Saudis based abroad and citizens the Gulf Cooperation Council (GCC) member states,[6] the Crown Prince enjoys considerable popularity and backing. We argue that Saudi patriotism will gain even more traction if Saudi Arabia's image gains positive international recognition. Unlike nations forged through resistance to invasions or battles for freedom, Saudi Arabia's national identity could be sculpted by a leader's vision of peace, innovation, and global significance. While critics may doubt the success of Vision 2030, only time will provide a definitive answer.

Since the introduction of Vision 2030, several economic setbacks, including the decline in oil prices starting in 2014 and the challenges of the COVID-19 pandemic after 2020, have undoubtedly affected its ambitious trajectory. However, the Crown Prince's resilience is evident. He remains unwavering in his commitment to the Vision, adapting both political and diplomatic strategies to serve the best interests of the Kingdom. His resolute stance not only seems to bolster his popularity but also to foster a deeper connection between the nation's citizens and their leadership.

In Western contexts, national identity often emerges from significant, sometimes tumultuous events, uniting people in shared struggles. Yet, why can't a nation's pride and identity be shaped under different circumstances, guided by the vision and charisma of a leader?

---

6   Gulf Cooperation Council (GCC), a political and economic alliance of six Middle Eastern countries—Saudi Arabia, Kuwait, the United Arab Emirates, Qatar, Bahrain, and Oman.

11

Uniting the Kingdom: The Crown Prince's Vision for Saudi Arabia

In Western circles, the governance style of Saudi Arabia's Crown Prince is a subject of much speculation. To some, his leadership seems questionable, his societal reforms are construed as mere tools to consolidate power, and his public image remains less than flattering. Despite these external perceptions, those familiar with the intricacies of the Saudi nation will attest to his substantial popular support.

The Crown Prince's commitment to modernity has meant challenging deep-seated conservatism. Embarking on this transformative journey, he initiated dialogues with religious and tribal leaders to ensure that his vision for reform would gain traction. Reform is not instantaneous; upending a system rooted in time-honored traditions is a delicate endeavor. Any change risks resistance or backlash. However, modifications must mirror societal shifts, environmental adaptations, and the evolving aspirations of citizens. Without their support, national cohesion would be a distant dream. This is not to say he seeks or expects unanimous approval—a unanimous consensus is unattainable in any governance model. But prior to instituting reforms, it was imperative that the Crown Prince did not alienate influential conservative figures.

A public image must be cultivated—and the same goes for the spirit of governance. Everything hinges on finding the right balance. In theory, it sounds simple. But only on the surface. Governing is far more complex than it appears, as many factors must be considered, such as the specific characteristics of the national population, globalization, and the interconnectedness of domestic and international interests. In other words, a decision-maker takes risks when promoting new ideas. In essence, every policy proposition is a gamble: will the masses embrace the envisioned change?

Modernization, though ongoing, has garnered considerable support, especially from the youth—Saudi Arabia's most significant demographic. Two-thirds of its citizens are under thirty. As the growth rate of the national population moderates, it is evident that the bulk of young Saudis fall between fifteen and thirty years of age. This demographic, comprising teenagers, young adults, and early-career professionals, resonates with the societal shifts championed by the Crown Prince.

Saudi Arabia, contrary to some perceptions, is no isolated land. It is dynamically engaged with the global community. Modern technologies, especially digital communication platforms, have played a pivotal role in promulgating the nation's modernizing policies. The omnipresence of the internet and social media redefines governance paradigms. Anyone, anywhere, can transmit messages, echoing their sentiments to a vast audience.

Take 2011, for instance, when the Arab Spring cascaded across multiple nations, but seems to have had less effect in traditional monarchies such as one in the Kingdom of Morocco and in the GCC countries, including Saudi Arabia, for several reasons. One of the reasons may be a closer relationship between rulers and ruled. Social media platforms emerged as instrumental mechanisms of organization and communication. They united people, emboldening them to contest oppressive regimes where once they would have faced severe repercussions. These movements transcended personal apprehensions. Masses converged on streets, defying governmental diktats, propelled by the belief in collective strength. Rapidly, individual aspirations merged, culminating in formidable social movements, as personal fears dissolved in the face of collective resolve.

No statesman should overlook the sentiments of their constituents, even within a system that employs coercion. Barring a complete international isolation, people communicate and disseminate information via the internet. Those in power must acknowledge this reality while upholding the core principles of their governance approach.

Saudi Arabia is a focal point for global analysts due to its considerable influence. Geographically positioned in Asia, yet integrally connected to Europe and Africa, its significance in the oil sector is such that concerns about its stability ripple through global financial markets. The international community remains watchful of how Riyadh will foster conditions to allure global investors. The Arab Spring, which unfurled in regions proximate to Saudi Arabia, offers a poignant backdrop for understanding the Crown Prince's governance philosophy. Winning the trust and support of citizens means grasping their aspirations and addressing them. In governance, reciprocity is palpable: leaders who address citizens' needs are often rewarded with affection and loyalty.

Detractors from abroad may portray this as a meticulously devised ploy to feign freedom while consolidating authority. Such critiques, however, potentially underestimate the discernment of the Saudi populace. The nation boasts an educated citizenry engaged with global dialogues. A testament to this is the prolific use of platforms like Instagram, Twitter, and Snapchat among Saudis, with each platform boasting an estimated 10 to 15 million users. These metrics underscore the country's active engagement with global narratives. The Crown Prince traveled to the United States to meet founders and CEOs of world-renowned companies (including Apple, Cisco Systems, Facebook, Google, and Microsoft) based in the Silicon Valley. Keen to invest Saudi funds in a promising start-ups, these meetings also aimed at gathering information and advice to promote innovation, particularly in Saudi Arabia.

The pervasive digital landscape invariably impacts national governance strategies, particularly in populous nations like Saudi Arabia. Leaders face the arduous task of adapting their governance style to a constantly evolving digital milieu. The Crown Prince's ambitions to modernize the Saudi societal fabric duly factor in this digital dimension.

Yet, the digital realm is akin to a double-edged sword for any governing authority. The internet is a repository of both authentic information and misinformation. It is a formidable tool of influence but also a potential source of concern for governments. Ideas and sentiments, whether valid or not, spread at lightning speed. Decisions made at the highest levels of governance are immediately subject to public scrutiny, inviting both acclaim and criticism. To mitigate potential backlash and waning popularity, leaders must strike a delicate balance in their decision-making processes. In democracies where leaders are popularly elected, a dip in popularity could culminate in electoral defeat. Similarly, in constitutional monarchies, the mandate to govern is often contingent on sustained public approval.

In Saudi Arabia, the monarch holds the mantle of public power. The authority to make pivotal decisions rests with him. His legitimacy as a leader is not rooted in democratic elections; however, it is essential to exercise caution, as public opinion remains significant. Leadership demands not only the ability to lead but also the insight to navigate challenges, striving to strike a balance and achieve consensus. Since his ascension, the Crown Prince has immersed himself in the Kingdom's most critical and strategic sectors, including national defense and the economy. It is imperative for any leader to align these sectors with the populace's expectations, as a nation's primary concerns are security and economic prosperity. A citizenry plagued by insecurity and poverty is unlikely to rally behind its leadership.

Given the numerous crises in the Middle East and the societal disparities within Saudi Arabia, the Crown Prince is committed to instilling confidence in all. He perceives his role as the guardian of the Saudi nation, ardently defending it from external threats, addressing employment challenges, and remaining attuned to the public's aspirations and prevailing trends. His vision encompasses the Saudi Arabia of both today and the future. For this vision to materialize, he needs the public's trust and support. Successful governance hinges on a symbiotic relationship between rulers and their subordinates. When the populace feels genuinely valued and cherished by its leaders, they reciprocate with steadfast support.

The notion of a "clash of civilizations" has been broached before. The digital age brings with it mixed sentiments. While digital platforms can amplify authentic information, making it more accessible and comprehensible, they can also distort perceptions, especially of outsiders. Do we genuinely strive to understand others, embracing cultural diversity without prejudice? Samuel P. Huntington's thesis[1] depicted a world transitioning from ideological confrontations to cultural ones after the Cold War. Yet, amidst these cultural dynamics, powerful nations have historically sought to propagate their worldviews.

For centuries, this imperialistic mindset defined the colonial era. Nations ventured forth, annexing territories to impose new administrative structures, alter societal norms, and occasionally, propagate religious doctrines. Although the colonial empires receded in the latter half of the twentieth century, Western powers still endeavored to maintain their influence over the emergent, sovereign nations. The global landscape has since undergone monumental shifts, with Western hegemony increasingly challenged. Past narratives, once

---

1   Samuel P. Huntington, *The Clash of Civilizations and the Remaking of World Order* (New York, Simon & Schuster, 1996), 367.

accepted, are now met with skepticism by nations intent on charting their path, unburdened by external dictums. Other poles of domination have emerged or are in the process of defining their zone of influence.

Critics who cast aspersions on the Crown Prince and his governance often overlook the sentiments of the Saudi people. They are not a subjugated populace but one that genuinely supports their leader. Saudis rally behind him, resonating with his holistic vision. The societal reforms he has initiated dovetail with objectives to invigorate the national economy, reduce unemployment, and fulfill the people's aspirations.

In Western contexts, there's often skepticism regarding the authenticity of the privileges afforded to certain populations. The presumption is that these are merely tactics to blind the masses and solidify the authority of their leaders. Such a perception, however, appears overly simplistic when applied to an enlightened populace like that of Saudi Arabia—a nation that is globally connected and well-informed. The Saudis are acutely aware of their national landscape, and it is essential to respect the distinctive cultural nuances that set them apart from Western norms. The country's population actively endorses and comprehends the ongoing reforms, aligning themselves with the ambitious endeavor to transform Saudi Arabia into a global economic powerhouse. The unveiling of Vision 2030 surely elicited mixed reactions, ranging from palpable enthusiasm to reservations, especially regarding the potential diminution of the nation's cornerstone economic sector.

To actualize this vision, the Crown Prince undertook the daunting task of galvanizing his compatriots, articulating a governance blueprint attuned to the Kingdom's economic aspirations. It is noteworthy that this model also aligns with global trade imperatives. A strategy is only efficacious when it resonates with potential international collaborators, ensuring that engagement conditions align with their anticipations.

However, this does not imply that Saudi Arabia is relinquishing its sovereign decision-making. The Kingdom remains steadfast in its autonomy, dictating its operational parameters. Yet, there's an active endeavor to refine these parameters to allure foreign investments and expertise, a move poised to bolster the Saudi economy and elevate the standard of living for its nationals.

The empowerment of Saudi women, exemplified by granting them the right to drive, is often misconstrued in the West as a superficial concession masking a less progressive reality. Such critiques overlook the broader spectrum of liberties now accessible to Saudis. It is vital to recognize that profound reforms are not instantaneous; they necessitate meticulous planning and phased implementation. While Saudi Arabia's societal norms may deviate from Western paradigms, it is imperative to refrain from precipitous judgments. On what grounds and criteria do we appraise another culture's ethos? While the West might perceive the Crown Prince predominantly as a political figure, his role as a nation-builder cannot be understated. The profound societal transformations under his aegis are occasionally dismissed with the ancient adage *"panem et circenses"*[2] (bread and circuses). Such a characterization grossly underestimates a discerning populace that is astutely aware of global developments and is informed through diverse channels, debunking any notion of insularity.

In its Vision 2030 blueprint, Saudi Arabia envisions tourism as a pivotal pillar of its reimagined economic framework. The ambition extends beyond attracting religious pilgrims, aiming to welcome tens of millions of global tourists annually. The realization of this development plan necessitates cultivating an environment that entices tourists to Saudi Arabia. This outreach would be futile if the nation's image starkly contrasted with the expectations and inclinations of potential visitors; they would simply choose to go elsewhere. The Kingdom is actively sculpting its global image, ensuring it possesses the means to fulfill its lofty aspirations. The journey toward modernization is underway, but it is important to recognize that modernity is not universally championed within Saudi Arabia. There are factions that ardently uphold conservative values. From the Crown Prince's perspective, these conservative stances seemed incongruent with the strategic vision required for a seamless transition to a post-oil era. Decisions, albeit difficult, were imperative, and they needed broad acceptance. The Saudi populace admires this decisiveness in their Crown Prince. He is not merely appeasing them with superficial gestures; he's profoundly committed to the essence of these societal transformations, viewing them as vital to the national rejuvenation he envisions.

---

2   Literally, "bread and circus games." This quote is attributed to the satirical author Juvenal, who criticized the state of mind of his contemporaries in ancient Rome. With this expression, he blamed the people for only worrying about their stomachs and their leisure time. The emperors took advantage of this mindset. In other words, it would not take much to satisfy the masses.

12

The Pursuit of Excellence

Nations harboring bold economic development ambitions often employ language resonating with performance and excellence. Such terms inherently exude positivity, alluding to an invigorated momentum centered on obtaining tangible results and fostering commendable progress. While there's a temptation in many instances to perceive such proclamations with a shade of demagoguery, Saudi Arabia stands distinct. The Vision 2030 plan is not merely a lofty aspiration; it is grounded in pragmatism. This blueprint reflects a holistic understanding of diversifying avenues to fortify the nation's economic future. Saudi Arabia possesses the requisite resources and wherewithal to actualize its policy. Indeed, the financial magnitude of the Kingdom often becomes a topic of discourse, especially given the West's occasionally skeptical view on its investment endeavors.

A prominent case in point is the realm of football. The global football stage witnesses elite players and coaches gravitating toward the Saudi league, enticed by lucrative packages. But is this expenditure warranted? Critics are quick to question the lavishness of these transfer deals and salary structures. Is Saudi Arabia merely splurging without a cause? Contrary to such conjectures, these investments are strategic. The sudden influx of renowned sportspersons is not a mere pursuit of opulence. While these figures undeniably benefit from their association with the Saudi league, it equally propels the Kingdom's larger objectives.

The pursuit is not merely about accruing global talent. A lot of ink has been spilled on the acquisitions of football luminaries like Cristiano Ronaldo, Neymar, and Karim Benzema. Many perceive these signings as these maestros paving a path toward a lucrative swan song. Yet, they are more than just marquee players; they are emblematic envoys of global football. These sporting icons encapsulate a universal ethos Saudi Arabia eagerly wishes to embrace; a sentiment fervently championed by its Crown Prince.

Moreover, emerging talents, already decorated with significant accolades, are now aligning with clubs they might have overlooked in years past, irrespective of the handsome remuneration on the table. Football is emblematic of Saudi Arabia's overarching strategy: a relentless drive to harness premier expertise across various domains. It is a misconception to solely attribute the Kingdom's allure to its financial prowess. Beyond its material wealth, there lies a profound vision—to magnetize the world's best and foster the next generation of the nation's luminaries.

At the intersection of geographical magnificence and cultural opulence, Saudi Arabia envisions becoming a prime global tourist destination. Recognizing its untapped tourism potential rooted in its rich heritage, the Kingdom has earmarked tourism as a top national priority. Hosting prestigious events like the Dakar Rally in its expansive deserts for years has already given the nation unparalleled media attention, allowing foreigners a fresh perspective into the nation's grandeur. Vision 2030 articulates this dream lucidly, setting an audacious target to allure thirty million tourists annually.[1]

To manifest this vision, extensive groundwork is imperative. Preparing for a surge of tourists necessitates state-of-the-art accommodations, transportation, and other infrastructural facilities. This calls for robust investment. The December 1, 2024, launch of Riyadh's state-of-the-art metro system, a blend of advanced technology and sustainable development,[2] now offers residents of the capital an alternative mode of transportation that helps ease road congestion and daily traffic jams. Once completed, it will feature six lines serving eighty-five stations. This achievement is part of the massive King Abdulaziz Project for Riyadh Public Transport, aimed at modernizing the city and preparing it to host upcoming global events such as the 2030 World Expo and the 2034 FIFA World Cup. Additionally, unlocking the nation's tourism potential will pivot on its ability to enchant visitors with mesmerizing sites and top-tier services. In 2024, reports began circulating in the media regarding a

1   Vision 2030, 2016, p.19, https://www.vision2030.gov.sa/media/rc0b5oy1/saudi_vision203.pdf.

2   The network, spanning 176 kilometers, is the longest in the world for a fully driverless train system. The total estimated cost is $22.5 billion (Source: "Riyadh Metro, Saudi Arabia," August 3, 2023, https://www.railway-technology.com/projects/riyadh-metro-saudi-arabia/?cf-view).

major new project: Saudi Arabia is preparing to launch its luxury train, *Dream of the Desert*,[3] an exclusive travel experience traversing the heart of the nation. This five-star train is poised to join the ranks of the world's most illustrious rail journeys, akin to the legendary *Orient Express*. Developed through a partnership between Saudi Arabia Railways and the Italian luxury hospitality giant Arsenale Group, this initiative is part of a broader strategy to establish Saudi Arabia as a premier destination recognized for excellence in service and hospitality.

This drive toward excellence warrants equipping the young Saudi generation with world-class training, tailored to meet and exceed the expectations of the global visitors. Saudi Arabia's commitment to this mission is evident in its policies that emphasize high standards for performance. Excellence is not just an aspiration; it is a mandate. Striving for the best, refining it, and elevating it further enhances the nation's global reputation. An esteemed reputation further boosts its international standing. Riyadh understands the soft power this yields and has prudently allocated significant resources, viewing each expenditure as a long-term investment. These allocations are not whimsical; they're backed by comprehensive market research and feasibility studies.

Yet, it is simplistic to presume that financial might is the sole driver. True excellence is a blend of strategic recruitment to nurture future luminaries and an inherent culture of seeking unparalleled standards. Distinctiveness in the global arena emerges when one outperforms competitors. Vision 2030's blueprint, encompassing sectoral diversification, inherently includes collaboration with eminent experts from across the globe. The higher education realm, for instance, is an area of intense focus. While institutions such as King Abdelaziz University and King Saud University in Saudi Arabia are recognized as leading educational establishments in the Arab world, the 2022 Shanghai Ranking emphasizes a more extensive aspiration: for Saudi Arabia to establish itself as a shining beacon for higher education and cutting-edge research, even beyond the 100th world rank.[4]

3   Everett Potter, *"Saudi Arabia to Launch Dream of the Desert, the Middle East's First Luxury Train,"* February 13, 2024, https://www.forbes.com/sites/everettpotter/2024/02/13/saudi-arabia-to-launch-dream-of-the-desert/.

4   "2022 Academic Ranking of World Universities," Shanghai Ranking, 2022, https://www.shanghairanking.com/rankings/arwu/2022.

In a pattern mirrored globally, Saudi Arabia seeks collaborations with illustrious academicians to augment the stature of its universities. However, beyond such associations, the deeper objective is to instill in the youth an insatiable hunger for unparalleled excellence. This philosophy permeates not just research but all facets of higher education. The dual strategy focuses on both enticing international students and securing globally renowned experts. The Crown Prince's ambition is clear: a Saudi Arabia that is open, vibrant, and a magnet for global talent.

Saudi Arabia's potential for growth is significant, particularly when paired with state-of-the-art infrastructures and an unwavering commitment to enhancing educational quality. It must get rid of old teaching methods that did not fit in with the training requirements for many professional activities. For instance, the memorization model is unsuitable for jobs requiring analysis. Saudi Arabia is working to reform its school system to educate and train the younger generation to make the country benefit from their skills and increase their competitiveness.

While the socioeconomic fabric of Saudi Arabia reveals challenges in employment and public health, Vision 2030 offers a beacon of hope by fostering entrepreneurship. Recognizing that the backbone of robust economic systems globally is often their private sectors, the Kingdom is championing its citizens to embark on entrepreneurial journeys. However, a pertinent question looms: In which sectors should these nascent enterprises anchor? This is critical because private-sector expansion must cater to the actual needs of the Saudi populace in terms of goods and services. In March 2024, *The New York Times* reported that Saudi authorities, through the Public Investment Fund (PIF), intend to invest over $40 billion in artificial intelligence,[5] a rapidly growing field that is at the center of extraordinary technological advancements anticipated in the near future. Such a policy could, in time, position Saudi Arabia among the world's leading nations in emerging technologies. On the global front, businesses originating in Saudi Arabia will be vying for market share

---

5   Maureen Farrell, Rob Copeland, "Saudi Arabia Plans $40 Billion Push into Artificial Intelligence," *New York Times*, March 19, 2024, https://www.nytimes.com/2024/03/19/business/saudi-arabia-investment-artificial-intelligence.html.

amidst stiff competition. Their survival and growth will necessitate pinpointing unique market niches and constantly elevating their expertise.

Geographically, Saudi Arabia is a strategic nexus, located at the crossroads of three continents. This vantage point becomes particularly invaluable against the backdrop of evolving international dynamics and power play.

As the tussle between China and the United States intensifies over global economic dominance, the world witnesses the consequent ripple effects. While Washington endeavors to retain its supremacy, Beijing's ambitions lean toward pivoting the world's economic axis toward the East. Amidst these global fluctuations, Saudi Arabia perceives an opportunity, especially as Europe grapples with uncertainties surrounding its economic future in an increasingly competitive milieu. Concurrently, Africa, rich with untapped potential, emerges as a focal point of opportunities. As traditional ties with former colonial powers wane in certain regions, Saudi businesses might find fertile ground to fortify their strategic interests.

The term *tajdid*[6] is becoming increasingly prevalent in contemporary discourse, sometimes juxtaposed or conflated with artificial intelligence. However, its precise definition remains elusive. At the heart of major global powers, innovation is pivotal, for it offers a competitive edge—an advantage in possessing what rivals do not. Saudi Arabia, recognizing this, is channeling investments into pioneering projects spanning sectors like health, new technologies, energy, agri-food, and beyond.

However, leveraging inherent strengths is crucial. While Saudi Arabia's local climate may not immediately suggest agricultural prowess, innovation could alter this narrative. Given the significant investments being funneled into R&D by companies globally to counter climate-related challenges, Saudi Arabia's substantial investments in overseas agricultural land hint at its forward-thinking strategy. Focused on maximizing productivity while judiciously utilizing natural resources, including water, the Kingdom's agricultural vision is deeply interwoven with innovation.

Digital technology and emerging technologies present unparalleled opportunities for progress and innovation. Three decades ago, few could have

---

6   This is an Arabic word for an innovative approach involving an intelligible and constructive vision.

foreseen the meteoric rise of the internet, a platform that has since minted countless entrepreneurs and revolutionized global paradigms. The transformative power of the internet is evident not only in the plethora of jobs it has generated but also in the vast array of goods and services it has made directly available to consumers. During his official visit to Saudi Arabia in May 2025, President Trump was accompanied by several of the world's most influential business leaders, including Elon Musk, Mark Zuckerberg, and Sam Altman. Many of the trade agreements signed between the two countries focused on advanced technologies, which is why Donald Trump refers to Riyadh as an emerging "high-tech capital."[7] On this occasion, the Saudi Data and Artificial Intelligence Authority signed four memorandums of understanding with US companies PureStorage, Waka.io, Palo Alto Networks, and DataDirect Networks. The Saudi Digital Government Authority, for its part, also signed one with tech giant Oracle to strengthen collaboration in cloud computing, artificial intelligence, and digital services.[8]

The landscape of communication has been dramatically reshaped with the inception of apps that enable global communication at little to no cost. It is worth reminiscing about the times preceding applications like Skype when international calls demanded a premium. Social media platforms, on the other hand, have fundamentally altered our interpersonal dynamics. They serve as conduits for individuals to interact globally, whether with acquaintances or strangers. Moreover, these networks provide avenues for job seekers, with companies advertising positions and employees disseminating internal opportunities.

Consumer behavior will inevitably evolve in tandem with technological advancements. A myriad of start-ups are spearheading research and development in diverse sectors. One notable example in Europe is the burgeoning hydrogen market, a pivotal component of the ongoing energy transition. The quest to decarbonize the European economy has thrust hydrogen into the limelight, prompting discussions about its production, storage, and transportation.

7　"President Trump Participates in a U.S.-Saudi Investment Forum," The White House, May 13, 2025, https://www.youtube.com/watch?v=wj1QOz3iuCE.

8　Mohammed Al-Kinani, "Saudi Arabia forges ahead in AI and tech through US partnerships," May 15, 2025, https://www.arabnews.com/node/2600839/business-economy.

As a testament to this movement, numerous innovative start-ups have surfaced, continually expanding the horizons of possibility. However, the frenetic pace of innovation has its downsides—today's breakthrough can easily be overshadowed by tomorrow's novelty like the "performance" detection of promising start-ups.

In essence, certain nascent sectors of innovation, while not universally recognized, harbor burgeoning opportunities pivotal for enhancing a nation's soft power. Companies are embarking on projects designed to gauge the potential of start-ups at their inception. Such services are invaluable both domestically and internationally. On the home front, nations value insights into internal advancements and the identification of promising ventures. On the global stage, discerning superior projects offers various benefits—investment prospects, early adoption advantages, the allure of relocating promising companies, the creation of technological partnerships, and more. The challenge, however, lies in astutely capitalizing on these opportunities. Saudi Arabia, aligning with its Vision 2030 objectives, is at the forefront of this endeavor.

The Kingdom is pursuing a policy of diversified investments. Some may appear to overshadow others, but any ambitious project requires the promotion of key sectors so that others can benefit from the resulting momentum. In this sense, sports embody this approach. Many question the relevance of Saudi Arabia's substantial investments in football, golf, rally racing, combat sports, and other high-profile activities. This sports-centered strategy has drawn international attention. Despite seeming extravagant, the amounts spent are strategic investments that generate positive spillover effects for other areas of the economy.

The promotion of a new golf tour, the LIV Golf Series, aimed at attracting the world's top players, has divided those directly involved. Some quickly agreed to compete in Saudi Arabia, while others chose to remain committed to their careers on the American and European circuits. Yet, in terms of the country's image, this is a victory. Saudi Arabia is not known for its golf culture, but drawing in big names who have won major tournaments (the Masters, the US Open, the PGA Championship, and the British Open) provides global exposure. People are talking about the Kingdom. One might argue that this is the aim of any sponsorship effort—but it's more than that. Saudi Arabia has succeeded in attracting the elite. That kind of pulling power requires effort and strategy. It's comparable to the challenge faced by the organizer of a tennis tournament that isn't part of the Grand Slams or Masters 1000: to fill the stands and attract broadcasters, you must convince several top-ranked players to participate. Is Saudi Arabia aiming to create the most competitive sports league in the world? That's probably not the ultimate goal. However, when considering a future bid to host a FIFA World Cup, it becomes crucial for any candidate nation to present itself in the best possible light and to offer high-quality domestic competitions.

A cultural opening concerns Western popular music. International stars have already performed in Saudi Arabia such as Janet Jackson, 50 Cent, Justin Bieber, John Legend, and David Guetta. In another area, the country plans to open several art museums. In 2023, for example, an agreement sealed with the French Centre Pompidou provides for the creation of a future museum of contemporary art in the AlUla region.[9] The Crown Prince places great importance on entertainment culture, a vision that led to the creation of Boulevard City[10] in Riyadh. This unique destination is designed for all generations and offers an unprecedented variety of attractions: restaurants, shopping centers, theaters, cinemas, street performances, video games, tennis courts, golf courses, go-karting, skiing, and many other activities concentrated within this urban space. This ultramodern area, covering approximately 900,000 square meters, opened in October 2019 and stands as one of Saudi Arabia's showcases—blending fun, modernity, and ambition.

The increased visibility of the domestic championship exemplifies the nation's strategic investment. This surge in global interest, evidenced by foreign media securing broadcast rights, elevates the championship's stature. Consequently, this not only amplifies its renown but also generates revenue for participating clubs. In essence, investments channeled into player transfers and salaries are not mere expenditures; they strategically position the league as a compelling watch on the global stage, especially with the participation of international football stars.

---

9   "Le Centre Pompidou signe un accord pour un futur musée d'art contemporain en Arabie saoudite," www.lefigaro.fr, March 15, 2023.

10   https://www.visitsaudi.com/fr/riyadh/attractions/blvd-riyadh-city, website visited on May 14, 2025.

Endorsing a competitive league aligns seamlessly with Saudi Arabia's broader initiative to captivate the global audience. Incorporating renowned players not only elevates the league's standards but augments the prowess of the national team, as evidenced by their commendable performance against Argentina in the 2022 World Cup hosted by Qatar. This proactive approach provides Saudi players with consistent opportunities to compete at elite levels, ensuring their holistic development.

This philosophy extends beyond the realm of popular sports and music into education and research. By enlisting distinguished foreign educators and professionals, Saudi Arabia is preparing its future, advocating for an investment approach that benefits its citizens holistically, especially in innovation and high-tech sectors. Detractors may perceive the Crown Prince's strategy as profligate, often questioning the tangible returns from such significant outlays.

Yet, a different perspective emerges when one delves deeper. While the financial commitments are substantial, they are by no means reckless. Every investment is calibrated against anticipated dividends. The hefty salaries extended to football luminaries from Europe's premier leagues frequently spark debates. However, if the ultimate goal is to host a World Cup, the potential economic windfall for a nation rapidly augmenting its tourism infrastructure becomes evident. The overarching strategy is clear: amplify Saudi Arabia's global prominence and influence.

The relentless pursuit of excellence, integral to Vision 2030's ambitious blueprint, necessitates the right resources and mindset. Attaining excellence is a journey, and to expedite this process, it is imperative to collaborate with the best, gleaning insights from their expertise and experiences. Such interactions are pivotal for any form of evolution, be it individual or collective. This involves enticing individuals recognized as pacesetters, ensuring that their skills and acumen benefit the nation.

The Crown Prince, with remarkable foresight, has integrated multiple facets to ensure Vision 2030's success. He comprehends that to magnetize the best talent, Saudi Arabia must present living conditions that resonate with the aspirations of its prospective residents.

While financial incentives undoubtedly play a pivotal role in attracting talent and investment, they are not the sole determining factor. Indeed, some individuals might be swayed by lucrative offers, perceiving them as a once-in-a-lifetime opportunity. Yet, the sustainability of any system hinges on more profound elements, particularly when the stakes are as high as redefining a nation's socioeconomic trajectory.

The reforms spearheaded by the Crown Prince are not just fleeting gestures but manifest deep-seated commitments to progressive change. Reverting to older paradigms after such transformational initiatives seems unfathomable. And for Saudi Arabia to truly resonate with the global populace—be it to entice professionals, tourists, or investors—its modernization endeavors must align seamlessly with international standards and expectations.

The enduring challenge, however, revolves around the complex dance of cultures. Saudi Arabia's pivot toward more progressive reforms is an overt invitation to bolster international trade, aiming for domestic and global dividends. The nation aspires to craft a sustainable economic blueprint while simultaneously safeguarding its strategic interests globally. And while its prodigious expenditures might dominate headlines, there's an underlying method to the perceived madness. The nation is not merely splurging without discernment; every investment is calibrated against anticipated returns. It is an unfortunate misinterpretation, with many external observers seemingly overlooking the nation's holistic growth strategy. Such misconceptions might stem from apprehensions regarding the audacious visions championed by Saudi Arabia's elite. Yet, what's consistently overlooked is the nation's sincere commitment to long-term economic evolution.

Drawing parallels with the tennis analogy, Saudi Arabia's strategy mirrors the ethos of only inviting top-tier players to ensure stellar tournaments. If a tennis event is graced solely by players ranked between 50th and 100th in the Association of Tennis Professionals (ATP) rankings, it does not inherently dilute the quality of the games. These athletes possess undeniable prowess, performing at elite levels. Yet, the allure of icons like Novak Djokovic, Jannick Sinner, and Carlos Alcaraz is irrefutable. They do not just bring their skills to the court; they also command unmatched global attention due to their illustrious careers. Similarly, Saudi Arabia is not merely focused on excellence in select domains. It endeavors to transcend mediocrity across the board, confident in its human capital that can cater to the most exacting global standards.

13

A Strategic Reorientation of Vision

Within the realm of epistemology and the broader social sciences, a paradigm is understood as a foundational model elucidating our perception of the world. The Crown Prince has interwoven himself into this global paradigmatic view, both in terms of domestic Saudi Arabian affairs and the nation's international positioning. It is worth noting that his initiatives, such as Vision 2030 and its related endeavors, underscore a pronounced governance (i.e., the mechanisms for steering public policies) acumen. These are not just strategic blueprints; they symbolize the profound transformation that the Kingdom is undergoing. Consequently, the Crown Prince is poised to etch an unforgettable legacy on both the national and potentially international stage.

Within the borders of Saudi Arabia, he has championed reforms of an unprecedented magnitude. For Western observers, the symbolic implications of these changes might be elusive. Yet it is evident that the Crown Prince's decisions are meticulously orchestrated, each seamlessly dovetailing into a grander paradigmatic view. Herein lies a model birthed, nurtured, and brought to fruition by a leader acutely aware of his monumental responsibilities and fervently proactive in sidestepping future challenges. The lasting legacy he bequeaths to his nation is undeniable. Beyond modernizing the economic and societal fabric, he's demonstrated unparalleled tenacity in safeguarding national interests. In him, one discerns the archetype of a visionary architect. Although the future never offers certainties, he has valiantly disrupted entrenched methods that seemed discordant with the contemporary economic and social zeitgeist. Merely lauding his audacity would oversimplify the Herculean endeavor of rallying support for such a groundbreaking vision of progress, all orchestrated for the nation's greater good.

However, by 2030, it remains uncertain whether the Kingdom will have fully realized the ambitions delineated in the Crown Prince's manifesto. It is pivotal to recognize the ethos propelling these endeavors, rather than fixating solely on empirical milestones. This is a gargantuan venture, perhaps not wholly grasped in its enormity.

Even among Saudi Arabia's most traditional segments, there exists an admiration for his work and a belief in the reformative merits he espouses. His leadership style resonates with inclusivity, fostering dialogue even amidst dissent. Saudi society's dynamics are multifaceted, extending beyond a singular leader's decrees. Numerous voices emerge, presenting concerns and seeking redress. The Crown Prince meticulously evaluates these myriad inputs, judiciously arriving at well-considered resolutions tailored to the situation's intricacies. To assert that he navigates these waters in isolation would be a grave misjudgment. He has never proclaimed an intent to entirely efface Saudi Arabia's traditional mores. Nonetheless, the Crown Prince and his collaborators have initiated transformative reforms, warranting due commendation.

From our perspective, his legacy will indelibly influence national history. He has broached challenges previously left unaddressed by any Saudi statesman. This observation is not a critique. For long spans, the nation thrived on its oil-centric economic model. In an era where bountiful revenues met the needs of a limited populace, why tinker with a winning formula? The landscape began shifting in the 2010s. To contextualize, the Nitaqat system was introduced in 2011. This new Saudization framework wasn't birthed on a whim. It arose from a recognition that employment regulations needed recalibration, in light of the Kingdom's evolving demographic and economic realities.

This policy shift indicates a gradual, judicious, and forward-looking perspective adopted by the nation's leadership. The Crown Prince, in his visionary capacity, has intensified these efforts, spearheading reforms of an unparalleled magnitude. No leader before him has championed, with such fervor, a sweeping transformation affecting every facet of societal life, at all levels. Such tenacity reveals a profound depth of thought and commitment. It showcases his adeptness as both a communicator and statesman. This approach does not just manifest domestically but resonates on an international stage, a crucial insight into his global strategy.

Acutely aware of economic dynamics, the Crown Prince acts proactively, seeking to forestall any transient or enduring setbacks. His gaze is fixed firmly on the future, laying down mechanisms to mitigate any adverse impacts from potential local or global crises. He envisions Saudi Arabia not just as a prosperous national economy, but as a global model. His ambitions, though vast, are underpinned by well-debated concepts. While his reforms are marked by their modernity, their primary aim is longevity. His objective? To set Saudi Arabia on a trajectory of enduring economic prosperity, enhancing its global stature.

Drawing inspiration from the legacy of King Ibn Saud, King Salman, and King Abdullah, the Crown Prince's resolve is unparalleled. He constantly challenges perceived boundaries, often taking initiatives that many deem insurmountable. His actions, especially in the Western international arena, can be misinterpreted. Yet, to comprehend his modus operandi is to recognize his unique position. When he graces forums like the G20, he stands apart. Most monarchies operate within a parliamentary framework, making Saudi Arabia a notable exception. Engaging with an elected leader differs markedly from interfacing with a monarch, particularly one representing a nation synonymous with its ruling lineage, the only existing case in the world other than the principality of Liechtenstein.

His Royal Highness Crown Prince Mohammed bin Salman bin Abdulaziz Al Saud indeed holds a unique standing among global leaders, which seems even more pertinent when considering his international strategy. He champions a new global paradigm for Saudi Arabia, asserting its autonomy with vehemence. Recognizing the Kingdom's economic and strategic leverage, he eschews any dialogue suggestive of subservience, even in a realm where power dynamics often dictate international discourse. To him, Saudi Arabia should be among the preeminent global actors. He staunchly opposes any affiliations or alliances that might relegate the Kingdom to a subordinate role. Such convictions underpin his decisive responses to international requests, such as rebuffing President Biden's appeal for OPEC to amplify its crude oil production—a move misaligned with Saudi interests.

To the casual observer, the assertive manner in which the Crown Prince communicates might be misconstrued as arrogance or disdain. However, it is neither theatricality nor haughtiness driving him. His sole role is that of a devoted leader passionately serving his nation. In doing so, he distinctly imprints his philosophies, broadcasting clear messages. Critics barely sway his convictions; he governs based on deep-seated beliefs and unwavering conscience. He embodies sovereignty, highlighting to those who try to dictate terms that he will not indulge in dialogue unless it aligns with his vision and respects the sovereignty and business autonomy of Saudi Arabia.

This methodology is far from erratic; it embodies a holistic, paradigmatic approach. Naturally, his decisions may not resonate with everyone, particularly considering Saudi Arabia's geopolitical significance and allure. But his message is unambiguous: he is receptive to discussions with all but demands reciprocal respect. Without it, he remains impervious to external pressures and demands.

An often-underappreciated aspect of diplomacy is the silent yet ever-present role of culture. Successful diplomacy hinges upon finding mutual ground, wherein both parties concede certain points to defuse tension or resolve conflict. The harmony achieved depends on the genuine intent of involved factions to collaboratively address the issue at hand. But is the cultural understanding of negotiation consistent worldwide? Likely not. Even when the apparent goal is compromise, is the result always equitable? Not necessarily; sometimes, the equilibrium is superficial.

In some cultures, negotiation revolves around achieving a certain outcome. The agreement might be inked under specific pretenses: one party may feel they've secured an upper hand, unbeknownst to the other. This deception creates an illusion of a balanced dialogue, where both sides assume they've met halfway. Yet, one party might be driven not by mutual benefit but by securing terms heavily tilted in their favor.

This underscores that beneath the veneer of diplomatic negotiations, power dynamics persist. A genuine understanding of and respect for cultural nuances are paramount; failing to recognize them can breed misjudgments and pitfalls. The Crown Prince's stance on the global stage is assertive, his robust personality shaping his discourse. Yet, he is not impulsively reactive. He bases his moves on pragmatic evaluations, assessing the resources at his disposal. In essence, his decisions harmonize his personal traits[1] with his perception of global dynamics, shaping strategic directives for the Kingdom.

Saudi Arabia retains its pivotal role in international oil matters even as it

---

1   When we talk about character, we are referring not only to the personality of Crown Prince Mohammed bin Salman bin Abdelaziz Al Saud, but also, implicitly, to the cultural dimension as elucidated in these lines.

champions a post-oil era. The ongoing global energy transition captivates the attention of the world's foremost elites. Current events underscore that petroleum, colloquially known as "black gold," is integral to the world economy. Such prominence empowers nations like Saudi Arabia, placing them in an influential bracket.

The Crown Prince capitalizes on this leverage, allowing the Kingdom to articulate its stances and counter external pressures to achieve the overall interest of his country. The evolving international milieu shapes his communicative strategies. The world is witnessing a paradigm shift: a power equilibrium is emerging between the United States and China. At the same time, regions, notably parts of Africa, increasingly distance themselves from Western influence. Some even display hostility toward the West. This global context informs the Crown Prince's matured perspectives, his grasp of international relations dynamics, and a more nuanced diplomatic approach. Alliances, in his view, are contingent upon the prospects they usher in.

This has led to a reevaluation of historical alliances, assessing their merits and shortcomings. The Crown Prince perceives Saudi Arabia's potential to play a pivotal role in the US-China rivalry, thanks to its strategic geographic location and international leverage. This unique position affords him the discretion to negotiate with partners most aligned with Saudi interests. This strategic advantage, however, is not without its costs.

Saudi Arabia's inclination to consider Beijing's diplomatic overtures stems from pragmatic considerations rather than mere discontent with Western alliances. The Kingdom values its autonomy in decision-making and conveys, unequivocally, its aversion to perceived Western hegemony.

This evolving perspective illustrates the waning appeal of the Western model of global supremacy, encompassing both hard and soft power. The once-resonant rhetoric has lost its sheen, and the erstwhile unchallenged Western dominance now faces a formidable contender. Saudi Arabia, in this shifting landscape, remains unwavering in articulating its stances, emphasizing its sovereignty and independence. The bygone era of unequivocal Western dominance is receding.

Saudi Arabia's geopolitical strategy responds to international developments and its national interests. Its diplomatic outreach to China and Iran has been met with skepticism in the West, being at odds with Western geopolitical objectives. For the United States, a diplomatic reconciliation between Riyadh and Tehran was unforeseen and less than ideal. The evolving dynamics underscore a nuanced reality: key Western institutions, such as the White House and the State Department, grapple with emerging geopolitical scenarios they no longer solely dictate.

Riyadh, the capital of the Kingdom of Saudi Arabia, discerns alignment in its interests with Beijing. Both the Saudis and the Chinese are building a foundation of mutual understanding, with their relations built on shared interests, especially in the arenas of maritime security and global trade. For Saudi Arabia, security concerns are paramount, given that its economic vitality is inextricably tied to its foreign trade engagements. Moreover, this security dimension resonates with the objectives delineated in Vision 2030, which aims to augment the country's global appeal. The détente observed between Riyadh and Tehran could portend a more stable milieu for the region surrounding the Strait of Hormuz—a critical nexus for global commerce, with hydrocarbons at its forefront. However, since the outbreak of the conflict between Israel and Hamas (and Hezbollah) on October 7, 2023, a new threat has emerged—maritime attacks by armed Houthi factions against Western military and commercial vessels in the Red Sea. This has prompted an armed response from the United States and the UK in Yemen. Unfortunately, these developments naturally undermine hopes for easing tensions in the region.

The Kingdom's diplomatic pivot has caught many off guard, often leading to misinterpretations. Few underscore the sagacity and strategic insight exhibited by the Crown Prince in his pursuit of national interests. The Crown Prince's methodology has irked many in the West. Their trepidation will persist unless they recalibrate their understanding of Saudi Arabia under his stewardship. The Crown Prince perceives a patronizing undertone in their approach, reminiscent of an antiquated sense of dominion, which now seems incongruous in the current international arena. He is amenable to dialogue but demands respect for him and his country. No external entity will impose decisions upon him.

Vision 2030 embodies the Crown Prince's governance blueprint and the milestones he aims to achieve. It manifests an ethos of entrepreneurial autonomy, resisting extraneous pressures. The Crown Prince envisages Saudi Arabia as a formidable global actor, deserving recognition for the strategic counterbalances it holds. Attempts to undervalue or marginalize the Kingdom will compel the Crown Prince to invoke these counterbalances. Some have already experienced the consequences of underestimating him. The Kingdom will not kowtow to external mandates that disregard its intrinsic interests. This stance disconcerts traditional partners, leaving them grappling with its implications but with no intention of altering their relations with Saudi Arabia. For example, wasn't this President Joe Biden's ambition to "reevaluate"[2] his country's relations with Riyadh after a dispute over oil issues in 2022?

The underlying narrative, however, is clear: Saudi Arabia is resolute in charting its political and economic trajectory, curtailing external influence. This philosophy emanates from the Crown Prince, who remains undeterred by external critique. Despite being contested and often misunderstood, he remains steadfast, adhering to his envisioned path. His decisions, which may appear abrupt or startling to some, especially to those witnessing their influence wane, are predicated on pragmatism and an astute assessment of his surroundings. He is unwaveringly propelling an agenda to recast Saudi Arabia's global image, positioning it among the foremost diplomatic powers.

The Crown Prince's resolve to address international dilemmas resonates with the tenacity evident in every endeavor he undertakes. Undeterred by criticism, he is steadfastly guided by core principles and convictions. This patient endeavor necessitates that he assertively communicates his perspective, particularly when he deems his positions nonnegotiable. Such a pursuit demands immense time, vigor, and personal sacrifice. It is a journey toward ensuring that Saudi Arabia carves out a distinct identity, one characterized by resilience and determination, positioning the nation prominently on the global stage.

---

2   Ben Gittleson, Allison Pecorin, "Biden thinks US needs to 'reevaluate' relationship with Saudi Arabia: White House", ABC News, October 12, 2022, https://abcnews.go.com /Politics/biden-thinks-us-evaluate-relationship-saudi-arabia-white/story?id=91327505.

14

Humanitarian Endeavors in Islam

Islam is not merely a faith of introspection; it profoundly extends its care toward others. Central to its teachings, especially evident in one of its five pillars, *zakat* (almsgiving), is the spirit of benevolence for the less fortunate. Such dedication to humanitarian relief has been a hallmark of Saudi governance. Yet, how many in the Western world are aware that Saudi Arabia has extended its support to numerous Yemeni refugees escaping conflict,[1] offering them residency and rights nearly akin to its own citizens? Such humanitarian gestures often go unnoticed outside the confines of the Arab-Muslim world. Nonetheless, organizations such as the King Salman Humanitarian Aid and Relief Center (KSrelief),[2] the MWL and Al Rabita have championed numerous initiatives dedicated to education, health care, and aid for the marginalized. Founded in Mecca in 1962 by Prince Faisal of Saudi Arabia, the MWL ardently upholds values of peace, love, and tolerance.

This perspective is deeply rooted in Islamic teachings. Dr. Djelloul Seddiki, in a lecture at the Catholic School of Bernardins in Paris in September 2011, eloquently discussed Islam's tenets of tolerance.[3] His discourse resonated with the ethos of the MWL, highlighting the humanitarian principles championed by the Quran. Dr. Seddiki emphasized that Islam is both a spiritual belief and a communal way of life. This community, he noted, is anchored

---

1   Saudi authorities cite a figure of 600,000 Yemeni refugees in the context of "Saudi Arabia and the Yemen conflict. Humanitarian aid to the people of Yemen," available on https://www.saudiembassy.net/sites/default/files/FactSheet_Humanitarian%20Aid%20Yemen%20Fact_April2017.pdf, as of April 2017.

2   The King Salman Humanitarian Aid and Relief Centre (KSrelief) was established on 27 Rajab 1436 AH (May 13, 2015) under the initiative of H.R.H King Salman.

3   Djelloul Seddiki, "Islam et tolerance," lecture delivered at the Catholic School of Bernardins, Paris, September 2011.

in faith. He insightfully highlighted that this faith transcends mere religious understanding, extending its influence to every aspect of a believer's life, encompassing personal, social, and political realms. Such a perspective draws inspiration from the exemplary community of Medina, established by Prophet Muhammad in 622 AD. This innovative community departed from the tribal norms of the time, prioritizing faith over bloodlines, marking the decline of clan-based affiliations.

Yet, this Islamic community model is distinct from Western notions of a nation,[4] which often coalesce around language, cultural heritage, and other factors. Islam emphasizes not just a righteous demeanor but also an ethical way of life, leading believers toward a global community or *ummah*. Here, faith is the primary criterion for inclusion. The deep conviction in the truth of Islam fortifies the bonds of Muslim unity, transcending mere legal or social structures. It is noteworthy that while political unity has been elusive, Islam's religious unity has remained steadfast. Despite historical schisms, the unyielding faith has fostered a resilient identity, unaffected by the ebbs and flows of history or the amalgamation of varied civilizations.[5] The Quran reinforces that

---

4   Different perceptions of a nation exist in the West. In France, the philologist, philosopher, and historian Ernest Renan delivered a significant lecture at the Sorbonne in 1882, titled "What is a nation?" In this landmark lecture, he associated the nation with a soul, a spiritual essence, defining it primarily as a collective will to live together, encapsulated in the concept of a "daily plebiscite." Renan's thinking emerged in the wake of the collapse of the Second Empire led by Napoleon III, following a military defeat against Prussia in 1871. Traditionally, the French national vision, as articulated by Ernest Renan, has been juxtaposed with the Prussian vision, which emphasizes common characteristics within a society, such as language, ethnicity, or religion. The concept of a nation remains challenging to define because national identity varies depending on peoples, their cultures, and their historical backgrounds. Furthermore, significant societal changes, including migratory movements that have characterized many regions across the world, have evolved over time. Another example of contrasting perspectives can be found in the reaction of the German philosopher Johann Gottlieb Fichte, who presented his "Addresses to the German Nation" during conferences held in the aftermath of the Battle of Jena in 1806. In these addresses, Fichte called upon the German people to rise in the name of freedom against the empire conquered by Napoleon I, urging collective resistance against the oppressor. In the Arab-Muslim world, the spiritual dimension plays a significant role, as acceptance into the community is often based on faith.

5   Djelloul Seddiki, "Islam et tolerance," lecture delivered at the Bernardins Catholic School, Paris, September 2011.

the Prophet did not introduce a new religion, but rather, he revived the foundational faith innate to humanity.[6]

Sura 29, verse 46 succinctly articulates the universalist sentiment of Islam: *We believe in what has been revealed to us and what was revealed to you. Our God and your God is only One. And to Him we fully submit.* This verse underlines the inherent ecumenical spirit of Islam. At its core, the Quran emphasizes the unity and oneness of God. The Divine Revelation is directed at humanity, charged with the duty to internalize and actualize Quranic tenets. Such doctrines establish that Islam champions tolerance unequivocally. Humankind's sojourn on Earth ought to be characterized by altruism, assisting those in need regardless of their religious affiliations. It is thus logical that entities like Saudi Arabia and the MWL ardently pursue endeavors in education, health care, and myriad other spheres.

Islam's central message is one of peace and tolerance, invoking the same Divine Entity to address the universal brotherhood of believers who acknowledge the Revelation of the singular God. Reference to Sura 2, verse 256 reveals that there is *no compulsion in religion.* God's intent behind the diversity of humankind and nations is not to sow discord but to engender richness in experiences, fostering mutual understanding.[7] This sentiment is reinforced by Sura 49, verse 13: *O humanity! Indeed, We created you from a male and a female, and made you into peoples and tribes so that you may get to know one another. Surely the most noble of you in the sight of Allah is the most righteous among you.* Al-Hujurât advocates unequivocally against discrimination, echoing the hadith that asserts the insignificance of racial or tribal distinctions, emphasizing piety as the sole distinguishing factor. The Quran's message is truly universal, incorporating Biblical prophecies and acknowledging Jesus, the son of Mary.[8] Sura 5 (Al-Ma'idah), for example, states in various verses that *Indeed, we revealed the Torah, containing guidance and light . . .* (5: 44) *and . . . we sent Jesus, son of Mary, confirming the Torah revealed before him. And We gave him the Gospel containing guidance and light and confirming what was revealed in the Torah—a guide and a lesson to the God-fearing* (5: 46).

---

6   Ibid.

7   Ibid.

8   Ibid.

The Quran persistently promotes a vision of peace and acceptance. While it extols the virtues of peace, it also underscores the significance of charity (*zakat*), one of the five pillars of Islam. Believers are exhorted to champion peace. Prophet Muhammad's teachings underscore that a person truly embracing the faith is one who upholds justice, propagates peace, and practices charity, even if their means are limited. In the Quran, references to peace and its cognates appear an overwhelming 136 times, in stark contrast to the mere six mentions of war (*harb*). The Quranic interpretation of peace carries theological implications of salvation, making it imperative for true belief. This is linked with justice, faith, tolerance, and interreligious discourse.[9] Moreover, the Quran actively promotes nonviolence. As noted in Sura 60, verse 8: *Allah does not forbid you from dealing kindly and fairly with those who have neither fought nor driven you out of your homes.* Such sentiments are further echoed in verses such as 17:33, *Do not take a human life—made sacred by Allah* and 5:32 *whoever takes a life—unless as a punishment for murder or mischief in the land—it will be as if they killed all of humanity; and whoever saves a life, it will be as if they saved all of humanity,* emphasizing the sanctity of human life and the righteousness inherent in rejecting violence.[10]

Grounded in the sagacious Quranic directives centered on respect and benevolence toward others, the MWL encompasses a distinct humanitarian dimension in its mandate. The League extends its support to underprivileged and marginalized communities across various countries. Notably, it advances educational programs, extends health care to those battling diverse illnesses, spearheads land irrigation initiatives, aids victims of natural disasters, and provides succor to orphans, refugees, and the infirm across ninety-five countries.[11] While the aforementioned endeavors are but a snapshot of MWL's extensive humanitarian endeavors, they encapsulate the spirit of Quranic teachings on peace and charity.

Underpinning the MWL's operational directives is the leadership and vision of its Secretary General, Sheikh Mohammad bin Abdulkarim Al-Issa.

---

9   Ibid.

10   Ibid.

11   "Humanitarian Aids," Muslim World League, https://themwl.org/en/taxonomy/term /168, consulted on August 2, 2023.

Appointed on August 12, 2016, the same year he was designated as the Chairman of the International Body of Muslim Scholars and became a member of the Senior Scholars Organization in Saudi Arabia, Sheikh Al-Issa revitalized the MWL.[12] This period also marked the inception of the Crown Prince's Vision 2030 program. The MWL's mission, under Sheikh Al-Issa's aegis, "aims to present the true Islam and its tolerant principles, provide humanitarian aid, extend bridges of dialogue and cooperation with all, engage in positive openness to all cultures and civilizations."[13] This renewed vigor aligns seamlessly with the Crown Prince's emphasis on genuine Islam. Committedly, the organization staunchly opposes all extremisms and terroristic tendencies, advocating instead for unity, solidarity, and a humanistic Islam that transcends faith or cultural boundaries.

In this sense, Sheikh Al-Issa embodies a perfect partner for the Crown Prince's diplomatic designs. Sheikh Al-Issa is renowned for his work dedicated to interreligious dialogue. On January 23, 2023, he visited the infamous Auschwitz-Birkenau death camp as part of an interfaith visit that included a Muslim delegation, a powerful gesture that called for respect of other religions. He is seen in Israel as an open-minded man, praised for his efforts in favor of the normalization of diplomatic relations with Saudi Arabia.[14] The Crown Prince entrusted him with the distinguished responsibility of delivering the main hajj sermon in July 2022, an intervention once again welcomed by Israel[15] and perceived as a clear commitment to continuing the diplomatic efforts then under negotiation. His speech revolved around the five pillars of Islam and called for "acceptance, harmony and compassion."[16] Sheikh Al-Issa is also known to have invited rabbis to Saudi Arabia, himself having previously visited the United

---

12   "Mohammad bin Abdulkarim Al-Issa," Muslim World League, https://themwl.org /en/SG2019, accessed August 2, 2023.

13   "Introduction to Muslim World League," Muslim World League, https://themwl.org/ en/MWL-Profile, website consulted on August 2, 2023.

14   Prior to the occurrence of the events of October 7, 2023, in Israel and the consequences induced by the prolongation of hostilities which led to the suspension of the diplomatic process of normalization between Saudi Arabia and Israel.

15   "Un cheikh connu pour sa visite à Auschwitz prononce le principal sermon du Hajj," July 10, 2022, *The Times of Israel,* https://fr.timesofisrael.com/un-cheikh-connu -pour-sa-visite-a-auschwitz-prononce-le-principal-sermon-du-hajj/.

16   Ibid.

States at the invitation of Jewish universities such as Yeshiva University in New York, the sign of a clear desire to maintain a permanent and open dialogue with other religions.

Saudi Arabia's dedication to humanitarian causes is not limited to the MWL. Other notable Saudi establishments, such as the King Salman Humanitarian Aid and Relief Centre (KSrelief), have made significant contributions in this domain. In 2022, KSrelief's general supervisor, Abdullah bin Abdulaziz Al Rabeeah, disclosed the center's involvement in over 2,000 humanitarian projects across 84 nations,[17] committing funds upward of $6 billion. Collectively, over the past 25 years, the Kingdom has generously disbursed almost $95 billion in diverse aid to 174 countries.[18] Yemen, in particular, stands out as a primary recipient of Saudi assistance since KSrelief's inception, with over 700 humanitarian initiatives underway.[19] While the Saudi military intervention in Yemen has attracted Western critique, the Kingdom's substantial humanitarian involvement therein unmistakably signals its genuine concern for Yemen's civilian populace.

KSrelief's scope of intervention is very broad. This assistance has benefited approximately 415 million people in need around the world.[20] Its operations include both long-term programs and emergency responses to specific events. KSrelief has intervened on numerous occasions to deliver food, medicine, shelter, and financial aid to populations affected by war, such as in Ukraine, Yemen, Sudan, and Gaza, as well as by natural disasters—including the deadly earthquake that struck Türkiye and Syria in 2023 and cyclones Chapala and Megh that impacted Socotra Island. The organization funds specific programs such as the reintegration of child soldiers in Yemen, the MASAM demining project launched in 2018, and women's economic empowerment initiatives in Taiz. Various medical initiatives have also been implemented, including the Noor Program to combat blindness in Sudan, a vision screening campaign in

---

17   Rashid Hassan, "Yemen biggest recipient as Kingdom aid budget reaches $94bn," June 1, 2022, Arab News, https://www.arabnews.com/node/2094571/saudi-arabia.

18   Ibid.

19   Ibid.

20   "415 Million Lives Touched: KSrelief, with Tremendous Impact in 55 Countries, Marks World Health Day," April 7, 2024, https://www.spa.gov.sa/en/N2080060.

Bangladesh, support for the global eradication of polio, and the establishment of prosthetics centers in Yemen.

For many geopolitical experts, the provision of humanitarian aid by Saudi Arabia can be viewed as a strategic move to enhance its soft power globally. While this perspective undoubtedly contributes to the Kingdom's global image, it is essential not to underestimate the profound influence of Islam in shaping this commitment. Saudi Arabia's philanthropic initiatives, championed by its Crown Prince, are rooted in the fundamental teachings of Islam. Recognizing the significance of Islamic values is paramount when evaluating the Kingdom's dedication to global humanitarian causes.

Overlooking the profound influence of these sacred texts in shaping decisions related to humanitarian assistance and peace advocacy indicates a lack of understanding of the motivations driving Crown Prince Mohammed bin Salman bin Abdulaziz Al Saud. Humanitarian commitments are of paramount importance to him, given his leadership over a nation that houses two of Islam's most revered sites. His advocacy for peace is an extension of the same foundational principles.

15

Charting Sustainable Peace
in the Middle East

In the dynamics of international relations, the ever-present juxtaposition between dominant powers and those with less influence remains a constant. Throughout this volume, our intention has been to elucidate the motivations and vision of Crown Prince Mohammed bin Salman bin Abdulaziz Al Saud. It has become evident that the initiatives he has spearheaded are often misinterpreted or underestimated, particularly by Western counterparts. If Saudi Arabia's priorities are evolving away from its traditional allies, it necessitates a deeper examination into the reasons behind such a shift. It seems plausible that the Crown Prince has felt slighted and disheartened by critiques from entities he envisioned as collaborators. Such disparaging sentiments undoubtedly hindered the cause of the critics. The Crown Prince's reactions, however nuanced, are wholly understandable given the circumstances.

Saudi Arabia's global aspirations should align with its rightful ambitions. Influence in the international arena is not achieved arbitrarily, particularly from Saudi Arabia's vantage point. Only a select number of countries, the colossal political and economic giants, can impose their diplomatic weight with relative ease. The Crown Prince has unambiguously articulated his vision for Saudi Arabia's development and its prospective role in the global arena. Achieving recognition and credibility on the international stage requires significant efforts and time.

Saudi Arabia's expectations to establish itself as a credible diplomatic entity entails a robust track record: A nation once involved in combating the Houthis, an internationally organization recognized as terrorist by President Trump himself, or maintaining a strained relationship with countries like Iran, faces an uphill challenge in presenting itself as a beacon for peace. However, the March

2023 tripartite agreement between China, Riyadh, and Tehran serves as a testimony to the realm of possibilities.

This agreement was a revelation. The West was suddenly confronted with China's proactive involvement in diplomatic realms it previously seemed indifferent to. The consensus is that China executed a masterful diplomatic maneuver, bridging the divide between two historically adversarial nations. Trade considerations undoubtedly influenced the trajectory and outcomes of these discussions. Yet, the essence of this accord underscores the pragmatism exhibited by both the Crown Prince and Iranian leadership. It demonstrated their mutual recognition that embarking on peace talks could usher in multifaceted benefits. So far, the war in Gaza does not seem to have called this new diplomatic order into question.

After the landmark meeting in Beijing, both Riyadh and Tehran accelerated their efforts to reinstate diplomatic and trade ties, aiming to address the prolonged conflict in Yemen. This situation bears uncanny similarities to the proxy battles that defined the Cold War era. In essence, Yemen has been ensnared in an intense internal conflict between the incumbent government and the Houthi faction,[1] labeled as "terrorist entities" by Sana'a, the Yemeni capital, and allegedly backed by Iran. Conversely, the governmental forces are bolstered by Saudi Arabia and its international allies. Saudi Arabia's direct military intervention against the Houthis marked a significant escalation in the conflict.

The reinvigorated dialogue between Riyadh and Tehran remarkably influenced the trajectory of the Yemeni crisis. Merely weeks after the official declaration of the normalization of bilateral ties, global media outlets reported the potential for a peace accord between Saudi Arabia and Yemen (the Houthi factions), marking the culmination of years of hostilities. This development has multifaceted implications.

First, the durability of the tripartite agreement: This progress underscores the enduring nature of the pact forged in Beijing. Both Riyadh and Tehran

---

1   The Houthi people are a Shiite tribe named after its founding members. Part of the group took up arms against the Yemeni government following Houthi demonstrations in 2004. The central authorities perceived them as a challenge to the governing authority. The situation escalated into the Saada War between 2004 and 2014 which resulted first from a feeling of marginalization experienced by the Houthi ethnic group, and then into civil war from 2014 onward.

are evidently committed to overcome their disputes, and it is incumbent upon them to adopt measures that align with their mutual aspirations.

Second, Saudi Arabia's commitment to peace: This shift also reflects Saudi Arabia's unwavering commitment to its international pledges, underscoring its proactive approach toward establishing peace. Such actions invariably reinforce its global standing.

Third, China's growing regional influence: It is undeniable that China maintains a vigilant watch over the Arabian Gulf's geopolitical developments. In a region marred by persistent crises, Saudi Arabia's role in potentially resolving two major conflicts is laudable. Its evolving rapport with Iran and its swift pursuit of a diplomatic resolution with Yemen (the Houthi factions) have painted Saudi Arabia in a new light as a nation genuinely committed to dialogue and peace.

By early 2023, few experts had anticipated such a swift rapprochement between Saudi Arabia and Iran. While China's mediation, championed by President Xi, was pivotal, the fruition of this initiative would have been improbable without the earnest cooperation of both Middle Eastern nations. As discussed previously in this volume, the Middle East and the Arabian Peninsula have been beleaguered by myriad tensions and conflicts, with some enduring for decades, underpinned by various causes. The de-escalation of a dispute involving two traditionally adversarial states necessitates the acknowledgment of the sagacity and pragmatism of the involved parties. It epitomizes a positive development too rare among bad news not to be mentioned.

At present, there's no assurance of achieving sustainable peace between Iran and Saudi Arabia. However, their ongoing efforts to alleviate the profound and intricate regional tensions are commendable. The Kingdom of Saudi Arabia's global image has undergone a transformation. Riyadh has on two occasions showcased its capacity to be an effective mediator in conflict resolutions, thus garnering newfound credibility, which is further enhanced by its resolute commitment to fostering peace. This transition has been overseen and directed by the Crown Prince, prioritizing national interests.

The pursuit of peace, once merely an objective, seems to be evolving into a Saudi forte in a region that desperately craves stability, peace, and serenity. The challenges are not limited to the Middle East. Various African nations, especially those proximate to the Saudi shoreline, face similar tumults. The

Horn of Africa, particularly Somalia, exemplifies this instability. Somalia, a nation grappling with its internal strife, is regularly beleaguered by terrorist factions orchestrating lethal assaults. Ethiopia's tense internal conflicts, the latest of which has plunged the Tigrayan population (an ethnic minority that was subjected to severe repression orchestrated by the government between 2020 and 2022) into mourning, underscore the fragile nature of national stability, not to mention its tenuous relationship with neighboring Eritrea. Sudan has been currently undergoing fratricidal fights since April 2023, with conflicts between national forces and paramilitary units, even within urban centers such as the capital Khartoum. This conflict has propagated to other areas, plunging the nation back into pandemonium. Civilians simultaneously bear the brunt of these conflicts, and a looming food crisis exacerbates their plight. Furthermore, Sudan's historical backdrop is marred by prolonged civil unrest in Darfur, once again the scene of deadly conflicts, the main victims being civilians, and the subsequent civil war that consumed the newly formed Republic of South Sudan between 2013 and 2020. The situation persists to this day.

Upon analysis of the sociopolitical landscape of the Maghreb and Mashreq regions, it is evident that numerous states, including Tunisia, Libya, and Egypt, have undergone significant internal upheavals, most notably during the Arab Spring. A shared narrative among these nations is the termination of their long-standing leaderships.[2] While some semblance of stability has been reclaimed in these countries, the foundation remains tenuous. Libya, for instance, continues to be plagued by internal conflict long after the 2011 death of Gaddafi. Algeria's political scene was shaken when President Abdelaziz Bouteflika, despite his deteriorating health, sought another term. This ambition was short-lived, leading to his eventual political isolation and a transition fraught with challenges. Rising public discontent and political vendettas augured a looming national crisis.

In sub-Saharan Africa, multifaceted and diverse crises resonate with those in the Middle East. When coupled with disturbances in the Levant and the Arabian Gulf, the cumulative area is larger than 10 million square kilometers—an

---

2   Zine el-Abidine Ben Ali presided over Tunisia from 1987 until 2011. Colonel Muammar Gaddafi ruled Libya from 1969 to 2011, and Hosni Mubarak led Egypt from 1981 to 2011.

expanse surpassing the United States, China, or Canada.[3] Within such a vast region, myriad crises obstruct the path to lasting peace, leading many to question: Who will emerge as the peacemaker?

Saudi Arabia's involvement in the evacuation of thousands of foreign nationals from Sudan, coupled with its mediation role during the crisis, underscores once again Riyadh's commitment to asserting itself as an essential regional partner. Notably, other global powers have recognized and applauded this activism, refraining from challenging the legitimacy of Saudi interventions. Such actions recall Qatar's evacuation endeavors in Afghanistan amidst the Taliban's return to power in 2021.[4]

These proactive measures by Riyadh position it as a promising avenue for dialogue, potentially advantageous for nations looking to defend their strategic interests. Given the diminishing influence of the United States in African and Middle Eastern crises and the rising involvement of Russia and China, it becomes imperative to grasp Riyadh's appeal in such scenarios. By positioning itself as a beacon of stability and sustainable peace, the Kingdom is staking a claim in an arena that boosts its regional magnetism, particularly within Arab and Islamic cultures. World leaders will increasingly perceive the Crown Prince as the pivotal figure for negotiations.

The Kingdom's evacuation efforts from Sudan have positively enhanced its international reputation. While Western powers hesitated, Saudi Arabia acted decisively, offering sanctuary to foreign nationals, including Westerners, ensuring their safety.

In May 2023, then Syrian President Bashar Al-Assad's participation in the Arab League summit in Jeddah signaled Damascus's aspiration to reestablish amicable and enduring diplomatic ties with the affluent Arab monarchies of the Arabian Gulf. Syria, having been embroiled in conflicts for over a decade, is now in pursuit of financial allies for postwar reconstruction. Notably, Al-Assad was estranged from the Arab League since 2011, owing to the brutal civil war and crimes against civilians in insurrection against him by the

---

3   The United States has a surface area of 9.834 million square kilometers, China 9.597 million square kilometers, and Canada 9.985 million square kilometers.

4   Brendon Novel, "L'Arabie saoudite veut s'imposer comme un acteur incontournable," *La Presse*, May 4, 2023, https://www.lapresse.ca/debats/opinions/2023-05-04/crise-au-soudan/l-arabie-saoudite-veut-s-imposer-comme-un-acteur-incontournable.php.

regime's military and security apparatus. This rendezvous in Jeddah, against a backdrop of regional conciliation, left Al-Assad optimistic about new alliances before his regime collapsed in December 2024.[5]

Preceding this, on April 15, a conference in Jeddah, uniting the six states of the GCC alongside Egypt, Iraq, and Jordan, deliberated Syria's potential re-induction into the Arab League. Despite reservations by some members and Riyadh's decade-long severed ties with Damascus, Saudi Arabia advocated for Syria's reintegration. In the lead-up to this assembly, foreign ministers from both Saudi Arabia and Syria convened, setting the stage for this rapprochement between the two countries.

Riyadh's stance signifies its progressive efforts toward alleviating regional animosities. These strides coincide with the revival of dialogue with Iran and the anticipated de-escalation in Yemen.

Clearly, Saudi Arabia is proactively navigating multiple terrains. The Kingdom is demonstrating initiative, garnering respect and legitimacy. While it may not achieve resolutions in every crisis, its unwavering dedication to peace and stability is evident. The renewed discourse with Syria epitomizes a commendable diplomatic shift. Within a relatively brief period, Saudi Arabia has emerged as an ascending regional diplomatic entity. Addressing enduring crises in such a tumultuous regional milieu will probably enhance Riyadh's international stature, reflecting its competence in comprehending, articulating, and peacefully resolving complex issues marked by the regional seal.

We find ourselves at a crossroads in international relations, a juncture not solely defined by the escalating rivalry between the United States on one hand and China and Russia on the other hand. There are other pressing issues that demand our attention and reflection, including the burgeoning sentiments of disapproval mainly directed at France, evident in the popular discourse of Niger, Burkina Faso, and Mali under the impetus of newly installed military regimes. Observing Saudi Arabia's stance on several protracted crises and conflicts, it is evident that the Crown Prince possesses a profound understanding of the regional dynamics surrounding his nation. He comprehends the

---

5   On December 8, 2024, the Syrian regime led by President Bashar Al-Assad collapsed following a major offensive by opposition forces in the country's main cities, including Damascus.

imperatives that require strategic investment to bring stability to a region historically plagued by unpredictability.

This neverending regional instability invariably hampers economic growth. For Saudi Arabia to fully realize its economic potential, its neighboring countries must also flourish economically. However, achieving such prosperity becomes a daunting task when regional disturbances stifle economic endeavors. Hence, the pursuit of peace and stability becomes not only a desire but a necessity. The pressing need of the hour is to leave behind historical animosities that have caused untold suffering and devastation. While articulating this may seem straightforward, actualizing it is undeniably challenging. Yet, the Crown Prince is resolutely committed to this mission. Although he does not purport to hold solutions to all quandaries, Saudi Arabia's initiatives in 2023 furnished him with undeniable credibility. A palpable movement toward alleviating Middle Eastern tensions is emerging, with the Crown Prince positioned at its helm. A tangible process of tension reduction was underway in the Middle East until the Hamas attack on Israel on October 7, 2023, disrupted the progress.

These developments align seamlessly with the Crown Prince's overarching message to all the actors of the region. The essence of dialogue and mutual respect between nations is nonnegotiable. It is imperative to reevaluate long-held beliefs and positions, to set aside past grievances, and to collectively envision a future unburdened by the tragedies that have marked our history. The hour beckons for initiating meaningful discourse, for the Crown Prince to solidify his role as a credible and respected ambassador for peace. His approach, characterized by methodical deliberation, deserves commendation, especially considering the encouraging progress achieved in a relatively short time frame. Admittedly, the path to sustainable peace is fraught with challenges, but the endeavor, demanding as it may be, holds the promise of a future worth striving for.

16
Advocating for a Sustainable Future

A ccording to the English philosopher Thomas Hobbes, *homo homini lupus est*,[1] which means that man is inherently the worst enemy of his fellow man. In the realm of international relations, few endeavors are as noble as championing peace. While interpretations of peace vary, it is crucial to recognize that a harmonious state is often elusive in our global landscape. Some view peace as a mere interlude between wars. However, such a perspective does not align with the United Nations' goal of sustaining peace. An overview of historical narratives reveals a recurring pattern of conflict. This observation harks back to philosophical musings on the nature of humanity, both in its natural state and within the constraints of societal laws. Regardless of the context, human interactions remain complex, even when guided by societal norms.

Tragically, the contemporary era is no exception. Countless advocates for peace face dire consequences for their endeavors, especially when their pursuits conflict with dominant vested interests. Many entities would rather confront adversaries than engage in constructive dialogue. The Crown Prince of Saudi Arabia stands as an exemplar of advocacy for peace who is acutely aware of the human cost of conflict. Recognizing the manifold benefits of peace— particularly the conducive environment it creates for economic and societal growth—is paramount. Wars inevitably impede progress. Given the volatile milieu of the Middle East, where local and regional crises abound, the prevailing unrest adversely affects all regional states, including the more stable ones.

The Crown Prince's vision for national development will find a volatile Middle East incompatible. To appeal to global investors, the region must project an image of stability and security. Thus, mitigating hostilities and ensuring lasting

---

1   Thomas Hobbes, *Leviathan or The Matter, Forme and Power of a Commonwealth Ecclesiasticall and Civil*, London, 1651.

peace become imperatives. The Crown Prince believes that attracting foreign collaboration to Saudi Arabia hinges on the broader region's sociopolitical stability.

Sustainable peace stands as the cornerstone for revitalizing a region marred by frequent upheavals. The ongoing tension between Israel and the Palestinian Authority, among other regional conflicts, underscores this need. The Crown Prince's conviction lies in the potential of sustainable peace to unlock the region's vast economic possibilities.

In essence, Saudi Arabia's approach signifies its necessary interconnectedness with the global community. To realize its ambitious Vision 2030 plan, a stable regional setting is indispensable. This perspective does not diminish the country's genuine dedication to peace; it only solidifies Saudi Arabia's stature as an international proponent of harmony.

The global news landscape remains rife with conflicts, with the Ukrainian crisis dominating Western media. Europe's proximity to the battleground heightens its apprehension. The conflict, initiated by Russia in February 2022, has been marked by the devastating realities of warfare. The Western world's backing, sometimes difficult, for Ukraine was evident in its financial, logistical, and strategic support. The international community has roundly criticized Russia's actions in different ways, resulting in particular in substantial economic sanctions. As of March 2023, President Putin faces an arrest warrant from the International Criminal Court (ICC) in The Hague, charged with the grave offense of unlawfully deporting Ukrainian children.

The prevailing Western stance on the conflict between Russia and Ukraine does not resonate universally. Many nations remain noncommittal, neither endorsing Russia nor Ukraine, with numerous countries refraining from censuring Moscow and some even supporting Russia, including China, North Korea, Iran and, more recently, several African countries. This conflict underscores the subtle undercurrents of global power dynamics, where silence often speaks louder than words. Each nation's position offers insights into its worldview and its proximity to one or other of the protagonists and their respective allies.

Saudi Arabia presents a compelling case study. Adopting a prudently balanced stance, Riyadh extended humanitarian assistance to Kiev[2] without

---

2   In October 2022, a global agreement was reached on $400 million in humanitarian aid from Saudi Arabia to Ukraine.

overtly criticizing Moscow. Such an approach epitomizes nimble diplomacy, which aims to maintain equal relations with all concerned parties. This tact was brought into sharper focus in August 2023 when Saudi Arabia announced its intent to host multiparty discussions aimed at fostering a peace blueprint.[3] Other negotiations initiated by Vladimir Putin a few weeks after the start of the Russian attack were reportedly unsuccessful, being refused by Ukraine, obviously on the advice of Western allies. This context underscores Saudi Arabia's ambition to ascend as a pivotal mediator on the global stage. While many nations, including China, have endorsed this dialogue in Jeddah, Russia's conspicuous absence from the assembly—in contrast to other BRICS nations—underscores its reservations. Since October 2023, war has been raging as well in Gaza.

Regardless of the outcomes from the discussions in Jeddah, Saudi Arabia and its Crown Prince have achieved a significant diplomatic feat by convening this conference. Garnering the endorsement of approximately thirty nations for this dialogue testifies to Saudi Arabia's burgeoning repute as a credible mediator in resolving contemporary crises. While Moscow may harbor reservations, it will need to engage with Riyadh, particularly if it wishes to retain its influence over pivotal Middle Eastern affairs. Riyadh's strategic positioning in global diplomacy is becoming increasingly formidable.

Saudi Arabia's rapid evolution in addressing pressing diplomatic challenges is remarkable. Within a short span, the Kingdom has rekindled ties with Iran, initiated dialogues with the Houthi factions of Yemen (a nation it aids in reconstruction), championed Syria's readmission to the Arab League on May

---

3   In reality, this conference is a continuation of what has already been undertaken between Saudi Arabia and Ukraine. Saudi Arabia effectively invited President Volodymyr Zelenskyy to take part in the Arab League summit held in Jeddah in May 2023. The Ukrainian head of state accepted the invitation, clearly delighted to see Saudi Arabia as a credible partner in finding a peaceful solution to the armed conflict that has been raging since February 2022, particularly in Eastern Ukraine after the annexation of Crimea in 2014. Since then, the Ukrainian head of state visited Saudi Arabia twice more, most recently on June 11, 2024, to discuss with the Crown Prince the final preparations for the first Summit of Peace in Ukraine, held in Switzerland on June 15 and 16, 2024, and attended by ninety-two countries and eight international organizations (the Council of Europe, the Ecumenical Patriarchate, the European Commission, the European Council, the European Parliament, the Organization of American States, the Organization for Security and Cooperation in Europe, and the United Nations).

7, 2023, orchestrated evacuations from Sudan, and organized an international conference held on August 5 and 6, 2023, in Jeddah to find a peaceful solution to the war in Ukraine. Saudi Arabia's ascendancy as a peace broker has been meteoric and evidently strategic. This series of diplomatic successes has significantly augmented the Crown Prince's international clout.

Historically, Saudi Arabia's influence was predominantly tethered to its oil reserves. Yet, mirroring its aspirations to diversify its domestic economy, the nation is now striving for a diplomatic influence that transcends its oil-centric legacy. The rapid strides in this direction bear testament to the Crown Prince's astute leadership. He is not merely outlining a vision but actualizing it. The world is beginning to recognize and accept Saudi Arabia's role as a key facilitator of peace.

Crown Prince Mohammed bin Salman bin Abdulaziz Al Saud has emerged as an undeniable builder for Saudi Arabia. The sheer scope and scale of the reforms and strategies he has envisioned and executed exemplify his far-reaching ambitions for the nation. He has not merely made decisions but has stood by them, consistently showcasing an acute grasp of the complex interplay of diplomatic and economic factors on the global stage.

One of the most notable dimensions of his leadership has been the strengthening of ties with Beijing, a move that signals a significant recalibration of global power dynamics. This strategic alignment has positioned Saudi Arabia as a nation fervently seeking peace, drawing international attention and admiration. Furthermore, the Crown Prince's subtle implementation of a soft-power strategy, while not immediately recognized, has now set the stage for Saudi Arabia to become a pivotal player on the global diplomatic landscape.

Parallel to these diplomatic triumphs, the Crown Prince is spearheading multiple economic development initiatives. It is as if he had foresight into the diplomatic successes that lay ahead, prompting him to intensify domestic reforms aimed at enhancing Saudi Arabia's global appeal.

The momentum in Saudi Arabia is palpable. The years 2024 and 2025 marked a transformative chapter in the nation's global standing, one that few could have predicted, except perhaps for its visionary leader. For the first time, Saudi Arabia is shedding its identity solely tied to oil, as it crafts an innovative economic model, striving to diminish its reliance on petroleum.

The meteoric rise of Saudi diplomacy naturally gives rise to speculation.

Will Saudi Arabia continue its active role in brokering peace on the global stage? The evidence suggests a resounding yes. Retreating from such a newly established diplomatic prominence would be incongruous. The intertwining of domestic reforms with international diplomacy is clear—one cannot thrive without the other. The Crown Prince seems to recognize that the nation's economic future is inextricably linked to a more stable Middle East. Under the leadership of the Crown Prince, Saudi Arabia is not just evolving; it is being reimagined. And the world is taking note.

The Crown Prince astutely leverages the opportunities outlined in Vision 2030 to guide his nation toward its aspirations, among which is the nation's strategic geographical position. Located at the nexus of Asia, Europe, and Africa, Saudi Arabia holds a pivotal role. In an environment where many expect aggression, the Crown Prince's commitment to peace stands out as a beacon. He swiftly distanced the nation from crises that previously ensnared it. The deeper we delve into his leadership, the clearer it becomes that he possesses many undisclosed strategies. For now, he meticulously navigates the international stage, aligning with China's interests, particularly as Beijing values peaceful trading partners. Their collaboration emerges just as the United States and Europe grapple with diminishing influence.

When Beijing facilitated rapprochement between Riyadh and Tehran, the global community recognized an extraordinary shift. Saudi Arabia's turn to diplomacy was not mere happenstance. The Kingdom was positioning itself as a formidable force in international diplomacy. If its sincere pursuit is peace, it garners our support. These developments indicate a possible aspiration: Riyadh becoming a keystone in conflict resolution.

In the realm of international relations, major political and economic entities often sculpt the global narrative. Crown Prince Mohammed bin Salman bin Abdulaziz Al Saud challenges conventional paradigms, emerging as a central figure in the current global dynamics. His rapid ascent, despite international criticism, is noteworthy. He crafts a legacy based on transforming Riyadh into a hub for tourism, innovation, and economic progress.

Simultaneously, as already indicated, he exhibits adept tactical and strategic skills, balancing national economic interests against the backdrop of US-China competition. He communicates with precision, ensuring his messages reach their intended recipients timely and effectively. He remains unwavering, refusing to be swayed by external pressures. Saudi Arabia is resolute in implementing policies it deems beneficial for its national and regional interests. The Crown Prince's intellectual prowess becomes more evident as we observe Riyadh championing peace as its new mandate. The Kingdom's investments not only bolster its policy initiatives but also fit into a broader global strategy.

Let us contemplate a transformative hypothesis: What if, under the leadership of the Crown Prince, the Middle East were to overcome its long-standing crises, effectively reshaping the prevalent diplomatic landscape dominated by the West? If he were to achieve in a short span what many have grappled with for decades, it would thus indubitably cement his global stature and position Saudi Arabia among the elite echelons of global superpowers. In 2025, could we be at the cusp of a monumental paradigm shift in international relations whereas the major Western powers, led by the United States, are failing to adopt solutions that will put an end to the conflicts that are bloodying Gaza, Ukraine, and parts of Africa, among other places?

The prioritization of lasting peace by nations as a core tenet of their national and regional agendas is indeed commendable. In the context of Saudi Arabia, efforts are unfolding at an unprecedented pace, echoing the vision of a leader poised to govern these vast territories at the heart of the Arab and Muslim world. It is easy to overlook the Crown Prince's age amidst his expansive achievements and ongoing initiatives, yet he is only forty.

17

Toward a New Energy Paradigm:
Civil Nuclear Power

The allure of exploiting an invaluable resource to maximize profits is a powerful temptation for any holder of such wealth. In the case of Saudi Arabia, oil has long defined the nation's economic model, underpinning its omnipresence in global markets. Despite the international community's concerted efforts to promote sustainable energy solutions as a countermeasure to greenhouse gas emissions, crude oil remains the most coveted natural resource. Its centrality is starkly evident when any systemic disruption in its market triggers global anxiety. Annual production and consumption figures underscore its enduring dominance in the global energy landscape. Saudi Arabia, with its vast reserves, is poised to trade on this resource for decades. Yet, the Crown Prince envisions a different trajectory, advocating for a diversified economic model centered on a groundbreaking venture for the nation: nuclear energy.

When nuclear power is mentioned, it invariably stirs debate between its proponents, who champion its role in generating electricity, and detractors, who underscore the risks—ranging from reactor accidents to the complexities of nuclear waste management. The collective memory remains haunted by events like the Fukushima disaster of March 2011, when a powerful earthquake and subsequent tsunami devastated a nation renowned for its stringent safety protocols. The nuclear sector is, undeniably, fraught with risk. Consequently, the Crown Prince's ambition to introduce nuclear technology for civilian purposes in Saudi Arabia invites skepticism. What, many ask, is the genuine utility of such an endeavor?

The answer appears clear: if Saudi Arabia aims to reduce its economic and energy dependence on oil, its alternatives are limited. While renewable energy will play a role in meeting some of the nation's electricity needs, nuclear power emerges as the most competitive solution to achieving an energy transition.

Emerging and ambitious economies are currently leading the global push for the construction of nuclear plants, with China and India as prominent examples. These two demographic giants, often criticized for their reliance on polluting fossil fuels, have launched substantial renewable and nuclear energy programs to curb their consumption of oil, natural gas, and coal. Their challenge is particularly acute, given their surging energy demands.

In the context of Saudi Arabia and its Vision 2030 reforms, domestic energy needs are projected to rise in tandem with population growth, increased consumption of energy-intensive goods and services, and industrial development. In this scenario, reducing oil's share in the national energy mix requires a robust alternative. Nuclear power stands as the most viable alternative to oil and natural gas, particularly in the realm of electricity generation. Saudi Arabia, blessed with exceptional solar irradiance, is also developing photovoltaic parks, with ambitions to produce several thousand megawatts annually. However, the Kingdom's harsh climate drives significant energy consumption, particularly for air-conditioning systems—levels that cannot yet be reconciled with the current scale of renewable energy production, especially in a model that seeks to minimize reliance on fossil fuels.

As of 2022, the International Energy Agency (IEA) reported that 99.4 percent of Saudi Arabia's electricity production derived from oil and natural gas,[1] with these sources comprising 99.9 percent of the nation's total energy output.[2] These figures starkly illustrate the Kingdom's dependence on its hydrocarbon wealth, which, while foundational to its prosperity, exposes the economy to potential volatility from price downturns—a vulnerability previously demonstrated. The Crown Prince recognizes the necessity of reimagining the national economic model to prepare for the post-oil era. This transition will span decades and demand substantial financial investments to establish a competitive nuclear energy infrastructure capable of fulfilling multiple objectives.

Beyond its economic implications, nuclear power is also a strategic tool for regional geopolitical stabilization. Saudi Arabia aspires to achieve energy

---

1   Natural gas accounts for 58.2 percent of electricity production, while oil represents 41.2 percent. (Source: "Saudi Arabia. Energy Mix," accessed January 6, 2025, https://www .iea.org/countries/saudi-arabia/energy-mix).

2   Ibid. Oil dominates all other natural resources in energy production, accounting for 87.3 percent compared to 12.6 percent for natural gas.

independence by producing sufficient electricity for domestic needs and export. Furthermore, nuclear energy offers a solution to another critical challenge: carbon-free desalination of water. Fresh water, a highly sought resource in this arid region, is traditionally obtained through energy-intensive processes reliant on fossil fuels. Scaling such efforts would amplify carbon emissions and environmental impact. The International Atomic Energy Agency (IAEA) identifies nuclear technology as a viable alternative for nations with growing freshwater needs, particularly those with populations in tens of millions or more.[3]

Saudi Arabia has demonstrated a keen interest in acquiring the expertise necessary for enriching uranium domestically—a critical material for the operation of nuclear reactors. Traditionally, nations embarking on civilian nuclear programs procure enriched fuel from established suppliers. However, Riyadh's efforts to develop domestic uranium enrichment capabilities, coupled with the sophisticated technology required, have prompted the Kingdom to seek partnerships with international actors in the nuclear sector and to invest in the training of Saudi engineers. Crown Prince Mohammed bin Salman envisions not only the acquisition of advanced technology but also the assimilation of technical expertise as part of this ambitious initiative.

This comprehensive strategy aims to position Saudi Arabia as a pivotal player in global energy exports while simultaneously diversifying its portfolio of energy products. By freeing up crude oil consumed for domestic electricity generation and water desalination, nuclear energy could bolster the Kingdom's long-term oil revenues. This aligns with Saudi Arabia's aspirations to become a leading global supplier of clean or low-carbon energy, including hydrogen—a burgeoning energy solution—and electricity derived from nuclear power.

From a geopolitical standpoint, access to civilian nuclear technology represents a strategic lever within a rapidly evolving Middle East. This pursuit aligns with the broader goal of recalibrating regional power dynamics. Neighboring states such as Israel and Iran already possess advanced nuclear programs in varying capacities. Should Saudi Arabia succeed in establishing a

---

3   Omar Yusuf, "Harnessing Nuclear Power for Desalination to Secure Freshwater Resources," https://www.iaea.org/bulletin/harnessing-nuclear-power-for-desalination-to-secure-freshwater-resources, website consulted on January 6, 2025.

fully domestic nuclear fuel cycle, it would enhance its strategic stature and potentially alter the regional balance of power. While Riyadh officially denies any intention to develop a military nuclear program,[4] the capability to enrich uranium could be perceived, both regionally and internationally, as a form of latent deterrence. This prospect underscores the potential diplomatic ramifications of the Kingdom's nuclear ambitions, particularly in a region marked by chronic instability.

At present, Saudi Arabia is engaged in discreet negotiations with several international stakeholders, including the United States, Russia, and South Korea, regarding nuclear technology cooperation. Officially, these discussions focus on peaceful nuclear collaboration across three key areas: reactor construction, technology transfer, and workforce development. Unofficially, other considerations influence dialogue. By leveraging international competition among suppliers, Saudi Arabia seeks to secure favorable terms that might include the right to enrich uranium on its territory, advanced reactor designs such as small modular reactors,[5] and provisions for comprehensive knowledge transfer.

Parallel to these negotiations, Saudi research entities, notably the King Abdulaziz City for Science and Technology (KACST), have quietly developed expertise in nuclear science. Some analysts speculate that this reflects

---

4   The levels of uranium enrichment vary depending on whether the program is civilian or military. In a civilian nuclear program, fuel must contain between 3 percent and 5 percent uranium-235, the only isotope capable of undergoing nuclear fission to release energy. Naturally occurring uranium consists of more than 99 percent uranium-238 and less than 1 percent uranium-235. Uranium is considered "low-enriched" when the concentration of uranium-235 remains below 20 percent. Military-grade enrichment, by contrast, yields highly enriched uranium (HEU). For nuclear weapon development, the enrichment level approaches 90 percent, requiring a significantly more complex refinement process than that of low-enriched uranium. To prevent nuclear proliferation, the International Atomic Energy Agency (IAEA) enforces rigorous oversight of uranium enrichment activities.

5   Small modular reactors (SMRs) are defined by the IAEA as advanced nuclear technologies with a generation capacity of 300 megawatts electric (MWe), roughly one-third the capacity of a conventional 900 MWe nuclear reactor. (Source: Joanne Liou, "What Are Small Modular Reactors (SMRs)?" September 13, 2023, https://www.iaea.org/newscenter/news/what-are-small-modular-reactors-smrs). However, some reactors exceed this threshold —for instance, Finland's Olkiluoto European Pressurized Reactor (EPR), originally "European Pressurized Reactor" and later rebranded "Evolutionary Power Reactor," boasts a production capacity of 1,600 MWe. SMRs are primarily valued for their substantial low-carbon electricity generation potential.

a long-term vision to integrate nuclear research into the Kingdom's broader ambitions, including advancements in aerospace, high-tech industries, and the export of next-generation energy solutions.

Such a program would have profound implications for the international geopolitical landscape. First, it could potentially signal the end of the petrodollar era. If Saudi Arabia integrates a large-scale nuclear program with more flexible payment conditions for its oil or alternative energy sources, such as hydrogen—particularly in trade with China and other major Asian economies—it could accelerate the global departure from the petrodollar system. This shift would destabilize the foundations of global finance.

Second, it would herald a transition toward a new energy paradigm aligned with the objectives of international climate conferences advocating for the decarbonization of the global economy. In this context, Saudi Arabia's dominance in oil in the short term, coupled with its long-term investments in nuclear and hydrogen energy, would enable the Kingdom to remain one of the world's foremost energy suppliers, regardless of the pace at which fossil fuels are phased out.

Third, such a development would likely engender a profound geopolitical realignment. An advanced Saudi nuclear program—nominally focused on civilian applications yet underpinned by robust enrichment capabilities—could fundamentally transform the security architecture of the Middle East. It would enable Riyadh to exert pressure on global powers, compelling them to negotiate on entirely new terms. This would grant Saudi Arabia unprecedented diplomatic leverage. Fourth, achieving mastery over the full nuclear fuel cycle would confer technological prestige upon the Kingdom. Demonstrating expertise in nuclear technology—an area not traditionally associated with a nation better known for its oil reserves and desert sands—would solidify Saudi Arabia's position as a technologically sophisticated state.

While high-profile initiatives such as the Neom megaproject and the Kingdom's substantial investments in global sports dominate media coverage, Saudi Arabia's nuclear ambitions largely unfold behind closed doors. Announcements are typically limited to carefully worded official statements. Key developments, including the exploration of domestic uranium deposits, the establishment of advanced research and development laboratories, and the signing of framework agreements with leading nuclear exporters, seldom receive significant or detailed media attention.

Nevertheless, Saudi nuclear ambitions are closely monitored within diplomatic, defense, and energy circles. The day Riyadh secures a turnkey agreement for multiple reactors, national enrichment rights, and demonstrates tangible progress, the global community will recognize that the Kingdom has made a strategic leap. At that point, it will become clear that Saudi Arabia is not merely striving to remain relevant in a post-oil era but is positioning itself as an indispensable player in global security and high technology.

In the energy sector, this represents a "quiet revolution"—a determined pursuit of advanced nuclear capabilities, particularly in domestic uranium enrichment and the establishment of a fully localized fuel cycle. If successful, this endeavor would provide Saudi Arabia with a powerful new lever in energy markets while reshaping regional power dynamics. The Kingdom's pursuit of civilian nuclear technology is multifaceted and deeply strategic, marking a pivotal shift in its energy and geopolitical trajectory.

These ambitions, as articulated in Vision 2030 by Crown Prince Mohammed bin Salman, underscore Saudi Arabia's intent to secure enduring global influence. Beyond the era of crude oil, the Kingdom aims to emerge as a heavyweight in global security, energy innovation, and technological advancement.

18

October 7, 2023:
The Geopolitical Quagmire

On October 7, 2023, a significant geopolitical event unfolded, capturing the attention of international media. The terrible attack by the Islamic Movement Resistance (Hamas), with the support of Islamic Jihad, on an unprecedented scale, causing the death of almost 1,200 Israelis,[1] most of them civilians (over 800), wounding 7,500, and the capture of almost 250 hostages, many of whom have since died in captivity and a number released in a prisoner exchange during a brief ceasefire) was followed by a horrific war in Gaza that is still going on (having caused the deaths of almost 53,000 Palestinians,[2] mostly civilians including thousands of children, according to various reports to date, mid-November 2024, not to mention the serious food and medical crises afflicting the population).

Some of Hamas's open supporters celebrate the attacks, such as Iran, which expresses its satisfaction. The armed offensive was hailed. Some messages called for Israel to be fought relentlessly. On the other hand, others strongly condemn the events of October 7, 2023, comparing them to those of September 11, 2001, fearing an internationalization of the conflict while regretting the dramatic human cost paid by the Palestinian population since the Israeli offensive in Gaza. The situation worries even more because the outbreak of hostilities does not oppose two regular armies, but one country against a terrorist organization under sanctions by a number of Western countries and the EU.

Before the Gaza offensive was launched by the Israeli army, Tsahal, Israel

---

1   "Israël - Territoires palestiniens : l'espoir après l'annonce d'un cessez-le-feu," February 11, 2025, https://www.unicef.fr/article/israel-palestine-les-enfants-paient-le-prix-de-la-guerre/.
2   "Gaza: un cimetière à ciel ouvert," May 28, 2025, https://www.unicef.fr/article/israel-palestine-les-enfants-paient-le-prix-de-la-guerre/.

warned the civilians to evacuate targeted areas. The ensuing humanitarian crisis saw displaced individuals with limited refuge options, with neighboring countries like Egypt and Jordan hesitant to offer sanctuary. As for the West Bank, how could welcoming several hundred thousand or even millions of people in a territory of a few thousand square kilometers be possible without risking destabilization?

As the situation deteriorated, global perceptions became increasingly polarized; meanwhile, the number of attacks on Jewish and Muslim communities increases worldwide. In the West, support for the Palestinian population was sometimes conflated with endorsement of Hamas, leading to disturbing incidents of violence and growing anti-Semitic and Islamophobic sentiments. In France, a high school teacher was murdered by a man known to the intelligence services for his radical Islamist ideas. In Belgium, two Swedish supporters were shot dead by a lone gunman on the sidelines of an international soccer match. The investigation swiftly unveiled that the murderer had espoused the tenets of radical Islam. In the United States, a woman and her son, both of Palestinian origin and followers of the Muslim faith, were brutally attacked in their home. President Biden promptly denounced this "horrific act of hate,"[3] clearly attributing the crime to the ongoing Israel-Hamas conflict. The child died. More generally, tensions are on the rise. Anti-Semitic acts increase in alarming proportions in the West, while Islamophobia follows a similar trajectory. More than ever, the clash of civilizations seems to be at the heart of tensions. Above all, this new war does not only concern Israel and Hamas.

Meanwhile, the Islamic world mourned the Palestinian casualties, with widespread condemnation of Israel and fiery protests in various countries. People demonstrate in front of Israeli embassies in various Arab capitals. The distinction between anger over Israeli actions and support for Hamas became blurred, raising fears of further escalation. Everything seems confused. Any slightest event may ignite a firestorm at any moment.

Amidst this turmoil, Hezbollah in Southern Lebanon hinted at potential actions against Israel, with Iran's approval. Türkiye condemned Israel without denouncing Hamas's attacks. China initially maintained neutrality before

---

3   "Statement from President Joe Biden," October 15, 2023, https://www.whitehouse.gov /briefing-room/statements-releases/2023/10/15/statement-from-president-joe-biden-4/.

expressing support for Palestinian rights, conspicuously omitting any reference to Israel. Saudi Arabia, amidst negotiations for diplomatic normalization with Israel, suspended talks on October 14, 2023, reflecting the multifaceted nature of the crisis and its broader implications.

The Saudi response underscored the complexity of the situation, influenced by its diplomatic engagements with China and Iran, concerns about its standing within the Arab League, and the prevailing anti-Israel sentiment in the Arab-Muslim world. The Kingdom's cautious approach highlighted the precarious balance of regional and international dynamics in this escalating crisis.

Amidst this chaos, the United States, keen on preserving its influence in the Middle East, found itself in a delicate position. President Biden's decision to visit Tel Aviv on October 18, and attend a planned summit in Amman, which included Jordan, the Palestinian Authority, Egypt, and the United States, underscored this urgency. However, the summit was abruptly canceled following Palestinian Authority President Mahmoud Abbas's withdrawal in protest of the hospital attack, resulting in a diplomatic setback for President Biden. King Abdullah II of Jordan immediately canceled the event afterward. With the 2024 US presidential election approaching, Joe Biden grasped the potential impact of these developments on his reelection campaign, particularly regarding US influence in the Middle East compared to China's, a key topic of the future electoral debates.

For President Biden, the diminishing diplomatic influence in the Middle East underscores the challenges faced in dealing with the region, notably with Saudi Arabia. Despite his campaign promise to treat Saudi Arabia and the Crown Prince as "pariahs,"[4] he found himself compelled to visit the country in July 2022 to address economic and strategic concerns. The call to OPEC+[5] in October 2022 to boost crude oil production for lower prices did not yield the desired results, with OPEC+ opting to cut production, leading

---

4   David E. Sanger, "Candidate Biden Called Saudi Arabia a 'Pariah.' He Now Has to Deal with It," *New York Times*, February 24, 2021, https://www.nytimes.com/2021/02/24/us/politics/biden-jamal-khashoggi-saudi-arabia.html.

5   Authors' note: OPEC+ denotes a coalition of oil-producing nations comprising the fourteen OPEC members and ten additional partners, which include Russia, Mexico, and Kazakhstan.

to increased trading prices. This disparity highlights America's struggle to sway players challenging its leadership and influence—a narrative often exploited by then President Joe Biden's critics, including his predecessor Donald Trump, advocating a different foreign policy approach emphasizing renewed dialogue with former regional partners, particularly Saudi Arabia, and garnering favor among Republican voters for his party's nomination.

Meanwhile, the Israeli military's operations in Gaza from October 7 had resulted in a grievous human toll, with the UN Office for the Coordination of Humanitarian Affairs (OCHA) reporting a staggering number of casualties (on June 22, 2024, it announced more than 37,000 deaths, which have reached almost 53,000 in late May 2025, as already indicated, according to several sources including a large proportion of children and the loss of over two hundred members of UNRWA (United Nations Relief and Works Agency for Palestinian Refugees).[6] These figures fueled global demands for a humanitarian ceasefire, yet the conflict showed no signs of abating.[7]

In mid-November 2023, President Biden and Chinese President Xi Jinping met at the APEC[8] summit in San Francisco. While their meeting was cordial and yielded progress in areas like drug trafficking and military communications, it revealed the persistence of strategic divergences on major diplomatic issues, reflecting the deep-rooted Sino-American rivalry.

Emerging powers, navigating the complexities of global geopolitics, exhibited caution in aligning with the United States, trading with China, or

---

6   "Gaza: un cimetière à ciel ouvert," May 28, 2025, https://www.unicef.fr/article/israel-palestine-les-enfants-paient-le-prix-de-la-guerre/.

7   Several judgments have since been handed down by the International Criminal Court (ICC) and the International Court of Justice (ICJ). In May 2024, the ICJ ordered the Israel to cease its attack on Rafah, following a referral from South Africa. In the same month, ICC Prosecutor Karim A. A. Khan KC requested the issuance of arrest warrants for Israeli Prime Minister Benyamin Netanyahu, Israeli Defense Minister Yoav Gallant, and several leading Hamas figures Yahya Sinwar, Mohammed Diab Ibrahim al-Masri (also known as Mohammed Deïf), and Ismaël Haniyeh.

8   APEC stands for Asia-Pacific Economic Cooperation. It is an annual intergovernmental economic forum founded in 1989. It brings together twenty-one members: five from the Americas (Canada, Chile, Mexico, Peru, the United States), twelve from Asia (Brunei, China, Hong Kong, Indonesia, Japan, Malaysia, Philippines, Singapore, South Korea, Taiwan, Thailand, Vietnam), one from Eurasia (Russia) and three from Oceania (Australia, New Zealand, Papua New Guinea). The collegial meetings are intended to facilitate cooperation and exchanges and promote economic growth and investment.

engaging with Russia on energy matters.[9] This cautious approach underscored the multipolar nature of global politics. Notably, China's proposal to host an international peace conference on the Israel-Hamas conflict during a BRICS summit illustrated this new dynamic. Saudi Arabia exemplified a country engaging globally while pursuing ambitious future plans, representing a trend among nations seeking to assert themselves economically and diplomatically.

This multifaceted global response to the Israel-Hamas conflict diverted attention from other pressing global issues, including the Russian-Ukrainian conflict, tensions between Azerbaijan and Armenia, the crisis in Taiwan, and environmental challenges like climate change and genetic engineering. The Israel-Hamas conflict, thus, not only presented a direct security challenge but also had broader implications for global attention and resources. The future of this conflict remains uncertain, raising concerns about its potential duration, geographical spread, and broader impact.

In the realm of international diplomacy, the best of intentions often encounter the complex web of conflicting interests that define global politics, impeding progress toward peace and other noble objectives. This reality, however, does not inherently signify pervasive bad faith among nations, as frequently lamented by UN Secretary-General António Guterres in discussions on peace and climate change. The intricacies of human interactions and the fluid nature of strategic alliances contribute to a precarious geopolitical balance that is particularly pronounced in the Middle East, a region often likened to a powder keg due to its propensity for crisis and conflict. Every new crisis spreads like concentric ripples: from the immediate focus to the immediate periphery, to the exogenous environment afterward, which remains nonetheless connected to the situation. Saudi Arabia is close to the immediate focus, torn by external and contradictory interests relating to the crisis in the conflict zone.

In this uncertain geopolitical landscape, Saudi Arabia exemplifies the delicate dance of maintaining national interests while navigating international pressures. The Crown Prince, under the ultimate authority of King Salman,

---

9   Timothy Garton Ash, "In our new world disorder, the old bipolar frames of reference will not get us anywhere," European Council on Foreign Relations, November 17, 2017, https://ecfr.eu/article/in-our-new-world-disorder-the-old-bipolar-frames-of -reference-wont-get-us-anywhere/.

exercises considerable caution in his decision-making, adhering to the protocols of both Saudi and international political arenas. This prudence is driven by the need to uphold Saudi Arabia's interests, particularly in the context of Vision 2030, which aims to diversify and modernize the Kingdom's economy, including attracting foreign investment. The current geopolitical climate, especially the Israel-Hamas conflict, necessitates a measured approach.

The Crown Prince's diplomatic strategy embodies a careful balancing act, striving to maintain relations without causing reciprocal harm or hostility. His approach toward the Israel-Hamas conflict demonstrates a commitment to peace, despite the challenges and uncertainties inherent in such endeavors. The Crown Prince's efforts in seeking Russian involvement in peace negotiations with Ukraine, though unsuccessful, as already mentioned, have not diminished his pursuit of diplomatic solutions.

The resolution of the Israel-Hamas conflict, like many international crises, will likely require the participation of multiple external interlocutors, including Arab and Muslim leaders capable of engaging constructively with both Israel and Hamas. Such a scenario underscores the importance of consultation and collaboration, with the Crown Prince potentially playing a key role in facilitating dialogue and working toward a peaceful resolution.

19

New Pathways to Peace

More than one and a half years have elapsed since October 7, 2023, a date that marked a seismic shift in the geopolitical landscape of the Middle East, with far-reaching global repercussions. The conflict that has unfolded since then leaves many critical questions unanswered. Uncertainty reigns: How will the situation evolve? Will space be made for dialogue to ease tensions, and if so, will it succeed? What role will external powers play, especially those vying for influence in this strategically vital region?

At present, the outlook is grim. Beyond the ongoing armed confrontation, attempts at dialogue have thus far failed to align with a collective will to engage in meaningful negotiations. The absence of concrete and coordinated steps toward peace underscores the deep fractures in the international diplomatic community. Rather than striving for the elusive "ideal" solution to such a complex issue, policymakers are left to consider a more pragmatic approach: settling for the "least bad" option. This could serve as an interim measure, providing a necessary balance and a starting point for a longer-term process aimed at stabilizing and consolidating peace.

One political event, however, has the potential to redefine the dynamics of the Middle Eastern conflict: the US presidential election of November 5, 2024. The victory of Donald Trump, coupled with Republican majorities secured in both the House of Representatives and the Senate, signals the likelihood of a unified domestic political front for his administration, at least until the midterm elections of 2026. This political alignment offers Donald Trump an unusual degree of latitude to implement his foreign policy agenda, free from significant internal opposition.

During his campaign, he promised a sharp pivot in American diplomacy, beginning with the Middle East. He has already expressed a commitment to ending the ongoing war in the region. Achieving this goal, however, will require coalition-building with international partners. One of his initial actions has been to signal his intention to appoint Senator Marco Rubio of Florida as Secretary of State. Shortly after the election, Rubio issued a statement heralding a "new era" in American diplomacy, one that would be rooted in advancing the nation's core interests.[1] This declaration signals a dual message. First, it reflects Donald Trump's campaign pledge to "Make America Great Again" by reasserting US influence globally. Second, it underscores a departure from the Biden administration's approach to foreign policy, particularly as executed under Secretary of State Antony Blinken.

The contours of Donald Trump's foreign policy are likely to resemble those of his first term. He has already outlined key priorities: renewing economic competition with China, pursuing rapid resolution of the Ukraine-Russia conflict through direct engagement with Moscow, and demanding greater financial contributions from NATO allies. His stance on Iran remains uncompromising, particularly regarding its nuclear ambitions. These early signals suggest a return to a strategy centered on assertiveness and bilateral deal-making. In this context, it is plausible that Donald Trump will seek to reestablish close ties with Saudi Arabia and Crown Prince Mohammed bin Salman, building on his previous successes with the Abraham Accords.

The prospect of Donald Trump's return to the White House as the forty-seventh president will undoubtedly influence the geopolitical calculus in the Levant and the broader Arabian Peninsula. His administration's approach to the Middle East will likely prioritize revisiting and expanding the framework of the Abraham Accords, which he championed during his first term. This initiative, which brought unprecedented rapprochement between Israel and several Arab states, could serve as the foundation for renewed efforts to address the region's deep-seated conflicts.

Meanwhile, Donald Trump's broader foreign policy vision remains clear: restoring US global leadership by leveraging a transactional, interest-driven approach. His appointment of allies, such as Elon Musk before the deterioration of their personal relationship occurred, barely four months after Donald

---

1   Leo Sands, Karen DeYoung, "Trump taps Rubio for secretary of state. What are his foreign policy views?" *Washington Post*, November 13, 2024, https://www.washingtonpost.com/world/2024/11/13/trump-marco-rubio-secretary-state-foreign-policy/.

Trump's return to the White House, to roles addressing governmental efficiency and budgetary reform illustrates his intent to recalibrate both domestic governance and international engagement.

While the exact composition of his administration remains uncertain, the early contours of Donald Trump's foreign policy suggest a return to familiar strategies, albeit adapted to the current geopolitical realities. As the situation in the Middle East continues to evolve, the decisions of the next US administration will profoundly shape the prospects for peace in the region—and perhaps beyond. His early weeks as president thus need to offer some clarity whether his return to power will mark a turning point in efforts to resolve one of the most intractable conflicts of our time. In spite of his resolve to bring the war to an end, his aspirations for peace confront a diplomatic reality that may have been underestimated.

Donald Trump's appointment of Steven Witkoff[2] as Special Envoy to the region appears to be a calculated decision, selecting a representative whose lack of diplomatic experience complements his distinct approach to Middle Eastern affairs. This decision underscores a simplified dichotomy in his worldview, categorizing regional actors as either allies or adversaries, with Iran occupying the apex of the latter group.

The persistent volatility in the Middle East is rooted in unresolved historical disputes and the failure of prior dialogues and international frameworks. Numerous attempts by global and regional institutions to address coexistence issues have been undermined by competing interests and conflicting interpretations of historical events. The complex interplay of these factors—many traceable to early twentieth-century decisions—has left the region mired in instability.

One of the most pivotal periods in the region's history was marked by decisions and declarations that, however well-intentioned, laid the groundwork for enduring discord. Secret agreements and public declarations alike sought to reshape territorial boundaries in the aftermath of a global conflict, often with scant consideration for the complex realities and aspirations of the people on the ground. Subsequent efforts by international bodies to oversee the region's transition toward self-governance were unevenly executed, leaving

---

2   Steven Witkoff is a New York real estate mogul and longtime personal friend of Donald Trump, for whom he once served as legal counsel.

behind a legacy of mistrust and unresolved tensions that continue to reverberate through the corridors of history. The enduring influence of these early missteps illustrates a continuum of external interventions that have shaped, and often destabilized, the region over the past century.

Today, external powers continue to play a critical role, with the Middle East serving as a focal point for global rivalries, notably between the United States and China. Saudi Arabia exemplifies the region's strategic complexity. Its historical alliance with Washington has undergone significant shifts over the past decade, influenced by changing US administrations and Riyadh's evolving priorities. The announcement in March 2023 of a diplomatic agreement between Saudi Arabia and Iran, brokered by China, sent shock waves through Western capitals. This development underscored Riyadh's pursuit of a diversified geopolitical strategy that includes strengthening economic and political ties with Beijing, as evidenced by the promotion of Mandarin language education alongside English in Saudi schools.

Despite this recalibration, Saudi Arabia remains open to dialogue with its traditional Western allies. Crown Prince Mohammed bin Salman's remarks in a September 2023 interview with Fox News made clear the Kingdom's stance on Iran's nuclear ambitions: should Tehran acquire nuclear weapons, Riyadh would "have to get one, for security reasons, for balancing power."[3] This candid declaration underscores the high stakes in the region and Saudi Arabia's pivotal role in shaping its future.

The pathway to peace in the Middle East hinges on the involvement of external state actors capable of mediating and fostering dialogue among the region's key stakeholders. Saudi Arabia, with its economic leverage and diplomatic influence, is well-positioned to act as a leader in such efforts. However, any progress will require the resumption of normalization talks between Arab nations and Israel, a process impeded by internal and external challenges.

In Israel, Prime Minister Benjamin Netanyahu leads a national unity government constrained by domestic turbulence. Societal divisions and the religious dimensions of governance have curtailed his ability to pursue decisive

---

3   Peter Aitken, "Bret Baier interviews Saudi Prince: Israel peace, 9/11 ties, Iran nuke fears: 'Cannot see another Hiroshima,'" Fox News, September 20, 2023, https://www.foxnews.com/world/bret-baier-interviews-saudi-prince-israel-peace-ties-iran-nuke-fears-cannot-see-another-hiroshima.

foreign policy initiatives. As a result, the prospects for meaningful negotiations to halt hostilities remain dim, with internal debates likely shaping Israel's stance in the foreseeable future.

Nevertheless, the election of Donald Trump could herald a renewed diplomatic push. His prior role in orchestrating the Abraham Accords demonstrated his capacity to foster normalization agreements between Israel and several Arab states. It is plausible that his administration will seek to expand upon this framework, leveraging the accords to catalyze a broader peace initiative.

Saudi Arabia's evolving foreign policy also offers glimmers of hope. On November 29, 2023, the Kingdom publicly announced plans to increase economic cooperation with Iran, contingent on Tehran's commitment to de-escalating the conflict between Israel and Hamas. This announcement followed Riyadh's successful bid to host the 2030 World Expo, signaling a strategic effort to bolster its international standing.[4]

The enduring conflict in the Middle East stands as a stark reminder of the repeated failure of past United Nations resolutions and regional initiatives aimed at securing peace. Good intentions alone have proven insufficient. Recent events lay bare a much darker reality, fraught with the looming risk of escalation. This potential for wider conflagration threatens not only political and human stability but also poses significant economic repercussions, particularly for global investment policies. Amidst such pervasive uncertainty, the very notion of peace seems a distant ideal.

Yet, must the Levant remain condemned to perpetual cycles of antagonism expressed through armed conflict? Such a fate would exact a devastating toll on the region at every level. It is imperative to identify a mechanism for initiating collective dialogue, one that begins with de-escalating tensions as a prerequisite for fostering concrete negotiations which must ultimately aim for a cessation of hostilities, whether temporary or permanent, and lay the groundwork for lasting peace.

In a scenario where calm is eventually restored, the establishment of a regional framework inspired by successful international and regional

---

4   Sam Dagher, "Saudi Arabia Offers Iran Investment to Blunt Gaza War," Bloomberg, November 29, 2023, https://www.bloomberg.com/news/articles/2023-11-29/iran-saudi -proposals-seek-to-deescalate-tensions-amid-israel-hamas-war.

organizations could offer a pathway to stability. Models such as the Union for the Mediterranean, the foundational principles of the European Economic Community (EEC),[5] the Arab League, the Organization of Islamic Coopera- tion, and the Association of Southeast Asian Nations (ASEAN) illustrate the potential of dialogue and collaboration to transform rivalries into cooperative relationships. These entities emerged from historical rivalries, fostering instru- ments of cooperation to avoid repeating the mistakes of the past.

A similar framework in the Middle East could encompass both economic integration and a security alliance among member states. The organization's mandate would rest on reinforced cooperation between Middle Eastern, the Maghreb and Mashreq nations,[6] supported by external partners. Its structure would guarantee mutual defense, regional stability, and economic collabora- tion, with equal representation for all members to address shared challenges, from terrorism to the emergence of hegemonic powers or the threat of nucle- ar proliferation. Central to this alliance would be the principle of collective defense—an attack on one member would be considered an attack on all.

Such an organization would evolve through incremental stages. Initially, it would serve as a platform for consultation and cooperation during crises. Over time, it could develop into a mutual defense pact capable of addressing security concerns while laying the foundation for enduring regional stability. This pragmatic, step-by-step approach reflects a realist understanding of inter- national relations, acknowledging the fractured and highly competitive nature of the global environment.

In today's fragmented world, the pursuit of peace offers a powerful form of soft power for leaders willing to embrace its challenges. However, any such initiative requires broad-based support to gain legitimacy. The creation of a Middle Eastern alliance would be a long-term endeavor, yet it represents a

---

5   The European Economic Community (EEC) was the predecessor of the European Union. It was officially renamed following the Maastricht Treaty, or the Treaty on European Union, signed on February 7, 1992.

6   The Maghreb includes Algeria, Libya, Morocco, Tunisia. The Mashreq refers to the part of the Arab world that includes neither the Maghreb nor the countries of the Arabian Peninsula. The countries concerned are Egypt, Jordan, Lebanon, Palestine, and Syria. As for the Middle East, it encompasses the Mashreq, along with Israel, Iran, and the Arab countries of the Arabian Peninsula, namely Saudi Arabia, Bahrain, Kuwait, Oman, Qatar, the United Arab Emirates, and Yemen.

strategic necessity given the urgent need for a cohesive response to the region's instability.

While the initiative would face formidable obstacles—including historical rivalries, divergent political systems, and external interference—it holds the potential to redefine the diplomatic landscape. Success would depend on a willingness to prioritize dialogue and compromise over discord and confrontation.

This vision of a new regional organization requires collaboration between regional governments and non-state actors, including multinational corporations, civil society organizations, and religious institutions. Such an initiative would necessitate the backing of influential political leaders and the involvement of individuals committed to fostering dialogue through a multiparty framework that transcends the limitations of existing international institutions.

The Middle East needs moderate, visionary, and skilled leaders who are not only adept at governance but also open to dialogue. These leaders must demonstrate an understanding of the region's religious, cultural, and societal complexities and a commitment to addressing these differences through peaceful means. Establishing such an organization would symbolize a significant step toward dialogue and exchange—one that respects the sources of conflict without resorting to violence. As history has shown, peace cannot be purchased; it must be constructed.

Among the potential figures capable of spearheading such an initiative is Crown Prince Mohammed bin Salman of Saudi Arabia. His leadership could play a pivotal role in rallying public and private stakeholders around this vision. The upcoming presidency of Donald Trump, whose first term was marked by strong US-Saudi relations, could further facilitate this diplomatic endeavor. His return to office might present an opportunity to reestablish dialogue and collaboration with Riyadh, particularly in the context of normalizing diplomatic relations between Saudi Arabia and Israel.

Johann Friedrich von Schiller advocated that there are moments when it is necessary to leave behind old hopes in order to create new ones. In this spirit, true progress arises not from clinging to the remnants of shattered aspirations, but from daring to reimagine the future—where the weight of history becomes the foundation for building something greater, rather than a chain that binds. As the incandescent conclusion of summer 2025 approaches, Saudi Arabia remains enveloped in an aura of discretion.

20

Saudi Leadership:
The Missing Piece to Peace?

While diligently observing the tumultuous dynamics of its regional and global surroundings, Riyadh continues to act with calculated precision. Yet, its endeavors rarely reverberate beyond the Arab-Muslim sphere, overshadowed by the deluge of major international developments. These global events—marked by profound consequences—demand caution from the Saudi leadership. This caution is particularly salient as neighboring regions grapple with escalating conflicts.

During the summer of 2024, Israel intensifies its military campaigns, targeting and neutralizing senior Hezbollah operatives based in Lebanon. Concurrently, the war in Yemen persists with renewed vigor. External actors such as the United States, the United Kingdom, and Israel have joined forces against Houthi factions in response to maritime attacks in the Red Sea and drone strikes launched against Israel. Against this backdrop, the return of Donald Trump to the White House as of January 20, 2025, promises significant diplomatic progress in the region. Despite his aversion to direct military intervention, the president's assertive engagement with Middle Eastern complexities in his first term suggests an intention to rapidly reestablish dialogue with both Israel and Arab nations. This intention takes on heightened significance amidst a seismic geopolitical development on December 8, 2024: the collapse of Bashar al-Assad's regime in Syria—a pivotal event that warrants further examination.

One month earlier, on November 11, Riyadh hosted the Arab League and Organization of Islamic Cooperation summit. The gathering underscored Saudi Arabia's aspiration to fortify a unified Arab-Islamic stance on the Palestinian cause. Participants unanimously expressed optimism about Trump's forthcoming tenure, anticipating that his proclivity for negotiation might offer pathways to resolve the region's simmering conflicts.[1] Memories of his hallmark diplomatic achievement—the Abraham Accords, which normalized relations between Israel and several Arab-Muslim states—were invoked as a template for future cooperation.

From December 2 to 4, French President Emmanuel Macron embarked on a state visit to Saudi Arabia. French media closely followed the visit, highlighting the transformative economic, societal, and diplomatic initiatives championed by Crown Prince Mohammed bin Salman.[2] These reforms, encapsulated in the Vision 2030 agenda, have begun to reshape global perceptions of Saudi Arabia, which in the past were marked by significant misunderstandings.

Barely a week later, global attention shifted to Syria. The national army, weakened by relentless rebel offensives, capitulated as the forces of Hay'at Tahrir al-Sham (HTS)[3] seized control of the country's major cities. By early December, Damascus had fallen, and Bashar al-Assad fled to Russia in haste. The leadership vacuum left by Assad's departure raised urgent questions about Syria's future governance.

At the forefront of this transitional period stands Ahmed Hussein al-Charaa, also known as Abu Mohammed al-Joulani, the HTS leader. Once aligned with al-Qaeda and the Islamic State, al-Charaa redirected his ambitions in 2012 to lead the armed resistance against Assad, founding the al-Nusra Front, which later merged into HTS in 2017. Though his past affiliations evoke trepidation, some claim he has sought to moderate his image, emphasizing his commitment to protecting Syria's religious minorities and engaging constructively with the international community.

Despite these reassurances, al-Charaa's ultimate intentions remain opaque.

---

1   In the context of US-Saudi bilateral relations, economic considerations swiftly emerge as central to the forty-seventh President of the United States. While he is intent on securing a lasting resolution to the ongoing war between Israel and Hamas, only three days after his inauguration, Saudi Arabia announced on January 23, 2025, its commitment to invest $600 billion into the US economy over the course of Donald Trump's presidency—an unmistakable signal of a shared desire to refine and deepen their diplomatic and economic ties.

2   Mathilde Visseyrias, "Une incroyable transformation économique, sociétale et Culturelle: Comment les entreprises françaises profitent de l'ouverture de l'Arabie saoudite," December 1, 2024, https://www.lefigaro.fr/societes/on-assiste-a-une-incroyable-transformation -economique-societale-et-culturelle-du-pays-comment-les-entreprises-francaises-profitent-de -l-ouverture-de-l-arabie-saoudite-20241201.

3   Also known as the Organization for the Liberation of the Levant.

His apparent ambition to establish an Islamic state governed by sharia has sparked both domestic and international unease. The situation grew more volatile following an anti-Iranian demonstration that culminated in the storming of Tehran's embassy in Damascus—a visceral expression of long-simmering resentment toward Iranian influence in Syria.

The collapse of Assad's regime signals the end of an era, but the path forward remains fraught with challenges. Syria, scarred by thirteen years of civil war, faces profound questions about its political and societal trajectory. How will al-Charaa navigate this precarious juncture? Will he honor his public assurances, or will his governance align with theocratic principles? These pressing uncertainties demand careful observation as the region braces for yet another chapter of transformation in its complex history.

The dramatic developments in Syria during December 2024 signal a profound geopolitical realignment in the Middle East. For over fifty years, the country had been governed by the Al-Assad family, drawn from the Alawite sect, a minority within the Shi'a branch of Islam. Now, power has shifted to Sunni leadership, fundamentally altering the region's delicate sectarian and political balance. This transition disrupts Tehran's strategic ambitions to maintain a dominant Shi'a crescent stretching from Iran through Iraq and Syria to Lebanon's Mediterranean coast. The loss of Syria as a linchpin in this axis is likely to somewhat curtail Iran's influence across the region.

In a broader context, Syria's political transformation also revisits a controversial decision made by Bashar al-Assad in 2021. By abolishing the role of Grand Mufti and subsuming religious affairs under a government ministry,[4] Assad aimed to tighten his regime's control over the country's spiritual landscape. However, this move galvanized the Sunni opposition, which, through the Syrian Islamic Council, appointed Sheikh Osama al-Rifai as the new Grand Mufti. The son of the esteemed Sunni scholar Abdulkarim al-Rifai, Osama al-Rifai commands significant respect within the Sunni world. Known for his fierce critiques of the Assad regime, he supported the 2011 protests against Assad, enduring police violence for his stance.[5] Having lived in exile

---

4   "Syria's Assad scraps top Muslim cleric post and expands government powers," November 16, 2021, https://www.arabnews.com/node/1968901/middle-east.

5   "Syrian opposition appoints new Islamic mufti after Assad regime abolishes post," November 21, 2021, https://www.newarab.com/news/syrian-opposition-appoints-mufti-after-assad-abolishes-post.

in Saudi Arabia from 1981 to 2000 to escape the regime of Hafez al-Assad, al-Rifai is now positioned to play a pivotal role in shaping Syria's post-conflict religious and social framework. His stature as a scholar and advocate for Sunni unity makes him a central figure in the country's future.

The fall of Bashar al-Assad prompted a swift influx of foreign dignitaries into Damascus. Both the United States and European nations notably moved to engage with Syria's new leadership, eager to reestablish influence in a region increasingly dominated by Russia, China, and Türkiye. Although President Joe Biden appeared to retreat from the forefront following Donald Trump's electoral victory, the United States wasted no time in dispatching a delegation to Syria. This effort coincided with a significant bolstering of American military presence in the country, which doubled in size.[6] Western nations seem intent on regaining lost ground, leveraging diplomatic overtures to build ties with the emergent Sunni leadership.

Saudi Arabia has observed these developments in Damascus with measured interest, acutely aware of the potential for a regime change to recalibrate the region's geopolitical landscape. However, rather than engaging in overt political maneuvering, Riyadh has prioritized humanitarian efforts. On December 31, 2024, under the auspices of KSrelief, Saudi Arabia launched a comprehensive air and land bridge operation to deliver food and medical aid to the Syrian populace—a gesture of solidarity with the war-ravaged nation. This initiative, which went largely unnoticed in Western media, exemplifies Saudi Arabia's commitment to alleviating human suffering irrespective of political calculations.

Saudi Arabia's humanitarian contributions extend beyond these events. Despite Syria's suspension from the Arab League, Riyadh has consistently supported the Syrian people, including its substantial aid in response to the devastating February 2023 earthquake that claimed tens of thousands of lives in southeastern Türkiye and northwestern Syria. Between 2011 and 2024, Saudi humanitarian aid to Syria is estimated to have exceeded $857 million,[7] underscoring a commitment that transcends geopolitical rivalries.

---

6   Matthew Olay, "DOD Announces 2,000 Troops in Syria, Department Prepared for Government Shutdown," December 19, 2024, https://www.defense.gov/News/News -Stories/Article/Article/4013726/dod-announces-2000-troops-in-syria-department -prepared-for-government-shutdown/.

7   "Saudi Arabia Sends First Aid Shipment of the Airlift to Syria," January 1, 2025, https: //www.spa.gov.sa/en/N2236072.

The Crown Prince's emphasis on humanitarian intervention reflects a broader strategy grounded in human-centered diplomacy. Rooted in the Islamic principle of *zakat* (charity), this approach resonates with the cultural ethos of the Arabian Peninsula, where aiding one's neighbor is a moral imperative. Could this philosophy serve as a foundation for a new paradigm of regional engagement? Might it even hold the key to advancing peace in the Middle East?

As the year ends, one question looms large: Why has Saudi Arabia not been solicited to mediate a resolution between Israel and Hamas? By December 31, 2024, neither Egypt nor Qatar had succeeded in brokering a truce. Given the growing stature of Riyadh as a central regional actor and its commitment to prioritizing human welfare, might the Crown Prince's influence offer a path toward a negotiated settlement? With traditional mediators at an impasse, the potential for Saudi Arabia to assume a leading role in forging a long-term resolution to the region's enduring conflicts deserves serious consideration.

On January 15, 2025, a ceasefire agreement was reached between Israel and Hamas, raising profound questions about its implications. The announcement of the accord ignited a wave of collective relief across the Levant. Jubilant celebrations erupted as the warring parties consented to halt hostilities, with key provisions including the release of thirty-three hostages, held captive in Gaza since October 7, 2023, and a reciprocal release of Palestinian prisoners detained in Israel.[8] This agreement offered a glimmer of hope for an end to a humanitarian catastrophe that claimed tens of thousands of lives, though reports from just days earlier suggested that the official death toll might be significantly underestimated.[9]

---

8   The agreement stipulates the release of thirty Palestinian prisoners in exchange for a male hostage, whether alive or deceased; fifty prisoners for the release of a female hostage, whether alive or deceased.

9   A study published in the medical journal *The Lancet* on January 10, 2025, estimates that the reported death toll in Gaza is underestimated by 40 percent. Due to the ongoing war, the epidemiological surveillance services of Gaza's Ministry of Health have been significantly impacted, as the majority of their resources are directed toward urgent medical care. This reallocation of resources is likely to contribute to an underreporting of fatalities. Moreover, official statistics do not account for individuals reported missing in Gaza, a number estimated to be in the tens of thousands. These factors explain the study's significantly higher fatality estimate. It is also important to note that official death toll figures do not include indirect fatalities.

The international community hailed this diplomatic breakthrough. From Beijing to Brussels to Washington, leaders expressed cautious optimism. In the United States, analysts underscored the so-called "Trump Effect," a testament to Donald Trump's proclaimed resolve to prioritize Middle Eastern diplomacy, despite his presidency being set to commence officially just five days later. Mediators received widespread accolades for their steadfast efforts in navigating the grueling negotiations. By January 16, 2025, a palpable sense of hope permeated global discourse, though history's lessons on the fragility of such agreements loomed large. While the ceasefire was undeniably a step forward, the volatility of the region reminded all that even the smallest spark could reignite devastating conflict.

The timing of this accord added another layer of complexity to an already tumultuous geopolitical puzzle. It came a little over a month after the fall of Bashar al-Assad's regime in Syria and two months after Trump's electoral victory, which he accompanied with an ultimatum: failure to secure a diplomatic resolution to the Israel-Hamas conflict by his inauguration would bring "hell" to the Middle East.[10] Al-Assad's ouster marked a seismic shift in regional dynamics. His rule, widely viewed as an obstacle to peace, had drawn concerted efforts from diverse actors to support his downfall. Ahmed Hussein al-Charaa emerged as a favored successor, buoyed by Turkish backing in a coalition aimed at dismantling the Assad regime.

This realignment unfolded through coordinated actions: Türkiye supported fighters from Hay'at Tahrir al-Sham; Saudi Arabia and Qatar provided financial and logistical aid, including weapons and intelligence; Jordan trained and deployed special forces to assist rebel operations in the decisive capture of Damascus; and Israel supplied crucial intelligence, particularly concerning Syrian communication networks. The convergence of these efforts dismantled the Assad regime and set the stage for the broader geopolitical shift that culminated in the ceasefire agreement.

Lebanon welcomes the forthcoming truce with cautious optimism. The

---

10   Since his election on November 5, 2024, Donald Trump has consistently voiced his opinions on the ongoing conflict between the Israel and Hamas. He has attributed responsibility for the crisis to various leaders, including Joe Biden and Benjamin Netanyahu, as well as to the ongoing war between Ukraine and Russia, which he claims has exacerbated international instability.

Cedar Nation is undergoing a significant political transformation following the recent election of President Joseph Aoun. His American counterpart, Joe Biden, has spoken highly of him, emphasizing that he is Lebanon's first head of state unaligned with Hezbollah. Expectations are mounting for a political and economic renewal in this Mediterranean coastal state, accompanied by a potential shift away from Iranian influence—a scenario that would mark a weakening of Tehran's regional foothold. Meanwhile, Iranian officials have offered restrained commentary on the ceasefire, framing it as a victory for the Palestinian people in this conflict. This perspective, however, is unlikely to resonate universally across the international community, reflecting the deep divisions in how the crisis is interpreted on the global stage.

This chain of events underscores the profound interconnectivity of regional challenges and the cascading effects of pivotal developments. Yet, the landscape remains fraught with uncertainty. The durability of the ceasefire between Israel and Hamas is far from assured. Achieving a lasting truce will require additional measures and regional consensus to advance a process aimed at definitively ending armed conflict.

Conspicuously absent from these pivotal negotiations was the Crown Prince of Saudi Arabia, a figure whose involvement might have significantly altered the trajectory of the peace process. His absence deprived the region of a leader uniquely positioned to leverage Saudi Arabia's influence, resources, and strategic relationships to achieve a more robust and enduring resolution. With his capacity to bridge divides and marshal regional consensus, the Crown Prince's active participation could have elevated the ceasefire from a fragile agreement to a transformative milestone, reshaping the Middle Eastern landscape in ways that only a leader of his stature and vision could deliver.

Yet, it is not in this capacity that he has been entrusted with the role of mediator. On February 18, 2025, American and Russian emissaries convened in Riyadh to engage in negotiations concerning the war in Ukraine, with particular focus on an upcoming meeting between Donald Trump and Vladimir Putin—an event for which Ukrainian President Volodymyr Zelenskyy abruptly canceled his attendance, while European leaders, despite their open eagerness to participate, have not been invited. This dynamic underscores the assertion of dominant powers precisely where others' influence is receding. In this context, Saudi Arabia finds itself at the heart of decision-making, a position that stems from its diplomatic engagement with both the United States and Russia, as well as its previous efforts in brokering discussions with the Ukrainian presidency regarding the war. The strategic interests these nations maintain—or seek to develop—render the Crown Prince an indispensable diplomatic player with rising influence. During his May 13, 2025, speech in Riyadh, didn't Donald Trump indicate that he had lifted the sanctions against Syria after being persuaded by the Crown Prince to take such action?[11, 12]

The prospective negotiation of an end to the Ukrainian conflict presents thus an immense challenge—one that, if successfully navigated, could elevate the Crown Prince into the ranks of world leaders whose counsel would be sought in the resolution of global crises. Naturally, attention turns to the Levant, where the ceasefire between Israel and Hamas, though presently holding, will inevitably require further dialogue if a lasting peace is to be achieved. Given the geopolitical realignment orchestrated by Donald Trump and his stated vision for the region's future, Saudi Arabia holds key advantages that position it as a central interlocutor—one whose role extends beyond mere peacemaking to the shaping of a new regional order.

The Crown Prince makes no secret of his ambitions in the Middle East, a region he described as "the new Europe" during the *Future Investment Initiative Summit* held in Riyadh in October 2018. At this event, he articulated his vision for fostering cooperation among neighboring Arab nations, including Qatar—a country with which Saudi Arabia had severed diplomatic relations at the time.[13] While economic development forms the cornerstone of this vision,

---

11   "President Trump Participates in a U.S.-Saudi Investment Forum," The White House, May 13, 2025, https://www.youtube.com/watch?v=wj1QOz3iuCE.

12   Donald Trump spoke with several regional leaders before reaching the decision to lift sanctions on Syria in order to give the country "a chance at greatness," as he put it during his May 13, 2025, speech. He added that this is now "their time to shine." In that speech, he emphasized the importance of his conversation with the Crown Prince in convincing him of the opportunity to help Syria take a new political and societal direction—one that would also generate positive outcomes for the entire region by contributing to the stabilization of a country devastated by more than a decade of internal war.

13   "Saudi Crown Prince: The new Europe is the Middle East," October 24, 2018, https://english.alarabiya.net/features/2018/10/24/Saudi-Crown-Prince-The-new-Europe-is-the-Middle-East.

it is underpinned by a broader aspiration for peace. Through the prosperity he envisions and delineates, he forecasts a promising future for the region.

Central to his strategy is the ambition to position Saudi Arabia among the world's leading economic powers,[14] a goal that hinges on the nation's ability to attract foreign talent. The Crown Prince has pledged to welcome these individuals to facilitate the sweeping transformation outlined in the Kingdom's Vision 2030 plan. And his ambitions do not stop at the Kingdom's borders. His vision radiates across the Middle East, where he foresees a united, thriving region—not just playing catch-up with the rest of the world but stepping up as its next great frontier of prosperity, stability, innovation, and coexistence.

---

14   Ibid.

Conclusion

At a moment when global attention is keenly focused on Riyadh, a single fact emerges distinctly: The Saudi capital is making calculated strategic decisions that do not necessarily resonate well with everyone, especially given the global issues upon which it is taking a stance. This reminds many of the pivotal role the Kingdom played within OPEC starting in the 1960s. As a dominant force in the oil sector, Riyadh's voice was heeded with utmost care, given the potential ramifications of its decisions on oil production and export. The events of the Cold War era are still fresh in global memory, particularly the two oil shocks of the 1970s.[1] The aftershock of the 1973 embargo, which Saudi Arabia imposed on oil exports to the United States following the October War, was profoundly felt across the Western world. The event underscored the West's acute dependence on oil and ignited efforts to diversify the energy mix. Yet, throughout this period, Riyadh positioned itself as a leading voice among oil-producing nations and, importantly, as a nation unwilling to bow to undesirable external pressures. Oil became its most potent lever, compelling the world to heed its stance, backed by the security of its vast reserves. This is still the case.

Philosophically, the governance approach championed by the Crown Prince mirrors those of his predecessors. Forming strategic alliances does not equate to subservience. All alliances have boundaries. While communication styles may vary, when diplomacy strains, decisive actions become necessary to underscore that no agreement is set in stone, especially in today's fiercely competitive global landscape.

In the current era, despite the criticisms, oil remains a potent tool of influence. Saudi Arabia wields this advantage effectively, especially with nations reliant on its oil. Yet, wisdom in governance suggests that a nation should diversify its assets. Saudi Arabia epitomizes this strategy, possessing a

---

1   The oil shocks took place in 1973 and 1979.

multifaceted arsenal that it deploys based on present opportunities and to sustain its political, economic, and societal trajectory. While oil continues to play a central role in the Kingdom's strategic planning—fueling initiatives like the Vision 2030 program—the Crown Prince is deeply committed to rejuvenating the national economic blueprint. This is to ensure that the Kingdom does not fall into the precarious trap of economic reliance that could jeopardize its fiscal health in the long run. After all, a solely economic perspective does not ensure a nation's enduring prosperity.

To gain international prominence, it is imperative to address matters that extend beyond domestic concerns. Saudi Arabia's unique geographical positioning places it at the nexus of multiple global matters, be they economic, security-oriented, or otherwise. The Kingdom is proximate to Africa, a continent eyed keenly by many of the world's leading and emerging economies. It lies en route to China's audacious vision of reviving the Silk Roads. Moreover, it is in close proximity to several hotspots that perennially unsettle the geopolitical equilibrium of the Middle East. Collectively, these elements amplify Riyadh's stakes and engagement in global affairs, catalyzing its strategic recalibration.

True diplomatic gravitas is not merely attained by an expressed desire to mediate or intervene in global issues. Legitimacy demands more than just rhetoric—it calls for tangible actions. The Middle East, with its web of protracted conflicts, has witnessed myriad attempts at mediation, yet many have proven ineffectual. It is conceivable that Saudi Arabia, with its profound understanding of regional intricacies, could usher in an era of productive dialogue among key stakeholders. Being heard often starts with attentive listening, and nations like Lebanon and Syria are already tuned in to Saudi perspectives. While achieving enduring peace is a daunting ambition, it seems less quixotic when championed by an indigenous Arab leader, as opposed to external agents.

The endeavors embarked upon by the Crown Prince are monumental. To many in the West, the scale and depth of the societal modernization he is spearheading might be challenging to fully comprehend. This transformative agenda has garnered him immense admiration both domestically and across the broader Arab and Islamic spheres. He stands out as a progressive statesman, keen on striking a harmonious balance between forward-looking reforms and cherished traditions. A pragmatic visionary, he recognizes that meaningful change does not necessitate upheaval; evolution needn't erase the past or disorient a nation's societal compass.

In the realm of peace diplomacy, the Crown Prince understands that influence is often the fruit of patient negotiation. The Middle East's complex crises will not dissolve overnight. While shifts toward positive outcomes might be rapid, achieving lasting peace is a long-term endeavor. Such monumental tasks demand time, and in this context, he emerges as an architect of the future, championing the goals he's set for 2030. As tomorrow dawns, his aspirations will undoubtedly soar even higher.

Regional peace is a process, constructed incrementally. Saudi Arabia's role in this construction is indisputable. Let's hope such peace will also be a catalyst for economic vigor, benefiting not just Saudi Arabia but also the broader region, including the African continent. Amidst this volatile international backdrop, the Crown Prince persists in his enlightening endeavors— welcoming dialogue, but resolute in leveraging opportunities that advance the interests of his nation. His overarching strategy was solidified with the unveiling of the 2016 road map, delineating his vision for the nation's modernization. Since then, at mid-point, the path toward realizing Vision 2030 and its future projections has been charted, with already important achievements in several areas of endeavors.

While skeptics question the Crown Prince's capacity for success, doubting the plausibility and sustainability of this grand initiative, the verdict of time remains pending. The strategy interweaves diverse elements, demonstrating a meticulous and holistic perspective. It necessitated striking a balance, forging the right compromises to prevent friction with religious leaders or public sentiment. Even within a system led by a dominant figure, it is essential to be attuned to potential dissent and disquiet. It is crucial to discern if such sentiments pose a threat, potentially destabilizing governance. Governance transcends mere decision-making. It is about active engagement, especially vital in a society in flux, yet grounded in age-old traditions. Historically, Saudi leadership has valued the counsel of elders, religious heads, and clans. Their opinions carry weight. Would it serve the Crown Prince to disregard them? Likely not. Modernization does not necessitate severing ties with tradition, but rather assimilating it within a contemporary societal framework.

The fruition of Vision 2030 hinges on the diversification of the national economy, its global allure, and its capability to foster innovation. While this sounds straightforward in theory, its practical implementation demands meticulous planning. However, it is paramount to recognize that these objectives will materialize only if supported by a robust synergy of diverse elements, reminiscent of complex watchmaking. Here, craftsmanship edges on the realms of artistry. The challenge lies in harmonizing myriad variables to execute an ambitious socioeconomic blueprint, which might be enticing on paper, but its success is not guaranteed. Even the most meticulously crafted plans are not immune to unexpected outcomes.

The ultimate success of the Crown Prince's program hinges on a delicate balance. While it champions performance, it must first secure widespread conviction and support. Earning the endorsement of religious and clan leaders is paramount, as is persuading the general populace of the initiative's merit and significance. Rhetoric alone will not suffice; tangible actions will always resonate more profoundly.

The quandary of the economic future looms large. How can Saudi Arabia rejuvenate its national framework, ensuring abundant employment and career prospects for its citizens? By fostering an entrepreneurial spirit. By enacting legislation that prioritizes hiring Saudi nationals, as exemplified by the Saudization policy. And by intensifying efforts to attract international enterprises. Pursuing excellence becomes a linchpin; opportunities that elevate the Kingdom's global standing are meticulously evaluated. A measured yet resolute modernization is underway, with foresight toward a post-oil landscape. Investments are being directed toward burgeoning sectors such as tourism, health care, agribusiness, and notably all things innovation-related. This latter domain, in particular, garners global optimism. Ventures, whether nascent or mature, that have the potential to reshape the future are actively sought. Identifying the next big success—often termed "unicorns"—is an art and science, demanding unrivaled expertise. However, every illustrious venture has its origins, and Saudi Arabia, with its formidable resources, is well-positioned to invest. The challenge lies in discerning and capitalizing on the right opportunities, as countless enterprises vie for the Kingdom's patronage.

Governance, by its nature, is intricate. Domestically, authority manifests in a pursuit of equilibrium, melding the legitimacy of decision-making with the affection of the populace. A successful leader promulgates guidelines that garner widespread acceptance. On the international stage, strategic rivalry becomes paramount. Drawing an analogy, the global arena is akin to a boxing ring, segmented by weight categories. Not every nation contends in identical arenas; Saudi Arabia might not vie directly with superpowers like the United States and China. However, it can be the pivotal force that influences overarching dynamics. To sustain its influential stature amidst global issues, Saudi Arabia must diversify its credentials beyond oil, especially as the world gravitates toward decarbonizing its economy. The Kingdom must explore alternative avenues for international acclaim, seizing opportunistic ventures as they arise.

In the high-stakes realm of global competition, criticism is often relentless, especially when choices do not align with the preferences of the primary heavyweight contenders. For a nation like Saudi Arabia, the challenge lies in maintaining its autonomy, demonstrating that it is capable of making decisions it believes are right without succumbing to external pressures. Such an independent stance is a luxury not many nations can afford. Saudi Arabia has firmly planted its flag in the camp of autonomy and enterprise. This international policy has assumed even more significance since Prince Mohammed bin Salman bin Abdulaziz Al Saud began playing pivotal roles in defense, economy, and subsequently, the governmental helm. His influence is unmistakable, and it is polarizing.

To most of his Saudi constituents, he is seen as a visionary and statesman, deeply invested in their welfare. He's on a mission to reform the national economic framework, aiming for a more diversified and less oil-reliant economic landscape—a monumental task.

Some may find his tactics enigmatic, but his overarching objective is clear: he's determined to chart Saudi Arabia's destiny. He's engaging in arenas previously unassociated with the Kingdom. Consider peace: Who, if not a regional leader, is best positioned to fathom the complexities of the Middle East? While many have ventured and faltered in their peacemaking endeavors, what makes him any less qualified to strive for harmony? The benefits of such efforts would ripple beyond the immediate region to the global community. Should the Crown Prince successfully orchestrate diplomatic triumphs, one can only imagine the immense pride resonating throughout Saudi Arabia and the nation's enhanced global stature. Is his mission quixotic? Not in the least.

Diplomacy, at its core, acknowledges a fundamental truth: even the most compelling arguments fall on deaf ears if faced with parties not genuinely seeking peace. Diplomacy, after all, is human-centric. Historically, many diplomats and intermediaries have managed to defuse volatile scenarios, fostering tranquility in their wake.

As we draw our reflections to a close, the ever-unfolding and often disheartening state of international affairs brings renewed attention to the Kingdom of Saudi Arabia. As of February 18, 2025, it has emerged as the designated venue for preliminary talks between American and Russian emissaries, marking the first steps toward ending the war in Ukraine.[2] This development underscores the credibility afforded to Saudi Arabia by the United States, Russia, and Ukraine alike, as they seek a venue conducive to negotiating a truce, a ceasefire, or even a formal cessation of hostilities.

While the negotiations remain complex—laden with contentious points and conditions that must be carefully navigated before any meaningful progress can be achieved—the Saudi Kingdom, under the leadership of the Crown Prince, has assumed the role of mediator in a conflict where it maintains close and well-established relations with the principal actors. This diplomatic role confers upon Saudi Arabia an enhanced visibility and growing credibility on the world stage, positioning it as a potential intermediary in the resolution of other major international crises.

During his official visit to Saudi Arabia in May 2025, Donald Trump made no secret of his admiration for the work carried out by the Crown Prince, particularly regarding his efforts to promote peace in the Middle East and beyond. The US president urged Arab countries to recognize the importance of pacifying the region, for which he predicted a bright future—provided it can put aside its differences and prioritize humanity and peace, which he described as a "cultural and commercial crossroads of the planet."[3] For Trump, peace and

---

2   On 18 February 2025, the initial round of discussions took place in Riyadh, despite the last-minute absence of Volodymyr Zelenskyy. US Secretary of State Marco Rubio, White House National Security Advisor Mike Waltz, and Special Envoy for the Middle East Steve Witkoff met on this occasion with Russian Foreign Minister Sergey Lavrov and Kremlin Foreign Policy Advisor Yuri Ushakov.

3   "President Trump Participates in a US-Saudi Investment Forum," The White House, May 13, 2025, https://www.youtube.com/watch?v=wj1QOz3iuCE.

prosperity are inseparable foundations of what he envisions as a Golden Age for the Middle East. He expressed optimism and belief in lasting peace, while emphasizing that such an outcome will only be possible through the leadership of strong and determined figures committed to peace—his gaze turning notably toward the Crown Prince.

His actions remain largely misinterpreted by the West and elsewhere in the world. Such misconceptions may be emblematic of a prevalent lack of familiarity with Saudi Arabia's political processes and underlying thought paradigms. Central to this is the cultural context. Arab proverbs, teeming with wisdom, offer valuable insights. Two particular proverbs stand out, encapsulating the Crown Prince's mindset. They succinctly illustrate his approach to governance and leadership, underscoring his visionary spirit.

There are five levels to achieve wisdom:
be silent, listen, remember, act, study.

Write the bad things that have been done to you in the sand but engrave
the good things in marble.

Appendix 1
Kingdom of Saudi Arabia's Royal Family Tree

- **Abdulaziz bin Abdul Rahman Al Saud or Ibn Saud** *(King from 1932 to 1953).*
  —Had thirty-five sons with fifteen different spouses.
  —Had seven sons with his favorite spouse, Hassa bint Ahmed Al Sudairi.[1]
  —From his thirty-five sons, the following six reigned:
- **Saud** *(King from 1953 to 1964)*
- **Faisal** *(King from 1964 to 1975)*
- **Khalid** *(King from 1975 to 1982)*
- **Fahd** *(King from 1982 to 2005)*
- **Abdullah** *(King from 2005 to 2015)*
- **Salman** *(King since 2015)*

---

1   The seven sons in chronological order of birth: King Fahd (1921–2005). Sultan (1928–2011), Crown Prince from 2005 until his death. Abdul Rahman (1931–2017). Nayef (1933–2012), Crown Prince from 2011 until his death. Turki (1934–2016). King Salman (1935). Ahmed (1940).

List of Crown Princes Appointed Since the Creation of the Allegiance Council by King Abdullah in 2007[2]

Under King Abdullah Bin Abdulaziz[3] (2005–2015)	Under King Salman Bin Abdulaziz (Since January 23, 2015)
1. Crown Prince Sultan bin Abdulaziz (1928–2011) from 2005 to 2011. Crown Prince appointed before the creation of the Allegiance Council.	1. Crown Prince Moqren bin Abdulaziz (1945), Crown Prince from January 23, 2015, to April 29, 2015. Officially resigned from this position.
2. Crown Prince Nayef bin Abdulaziz (1934–2012) from 2011 to 2012.	2. Crown Prince Muhammad bin Nayef (1959), son of Crown Prince Nayef bin Abdulaziz. Crown Prince from April 29, 2015, to June 21, 2017. Removed from office by King Salman.
3. Crown Prince Salman bin Abdulaziz (1935) from 2012 until his enthronement on January 23, 2015.	3. Vice-Crown Prince then Crown Prince Mohammed bin Salman (1985), son of King Salman bin Abdulaziz. Vice-Crown Prince from April 29, 2015, to June 21, 2017, and Crown Prince since then.

2   The Allegiance Council appoints the Crown Prince according to certain rules established under the reign of King Abdullah. However, the King has the final say. He may opt for a different choice from that of the Allegiance Council.

3   Bin Abdulaziz means son of Abdulaziz.

List of Spouses and Descendants of King Salman

Spouses	Children
1. Princess Sultana bint Turki Al Sudairi, deceased in 2011.	Six children: 1. Fahd (deceased in 2001) 2. Sultan 3. Ahmed (deceased in 2002) 4. Abdulaziz 5. Faisal 6. Hassa (King Salman's only daughter)
2. Princess Sarah bint Faisal Al Subai'ai.	One child: 1. Saud.
3. Princess Fahda bint Falah Al Hithlain.	Six children: 1. Mohammed (Crown Prince) 2. Turki 3. Khalid 4. Nayef 5. Bandar 6. Rakan

Spouse and Descendants of Crown Prince Mohammed bin Salman

- **H.R.H. Mohammed bin Salman** married **Princess Sara bint Mashour bin Abdulaziz Al Saud** in 2008.

    The couple has five children:
- Prince Salman
- Prince Mashour
- Princess Fahdah
- Princess Norah
- Prince Abdulaziz

Appendix 2
Summary and Progress of Vision 2030[1]

- **FOREWORD by Crown Prince Mohammed bin Salman, Chairman of the Council of Economic and Development Affairs:**

It is my pleasure to present Saudi Arabia's vision for the future. It is an ambitious yet achievable blueprint, which expresses our long-term goals and expectations and reflects our country's strengths and capabilities.

All success stories start with a vision, and successful visions are based on strong pillars. The first pillar of our vision is our status as the heart of the Arab and Islamic worlds. We recognize that Allah the Almighty has bestowed on our land a gift more precious than oil. Our Kingdom is the Land of the Two Holy Mosques, the most sacred sites on earth, and the direction of the Kaaba (Qibla) to which more than a billion Muslims turn at prayer.

The second pillar of our vision is our determination to become a global investment powerhouse. Our nation holds strong investment capabilities, which we will harness to stimulate our economy and diversify our revenues.

The third pillar is transforming our unique strategic location into a global hub connecting three continents, Asia, Europe and Africa. Our geographic position between key global waterways, makes the Kingdom of Saudi Arabia an epicenter of trade and the gateway to the world.

Our country is rich in its natural resources. We are not dependent solely on oil for our energy needs. Gold, phosphate, uranium, and many other valuable minerals are found beneath our land. But our real wealth lies in the ambition of our people and the potential of our younger generation. They are our nation's pride and the architects of our future. We will never forget how, under tougher circumstances than today, our nation was forged by collective

---

1   Source: www.vision2030.gov.sa, https://www.vision2030.gov.sa/media/rc0b5oy1/saudi _vision203.pdf.

determination when the late King Abdulaziz Al-Saud—may Allah bless his soul—united the Kingdom. Our people will amaze the world again.

We are confident about the Kingdom's future. With all the blessings Allah has bestowed on our nation, we cannot help but be optimistic about the decades ahead. We ponder what lies over the horizon rather than worrying about what could be lost.

The future of the Kingdom, my dear brothers and sisters, is one of huge promise and great potential, God willing. Our precious country deserves the best. Therefore, we will expand and further develop our talents and capacity. We will do our utmost to ensure that Muslims from around the world can visit the Holy Sites. We are determined to reinforce and diversify the capabilities of our economy, turning our key strengths into enabling tools for a fully diversified future. As such, we will transform Aramco from an oil producing company into a global industrial conglomerate.

We will transform the Public Investment Fund into the world's largest sovereign wealth fund. We will encourage our major corporations to expand across borders and take their rightful place in global markets. As we continue to give our army the best possible machinery and equipment, we plan to manufacture half of our military needs within the Kingdom to create more job opportunities for citizens and keep more resources in our country.

We will expand the variety of digital services to reduce delays and cut tedious bureaucracy. We will immediately adopt wide-ranging transparency and accountability reforms and, through the body set up to measure the performance of government agencies, hold them accountable for any shortcomings. We will be transparent and open about our failures as well as our successes, and will welcome ideas on how to improve.

All this comes from the directive of Custodian of the Two Holy Mosques King Salman, may Allah protect him, who ordered us to plan for a future that fulfills your ambitions and your aspirations.

In line with his instructions, we will work tirelessly from today to build a better tomorrow for you, your children, and your children's children. Our ambition is for the long term. It goes beyond replenishing sources of income that have weakened or preserving what we have already achieved. We are determined to build a thriving country in which all citizens can fulfill their dreams, hopes and ambitions. Therefore, we will not rest until our nation is a leader in providing opportunities for all through education and training and high-quality services such as employment initiatives, health, housing, and entertainment.

We commit ourselves to providing world-class government services, which effectively and efficiently meet the needs of our citizens. Together we will continue building a better country, fulfilling our dream of prosperity and unlocking the talent, potential, and dedication of our young men and women. We will not allow our country ever to be at the mercy of a commodity price volatility or external markets.

We have all the means to achieve our dreams and ambitions. There are no excuses for us to stand still or move backward. Our vision is a strong, thriving, and stable Saudi Arabia that provides opportunity for all. Our vision is a tolerant country with Islam as its constitution and moderation as its method. We will welcome qualified individuals from all over the world and will respect those who have come to join our journey and our success.

We intend to provide better opportunities for partnerships with the private sector through the three pillars: Our position as the heart of the Arab and Islamic worlds, our leading investment capabilities, and our strategic geographical position. We will improve the business environment, so that our economy grows and flourishes, driving healthier employment opportunities for citizens and long-term prosperity for all. This promise is built on cooperation and on mutual responsibility.

This is our "Saudi Arabia's Vision for 2030." We will begin immediately delivering the overarching plans and programs we have set out. Together, with the help of Allah, we can strengthen the Kingdom of Saudi Arabia's position as a great nation in which we should all feel an immense pride.

● **Introduction:**[2]

The Kingdom of Saudi Arabia is blessed with many rich assets. Our geographic, cultural, social, demographic, and economic advantages have enabled us to take a leading position in the world.

To build the best future for our country, we have based our vision for the

---

2　Vision 2030, 85 pp., https://www.vision2030.gov.sa/media/rc0b5oy1/saudi_vision 203.pdf.

Kingdom of Saudi Arabia on three pillars that represent our unique competitive advantages. Our status will enable us to build on our leading role as the heart of Arab and Islamic worlds. At the same time, we will use our investment power to create a more diverse and sustainable economy. Finally, we will use our strategic location to build our role as an integral driver of international trade and to connect three continents: Africa, Asia and Europe.

Our vision is built around three themes: A vibrant society, a thriving economy, and an ambitious nation. This first theme is vital to achieving the vision and a strong foundation for economic prosperity. We believe in the importance of a vibrant society. Members of this society live in accordance with the Islamic principle of moderation, are proud of their national identity and their ancient cultural heritage, enjoy a good life in a beautiful environment, are protected by caring families, and are supported by an empowering social and health care system.

In the second theme, a thriving economy provides opportunities for all by building an education system aligned with market needs and creating economic opportunities for the entrepreneur, the small enterprise as well as the large corporation. Therefore, we will develop our investment tools to unlock our promising economic sectors, diversify our economy, and create job opportunities. We will also grow our economy and improve the quality of our services, by privatizing some government services, improving the business environment, attracting the finest talent and the best investments globally, and leveraging our unique strategic location in connecting three continents.

Our nation is ambitious in what we want to achieve. We will apply efficiency and responsibility at all levels.

Our third theme is built on an effective, transparent, accountable, enabling, and high-performing government. We will also prepare the right environment for our citizens, the private sector and nonprofit sector to take their responsibilities and take the initiative in facing challenges and seizing opportunities.

In each of these themes, we highlighted a selection of commitments and goals, as a reflection of our ambition and a representation of what we aim to achieve. This vision will be the point of reference for our future decisions, so that all future projects are aligned to its content. To clarify our next steps, we have already prepared the ground and launched some executive programs at the Council of Economic and Development Affairs. We will now launch a first portfolio of crucial programs with the aim to achieve our goals and honor our commitments. Sustainable success can only be achieved when built upon solid foundations. Our vision, grounded in our country's strengths, will deliver this stability and create a brighter future for our country and our people.

- **Progress:**[3]

On April 25, 2016, Saudi Arabia presented Vision 2030, an initiative that charts a new course for the nation's future based on the diversification of the economy.

Eight years later, this innovative project has already achieved 87% of its 1,064 initiatives completed or in progress, while 81% of the 243 key performance indicators for the third level have already achieved their targets, with 105 indicators exceeding the targets for 2024–2025.

Hereafter are some highlights of the Kingdom's remarkable growth in several sectors, such as tourism, an industry that Riyadh has been promoting for years in order to achieve Vision 2030 goals:

- ✓ The Kingdom welcomed 106 million visitors in 2023, including 27.4 million international tourists, making it the second-fastest growing tourism destination in the world.
- ✓ On the other hand, the number of "Umrah" participants from abroad soared to a record 13.56 million, surpassing the target of 10 million by 2023 and almost doubling the benchmark of 6.2 million.
- ✓ Cultural heritage preservation is another area of success. The number of Saudi sites on the UNESCO list increased to seven, surpassing the target of six by 2023 and bringing the Kingdom closer to its target of eight by 2030. The latest addition, the "Uruq Bani Ma'arid" reserve, further strengthens Saudi Arabia's rich cultural footprint.
- ✓ Riyadh's international position has been further strengthened after the Arab country was chosen to host Expo 2030, beating Busan (Korea) and Rome (Italy).

---

3   "Saudi Arabia's Vision 2030: Early Signs of Success," 16 Shawwal 1445–April 25, 2024, https://www.spa.gov.sa/en/N2089591.

- ✓ Domestically, Vision 2030's focus on improving the quality of life is yielding positive results. Life expectancy in the Kingdom has increased to 78, surpassing a baseline of 77.1 years, while the initiative hopes to reach 80.

- ✓ The percentage of population centers, including those in remote areas, covered by health services now stands at 96.41%, exceeding the target of 96% by 2023. In addition, Vision 2030 is delivering on its promise to increase home ownership rates.

- ✓ More than 66,000 Saudi families have received their new homes. By the end of August, more than 24,000 new homes had been inaugurated. The percentage of citizens owning their homes has reached 63.74%, exceeding the target of 63% by 2023, significant progress from a baseline of 47%, with the final Vision 2030 target set at 70%.

- ✓ In this regard, housing support services are also expanding. More than 96,000 citizens have benefited from these services, with financial support totaling SAR 4.1 billion.

- ✓ One of the cornerstones of Vision 2030 is diversification of the economy, boosting non-oil sectors away from exclusive reliance on crude oil. Last year, non-oil GDP reached 1,889 billion rials, exceeding a baseline of 1,519 billion rials and approaching the 2023 target of 1,934 billion rials.

- ✓ The final Vision 2030 target for non-oil GDP is SAR 4,970 billion. Moreover, the private sector's contribution to GDP has reached 45%, achieving the 2023 target.

- ✓ Vision 2030 is also making progress in reducing unemployment. The national unemployment rate among Saudi citizens has fallen to 7.7%, exceeding the target of 8% by 2023. This represents significant progress from a baseline of 12.3%, while the Vision targets 7%.

- ✓ Within employment, Vision 2030 emphasizes the empowerment of women as a key driver of national development. Female labor force participation has increased to 34%, approaching the ambitious long-term target of 40%. This represents a significant increase from a baseline of 22.8%.

- ✓ Other areas where Vision 2030 has achieved significant successes over the past year include education, technology, communications and green energy.

Appendix 3
Vision 2030–2024 Annual Report
(Executive Summary)[1]

Out of the 374 currently active Vision 2030 indicators, 299 have already met their original targets, and 257 have surpassed them. An additional 49 indicators have reached between 85% and 99% of the goals set in 2016 for achievement by 2030.

While a full list of indicators is not provided here, a selection of key achievements illustrates notable economic and social progress as of 2024:

- ✓ Credit ratings: The major credit rating agencies—Fitch, Moody's, and Standard & Poor's—have maintained their previous ratings and reaffirmed their confidence in Saudi Arabia's long-term fiscal and economic outlook.
- ✓ Economic growth forecasts: Leading international financial institutions expect strong economic growth in 2025 and 2026, with the International Monetary Fund (IMF) forecasting 3% and 3.7%, the World Bank 3.4% and 5.4%, the Organisation for Economic Co-operation and Development (OECD) 3.8% and 3.6%, and the Saudi Ministry of Economy projecting 4.6% and 3.5%, respectively.
- ✓ Pilgrims: The number of pilgrims reached 16.92 million, far exceeding the 2024 target of 11.3 million (with a target of 30 million by 2030).
- ✓ Women in the workforce: Women's labor force participation continues to grow, reaching 33.5% in 2024 (compared to a target of 35.9% for 2024 and 40% by 2030).

---

1   Vision 2030–2024 Annual Report (Executive Summary), 79 p., https://www.vision 2030.gov.sa/en/annual-reports.

✓ Home ownership: Residential ownership reached 65.4%, surpassing the 2024 target of 64%.

✓ Cultural heritage: Saudi Arabia gained UNESCO World Heritage recognition for eight historical sites, achieving this milestone six years ahead of schedule.

✓ Public Investment Fund (PIF): The PIF's assets under management reached USD 941.33 billion, exceeding the 2024 goal of USD 880 billion.

✓ E-Government Development: The Kingdom advanced 25 positions in the United Nations E-Government Development Index (UN EGDI), now ranking 6th globally—far surpassing the 2024 target of 26th place.

✓ Volunteerism: The number of volunteers reached 1.2 million, exceeding the 2030 goal of 1 million.

✓ Happiness Index: Saudi Arabia achieved a score of 6.6 in 2024, placing it 32nd globally. The goal for 2030 is a score of 7.54, which would place the country around 5th worldwide.

✓ Life expectancy: Life expectancy reached 78.8 years in 2024, approaching the 2030 target of 80 years.

✓ Healthcare coverage: 97.4% of the national population was covered by health-care services in 2024, exceeding the target of 96.5%.

✓ Physical activity among youth and adults: In 2024, 18.7% of youth (ages 5 to 17) engaged in at least one hour of physical activity per day (goal: 10% in 2024; 21% in 2030). Among adults, 58.5% exercised at least 150 minutes per week (goal: 53% in 2024; 64% in 2030).

✓ Higher education: Three Saudi universities are now ranked among the top 200 globally. The goal is to have five by 2030.

✓ Disability inclusion: Employment of people with disabilities remains a priority. In 2024, 13.4% of the workforce was comprised of individuals with disabilities (goal: 15% by 2030).

✓ SME employment: 7.86 million people are employed by small and medium-sized enterprises (SMEs), exceeding the 2024 target of 7.1 million.

✓ SMEs' contribution to GDP: In 2023, SMEs accounted for 21.9% of the national GDP (2023 goal: 20.2%; 2030 goal: 35%).

Glossary of Acronyms

AFP: Agence France-Presse
APEC: Asia-Pacific Economic Cooperation
ATP: Association of Tennis Professionals
AUKUS: Australia, United Kingdom, and United States. This is a tripartite military alliance between the United States, the United Kingdom and Australia. It was made public in September 2021. Its aim is to counter China's expansionism in the Indo-Pacific region
BRICS: Brazil, Russia, India, China, and South Africa
CIA: Central Intelligence Agency
COP: Conference of the Parties
EU: European Union
FDI: foreign direct investment
FIFA: Fédération Internationale de Football Association
G7 / G20: global economic forums bringing together the most industrialized countries
GCC: Gulf Cooperation Council
GDP: gross domestic product
IAEA: International Atomic Energy Agency
ICC: International Criminal Court
ICJ: International Court of Justice
IMEC: India–Middle East–Europe Economic Corridor
IPCC: Intergovernmental Panel on Climate Change
KACST: King Abdulaziz City for Science and Technology
MWL: Muslim World League
NATO: North Atlantic Treaty Organization
OCHA: Office for the Coordination of Humanitarian Affairs
OPEC: Organization of the Petroleum Exporting Countries
PBS: Public Broadcasting Service
PDVSA: Petróleos de Venezuela SA

PIF: Public Investment Fund
UN: United Nations
UNESCO: United Nations Educational, Scientific and Cultural Organization
UNICEF: United Nations International Children's Emergency Fund
UNIFIL: United Nations Interim Force in Lebanon
UNRWA: United Nations Relief and Works Agency
USA: United States of America
WTI: West Texas Intermediate

Index

Acknowledgments

We wish to extend our deepest gratitude to Dr. Djelloul Seddiki, former director of the Al-Ghazali Institute of Theology in Paris and the current director of Avicenna Virtual Campus Network's scientific programs at UNESCO, Paris. His indispensable insights have been a cornerstone in the development of this manuscript. Dr. Seddiki's profound understanding of theology, the intricacies of Arab-Islamic culture, and linguistic nuances has been invaluable. His guidance has illuminated our path, particularly when navigating topics that are susceptible to misinterpretation. His generous allocation of time and expertise has enriched this work immensely. The text is peppered with historical references, some of which remain elusive to the general populace. Many of these were incorporated thanks to the erudite discussions and suggestions he graciously provided. We are deeply indebted to him for his patience, wisdom, erudition, and above all, his cherished friendship.

About the Authors

Frederic E. Teboul is a seasoned global professional with a diverse educational background, encompassing public international law, political science, an MBA in business administration, and a PhD in economic development. Over a span of more than twenty-five years across four continents, he has developed a deep commitment to diversity and has also passionately contributed to international relations, development cooperation, philanthropy, advocacy, and peace initiatives.

As a geopolitician, serial entrepreneur, and respected international civil servant, primarily with the United Nations, Fred Teboul has successfully led four Nobel Peace Prize-winning positioning strategies for the United Nations (2001), former US Vice President Al Gore (2007), the European Union (2012), and former Colombian President Juan Manuel Santos (2016). His influential role extends to shaping international development and diversification strategies for private sector firms.

Significant global responsibilities across the public, private, philanthropic, and intergovernmental spheres mark Fred Teboul's leadership journey. His multilingual and multicultural aptitude has allowed him to excel in diverse environments. Renowned as a strategist, spin doctor, lobbyist, and kingmaker, he is highly regarded by former and current world leaders as well as high-networth stakeholders for his astute insights, negotiation, mediation, positioning strategy, and advocacy.

Not only is Fred Teboul the president of two corporations, he also serves as a trusted advisor to numerous governments, corporations, and foundations worldwide. Notably, he is co-authoring several books on the leadership style, innovative methods, political vision, and governance of world leaders, and presently cofounding "My Peace Center," showcasing his commitment to fostering a better world built on sustainable peace, social justice, and positive change.

Thierry Pastor has a degree in law and political science. As a spin doctor, seasoned political and strategic advisor, Thierry Pastor specializes in crisis management, energy geopolitics, and global security. His professional journey has taken him to diverse regions, including Eastern Europe, Central Asia, the Far East, and the Gulf.

A subject-matter expert of global trends and lecturer, Thierry Pastor has penned numerous political essays, shedding light on pressing political challenges and the intricacies of contemporary international relations, and more generally, to the comprehension of the factors that govern power relations in the world. He has devoted several essays to energy geopolitics, the analysis of political governance systems, the study of contemporary conflicts and their impact on the international relations' evolution. He defends a realistic vision of political analysis and global geopolitics.

Thierry Pastor is regularly consulted on issues related to peace-building and good governance, both by public and private institutions, for which he provides analysis and strategic solutions. He has been working closely with Fred Teboul for many years.